Pistols, Petticoats, & Poker

Pistols, Petticoats, & Poker

The Real Lottie Deno:
No Lies, or Alibis

By
Jan Devereaux

**With an Introduction by
Robert G. McCubbin**

ISBN-13: 978-0-944383-75-9
ISBN-10: 0-9447383-75-0

Library of Congress Control Number: 2008942708

Cover graphic design and photo by Ann Lowe
Front over pistol courtesy of Terry Humble
Remainder of artifacts courtesy of the Silver City Museum

First Edition: April 2009

High-Lonesome Books
P.O. Box 878
Silver City, New Mexico 88062
575-388-3763
Orders@High-LonesomeBooks.com
www.High-LonesomeBooks.com

Table of Contents

Introduction

While we all acknowledge and respect the contribution honest, hard working, law-abiding men and women made to the settlement of the Old West, it is the ones who spurned respectability or chose to live outside the law we find most interesting. We like to read about outlaws like Butch and Sundance, gunfighters like Wes Hardin and Doc Holliday, and sometimes, but not often, feisty frontier women. Not often because none of the women of the Old West attained a notoriety approaching that of Billy the Kid or Wyatt Earp or Jesse James. In fact, few are remembered at all today.

Calamity Jane and Belle Starr are about the only western women who come quickly to mind, and perhaps Annie Oakley although she really does not belong to the Old West. It takes delving a little deeper into frontier history to reveal the many frontier women that excite our interest. Some were outlaws, or the associates of outlaws: Etta Place, Pearl Hart, Rose of Cimarron, and Cattle Kate. Others made a name for themselves in the oldest profession: Mattie Silks of Denver, Julia Bulette of Virginia City, Tillie Howard of El Paso, Fannie Porter of San Antonio, and Doc Holliday's paramour Big Nose Kate. There were even a few who doubled as professional gamblers: Poker Alice, Madame Moustache and the woman whose life story you are about to read, Lottie Deno.

We can find fascinating stories of these women, but were they who we think they were? Are the stories we read about them true? Often the answer appears to be a resounding "no." In his outstanding biography of Calamity Jane, James McLaird demonstrates that having earned some undeserved notoriety when still quite young, Jane spent—wasted—the rest of her life vainly trying to live up to it. The facts leave no reason for admiration of poor ol' Calamity. Lottie Deno also attracted a lot of attention on the frontier of the 1870s and gained considerable notoriety as a prostitute and gambler. She was then forgotten for decades except in the memoirs of some oldtimers.

Unlike Calamity Jane, Lottie Deno took another path after her days on the Frontier. She spent the last half of a long life running away from her past rather than trying to call attention to it. Lottie yearned to be thought of as a "lady." She lived out her life in Deming, New Mexico, as Mrs. Frank Thurmond, without her contemporaries having the slightest knowledge of her past. She died a lady, respected by her friends and neighbors.

Despite author Devereaux's valiant investigative work, much of Lottie's early life remains a mystery. But, if anything, the mysteries of her origins intensifies our interest. Billy the Kid, the icon figure of the

I

Wild West, has experienced intense research for decades by countless historians and yet his name at birth and the date and location of his birth are still not known. Nonetheless, his life in the West fascinates us and interest in him continues to grow. In this book, Jan Devereaux brings Lottie Deno back to life, meticulously trailing her through the frontier towns and times in Texas and New Mexico. In the process she demonstrates that nearly everything that has been published about Lottie in recent years is either completely wrong or highly questionable (for openers, those charming photos we thought were the young Lottie, ain't her!). Demanding we discard most of what we thought we knew, this *tour de force* of in-depth research strips away the inaccuracies and the myths about Lottie Deno's life, not only revealing the fascinating truth about a spunky, resilient woman on the western frontier, but beyond that telling us a very great deal about the struggles "the weaker sex" encountered and surmounted to survive and succeed in the male-dominated world of the Old West.

Robert G. McCubbin
True West Magazine

Preface and Acknowledgments

The allure with Lottie Deno's story is mystery. More has been written and less known about Lottie than any woman traipsing through the Old Southwest's boomtowns. That she was a real person is unassailable. That her real name was not Lottie Deno is indisputable. That the Lottie Deno most people know is but an illusion is also irrefutable. Apathy and complacency are the handmaidens of mythology. Fluffed as it is, much of the folklore veiling Lottie has been accepted as fact. Pertinent questions have long passed by unasked and unanswered. Lottie Deno's stage-managed charade was a 20th-Century creation. Promenading and poker playing beneath a spotlight of melodrama, she was imaginatively transformed into an enviable model of what we would want a heroine to be. Fair-minded examination of evidence and employment of common sense converts the fabrication into truthfulness. Sans the lies or alibis the real Lottie Deno is far more interesting than the fictionalized Lottie Deno.

One of those myths is that the cash proceeds from an 1892 high-stakes poker game between Lottie Deno and a notorious frontier gambler philanthropically financed the construction of a church. Never mind the truth. By 1892 Lottie Deno had forsaken her previous life as a habitué of dubious nightspots. Her legendary adversary, an amoral cardsharp to be sure, had died five years earlier in a Colorado sanitarium. Discarding the fiction does not distract from the truth: Lottie did win money from the Georgia born gambling and gunfighting dentist, but at the time neither she nor he was charitably inclined.

Allowing that Lottie Deno dealt cards and exhibited a faro bank in many of the Southwest's frontier towns is easy. Evidence places her in such 19th-Century gaming nerve-centers as San Antonio, San Angelo, Jacksboro, Fort Griffin, Brackettville and bawdy El Paso in Texas, along with Silver City, Cambray, Kingston and Deming in the wild and woolly territory of New Mexico. Sustaining that Lottie was well acquainted with a conglomeration of the best-known buffalo hunters, gamblers, con men, gunmen, desperadoes, working-girls, pimps—and a few honest folks—is effortless.

Lottie's narrative is similar to many of her Old West contemporaries. A number of those characters earned biographic notice during life's twilight years, for the most part in the 20th-Century. Scores of those accounts have been exaggerated or counterfeited. Myth colliding with fact, or even believability, is sometimes common practice during the work of sculpting Wild West heroes and heroines. Often, too, central figures complicated the search for truth. James D. McLaird corroborated such in his splendidly researched biography of Martha Canary, *Calamity Jane: The Woman and the Legend*. "In later life, she earned a living by exploiting her national reputation telling her story on stage and selling her autobiography and pictures....Although Martha occasionally denounced the dime novel stories about her as lies, she spun similar yarns herself, expanding her role in events she knew only indirectly....Sadly, after romantic adventures are removed, her story is mostly an account of uneventful daily life interrupted by drinking binges."[1]

Dissimilar to Calamity Jane, Lottie Deno did not try to capitalize on a nickname or the odious connotations fostered by a livelihood earned in barrooms and bordellos. She waltzed in the opposite direction. Lottie Deno shunned notoriety, particularly if it hinted of misspent days in Texas frontier towns. Lottie Deno had not been the sole coquettish darling sitting at the gambling tables. In fact, it was other sporting girls that attracted the lion's share of attention. While traveling the Lone Star State's gaming circuit Lottie was seldom noticed by contemporary journalists. Newspapermen's failure to write feature stories about her card turning talents—making her a celebrity—leads to but one rational conclusion: She was not a gambling circuit megastar. There were no dime novel stories about Lottie Deno. Neither was she glamorized as a superwoman when 19th-Century entrepreneurs were hawking images of their luminaries on billboards and handbills for Wild West shows. Substantiation of facts reveal Lottie Deno's role on the stage of Western theatrics was more than a cameo appearance, but she did not acquire marquee eminence until after she had cut the pattern for dressing in decency. Lottie Deno was a capable gambler. There, too, is confirmation she was other things as well.

Much like Calamity Jane in the Rocky Mountain West, when Lottie Deno looked into a mirror during those days wasted in the Texas nightspots she did not see an unsullied halo. The reflection did reveal a rather attractive young girl, but that image could not replicate her insatiable lust for dollars. Emptying fellow's pockets by one means or another was Lottie's aspiration; it guaranteed survival.

There is inherent value in reconstructing Lottie Deno's story. For a substantial portion of her life Lottie was a vagabond. She was a single, but not necessarily lonesome woman, eking subsistence by whatever methods it took to put bread on the table. Therein is the quintessence of her intriguing tale. In many respects Lottie Deno was so representative of the young and spunky women amusing men in the Old West's indulgent emporiums. Those saloon girls are an emblematic component of every factual or fictional saga about the Wild West. Despite crushing barriers Lottie Deno climbed out of the muck. The overwhelming majority of her girlfriends did not. Those gals drowned in squalor and sleaze.

Over the years Lottie Deno has had an untiring string of publicity agents. Other women in similar circumstances have not. Unraveling fact from fiction is the undertaking at hand. Disentangling the snarl will not only reveal the real Lottie Deno, but it will demonstrate salient insights into sociological factors bearing on many 19th-Century girls tramping throughout the American West. Lottie was no angel but she did catch notice.

Adding to the din surrounding Lottie Deno's mysteriousness was the work of an admired turn-of-the-century writer who immortalized her as a fictional character in a popularized series of cliché and dialogue stuffed Western novels. Faro Nell's real life identity and that of her Beau Brummell, Cherokee Hall, was no secret.[2] As well, Lottie Deno's appearance at Fort Griffin, Texas, had made a lasting impression. After America's ongoing love affair with the "Western" intensified many of Shackelford County's oldtimers were interviewed. Several of those interviewees had known Lottie Deno. A few knew her quite well, perhaps better than they even wanted to admit. Twentieth-century scholars had been rushing about trying to preserve oral testimony before conversant historical informants were overtaken by time. Miss Lottie Deno soon became a fixture in Texas folklore. Afterward an enthusiastic and prolific writer, one who claimed to have known Lottie Deno in New Mexico during the territorial days, penned his profile. The Lottie legend swelled. Of more recent vintage it is asserted and often repeated that the very real Miss Deno was inspiration for an iconic fictionalized character in a long-running television program. And, as a rule it is an accepted belief that Lottie Deno was Hollywood's concept for the female lead in what has become a cult classic Western movie.[3] Even today Lottie Deno sometimes stands on a packed theater's stage clad in colorful period dress, but the truthfulness of her script—like her gorgeous hoopskirt costume—is but a prop.

Deficiency with much of the previous writings about the well turned-out Lottie is noticeable by nonappearance of citation to source materials. Depriving a reader of the capacity to explore is not appropriate, nor is it conducive to peeling away layers of misconceptions and misstatements. Such will not be the case in *Pistols, Petticoats, & Poker.* Sources are identified. A purchaser is entitled to see brick by brick the foundation supporting the real Lottie Deno's story. The rationale of this endeavor is not to close the book on Lottie and lock it tight. On the contrary, it is best to open it wide for a good going over. Lottie Deno was/is an enigma. Any attempt at retelling her story will harvest fair-minded questions. History may not change, but as fresh discoveries are unearthed interpretation of history does. Reviewing these pages might be beneficial for those having their own gems of supplementary knowledge; hopefully with a proper source citation. If so, the discernible gaps in Lottie Deno's biography may be cemented with the jewels of accuracy—as it should be!

Nonfiction writing by its very nature places the author in debt. It is a heartfelt pleasure to acknowledge the participation of the following persons and/or institutions in making this book possible: Robert G. "Bob" McCubbin, Santa Fe, New Mexico; Sylvia Ligocky, Deming/Luna Mimbres Museum, Deming, New Mexico; Terry Humble, Bayard, New Mexico; Donaly Brice, Texas State Library & Archives Commission, Austin, Texas; Jim Bradshaw, Nita Stewart Haley Memorial Library & History Center, Midland, Texas; Ray Marvin and Ruth Hay, Bandera, Texas; Rose Greenwalt, Frontier Times Museum, Bandara, Texas; Carolyn Marksberry, Clerk/Treasurer City of Warsaw, Warsaw, Kentucky; Ellen Clifford, Archivists, Sisters of Charity Of Nazareth, Nazareth, Kentucky; Steve Engerrand, Asst. Director, Georgia State Archives, Morrow, Georgia; Allan Carter, Historian, National Museum of Racing & Hall of Fame, Saratoga Springs, New York; David Sysma, Librarian, Waco Public Library, Waco, Texas; Lester Gailbreath, Superintendent [Retired], Fort Griffin State Park, Fort Griffin, Texas; Clifford Teinert, Fort Griffin, Texas; Robin Gillam-Crawford, National Ranching Heritage Center, Lubbock, Texas; Evelyn Lemons, Historian, Fort Concho National Historic Landmark, San Angelo, Texas; Ray Monroe, Park Ranger, Fort Richardson State Park, Jacksboro, Texas; Clarissa Chavira and Deborah Countess, San Antonio Public Library, San Antonio, Texas; Suzanne Campbell, West Texas Collection, Angelo State University, San Angelo, Texas; Shirley Timmons, Forensic Artist [Retired], Texas Rangers, Austin, Texas; Elizabeth Weinman, Register, Old Jail Art Center, Albany, Texas; Bill Haenn, Kinney County Tax Appraiser, Brackettville, Texas; Doris Sandoval, Kinney County Clerk, Brackettville, Texas; Sarah Terrazas, Bracketville Library, Brackettville, Texas; Jewel F. Robinson, Brackettville, Texas; Diane Dooley, Montell, Texas. Delyn Lewis, Director, G. J. Ritchie Public Library, Jacksboro, Texas; Douglas McElrath, Curator, Marylandia and Rare Books, University of Maryland Hornbake Library, College Park, Maryland; Leslie Bellais, Curator of Costumes and Textiles, Sate Historical Society of Wisconsin; Maureen A. Taylor, Photo Detective, *Family Tree Magazine*; Jesse Lewis, State Documents Coordinator, Indiana State Library, Indianapolis, Indiana; Scott Anderson, Assistant Archivist, Sharlot Hall Museum, Prescott, Arizona; Susan Berry & Polly Smidt, Silver City Museum, Silver City, New Mexico; Pete Crum, Silver City Public Library, Silver City, New Mexico; Cookie Stolpe, Miller Library, Western New Mexico University, Silver City New Mexico; Dorinda Holly, Luna County

Clerk's Office, Deming, New Mexico; George Hackler, Las Cruces, New Mexico; Julie Coley, Wichita Falls, Texas; Dave Johnson, Zionsville, Indiana; Robert K. DeArment, Sylvania, Ohio; Fred Nolan, England; Rick and Paula Miller, Harker Heights, Texas; Chuck Parsons, Luling, Texas; Ida Saunders, El Paso, Texas; Karen & John Tanner, Fallbrook, California; Nancy B. Samuelson, Sacramento, Califronia; Martha Fanning, Lueders, Texas; Tom Gaumer, Denver, Colorado; Craig Fouts, San Diego, California; Jim Earle, Creative Publishing, College Station, Texas; Bob Pugh, Trail to Yesterday Books, Tucson, Arizona; Sharon Cunningham, Dixie Gun Works, Union City, Tennessee; Scott Johnson, Bloomington, Illinois; Craig Johnson, Heyworth, Illinois; Julia Putnam, Albany, Texas; Joan Farmer, Albany, Texas; Ginger McCullar, Albany, Texas; Mike Tower, Elmore City, Oklahoma; Cheryl Lewis, Hamlin, Texas; Lanette and John Shanahan, Templeton, California; Marjorie and Jean Rappolee, Centerville, Texas; Edward Herring, Mount Hope, Alabama; Lawrence Vivian, Cibolo, Texas, and Willa Hancock, Cambray, New Mexico.

A "thank you" must be extended to Patrick Tidmore, San Francisco, California. Mr. Tidmore's grandmother, Susie Tidmore, was an especially close personal friend of Mrs. Lottie Thurmond at Deming, New Mexico. In fact, Lottie was the godmother to Susie's daughter Roberta, Patrick's aunt. Mr. Tidmore shared his vast collection of family photographs, many of which were of Aunt Lottie, as she was known by those who loved her. Several of those charming photographs by a circuitous route have heretofore been published, but there is little doubt that they originated from the scrapbook of Mrs. Tidmore. Other delightful images of Lottie and Frank Thurmond will be reproduced herein for the very first time, thanks to Patrick Tidmore's devoted commitment to preserving history.

Thanks must also be extended to Bob Alexander, Maypearl, Texas. He graciously lent a helping hand with identifying collateral source materials necessary for capturing the essence of Lottie Deno's real story. Such a valuable contribution ensured the endnote section of *Pistols, Petticoats, & Poker* would be rather comprehensive; which provides a polished key for those persons interested in follow-up research. Bob Alexander's overall knowledge of the Old Southwest is extraordinary. In addition to broadening Lottie's real story with ancillary background data, Bob held me accountable to a sensible—yet so simple—nonfiction writing guideline: Don't write if you can't cite!

Endnotes Preface and Acknowledgments

[1] James D. McLaird, *Calamity Jane: The Woman and the Legend*. 5.
[2] *Deming Headlight*, April 18, 1963. "Alfred Henry Lewis repeatedly and unmistakably described the Thurmonds in his books comprising the 'Wolfville' series. The Thurmonds were then known as 'Cherokee Hall' and 'Faro Nell.' Wolfville was an imaginary town, probably a composite of many wild and woolly towns of the early west." *The Ruidoso Monthly*, March 1991. "A fictionalized series of stories were written about Fort Griffin during the late 1890's titled The Wolfuill [*sic*] Series. The author, Dan Quin (pen name Alfred Henry Lewis), went to live in Deming on the ranch owned by Lottie's husband. There, on the commission of William Randolph Hearst, he authored the historic account of the days at Fort Griffin, giving the names Faro Nell and Cherokee Hall to Lottie and her Ace. The illustrator for the characters in Lewis' book was artist, Frederic Remington." 22. Actually, the author's name was Alfred Henry Lewis, who sometimes used the pen name of Dan Quin. For an exceptional examination of this subject [Lewis] see Robert K. DeArment's *Broadway Bat: Gunfighter in Gotham—The New York City Years of Bat Masterson*. 51-61
[3] *The Abilene Reporter-News*, November 23, 1971. Byline, Ed Syers, "Lottie Deno Added Color To Fort Griffin Gambling." "Well, this will report to you heretofore disillusioned romantics that Kitty is the genuine, authentic imitation we hoped. In fact, Texas fleetingly knew a woman [Lottie Deno] for whom Kitty might well have been modeled."; Cynthia Rose, *Lottie Deno: Gambling Queen of Hearts*, picks up on Syers' theme, declaring that Deno was model for *Gunsmoke's* Miss Kitty: "Although Lottie has been 'immortalized' in frontier novels and more recently in television and film (as 'Miss Kitty' in 'Gunsmoke' and 'Laura Denbo' in 'Gunfight at the O. K. Corral'), the true story is more fascinating than any work of fiction." From back cover; *Las Cruces Sun-News*, November 3, 1994. Byline, S. Derrickson Moore, "Know when to hold them, know when to fold them." "She [Lottie Deno] was the model for Gunsmoke's Miss Kitty...."; *Deming Headlight*, September 26, 1994. "....Lottie Deno, and her influence has made it onto the silver screen in the form of Miss Kitty on 'Gunsmoke' and Laura Denbo in 'Gunfight at the O. K. Corral.'; Vince Bergdale, "Lottie Deno: Queen of the Pasteboards." "*Trails' End Magazine*. August/September 1998. "The real life person that Miss Kitty of Gunsmoke was based on. Lottie was also a key figure in the 1957 classic western, *Gunfight at the O. K. Corral* starring Burt Lancaster and Kirk Douglas. Rhonda Fleming plays 'Laura Denbo' who falls in love with Wyatt Earp. Not true, and the true story was actually more exciting than the movie." 26.

Chapter 1

"Leading a Dual life"

Gone With The Wind's Scarlett O'Hara and Carlotta Thompkins were similar creatures of the Old South's plantation era. Scarlett and Carlotta were traditional Southern Belles. Both had precocious sisters, wardrobes of stylish fashions, and adoring fathers fond of good horseflesh. Each had a slave given over to prerogatives of their comfort and well-being. Scarlett, the central but fictionalized character in the Lost Cause Romance, returned to Tara the family's palatial estate after the Civil War. Carlotta, a real woman with alluring dark eyes, turned her back on the South during Reconstruction and ventured into the Southwest. Both girls were tough and self-reliant. Scarlett O'Hara was persistent because Pulitzer Prize winning writer Margaret Mitchell wanted her to be. Carlotta Thompkins was persevering because she had to be.

Throughout her imaginatively inspired life Scarlett O'Hara's surname would change as she married, then remarried and then remarried again. Carlotta Thompkins, too, would be recognized by diverse names, but those appellations were typically nicknames. More often than not they were not chosen by Carlotta, but were bestowed by others' quirky motivations. Old West history knows her best as Lottie Deno, riverboat gambling queen and frontier faro dealer. Lottie Deno was not ignored when America's pop culture ignited with insatiable desires for everything Western. Just as Scarlett was a polished literary figment, Carlotta was fictionally reborn, too. She became Faro Nell for Alfred Henry Lewis' well-liked string of *Wolfville* novels; pattern for Amanda Blake's character Miss Kitty in television's *Gunsmoke* series; and Rhonda Fleming's movie role as Laura Denbo in the *Gunfight At The O. K. Corral* was based on Carlotta's authentic life.[1]

Why did this Kentucky bred antebellum child deserve such credit? Perhaps it was due to Lottie's youthful good looks and saucy attitude; the symbolic saloon girl waltzing, wagering and whoring her way to stardom. Maybe it was owing to Lottie's proclivity for hanging out with the wildest of the wild folks in the Wild West. She was a desperate woman. Or did she attract attention because of that high-stakes Texas poker game? It was a noteworthy game, a girl beating the financial stuffin' out of Doc Holliday. Lottie Deno was at the right places at the right times for nurturing a thrilling Western: A true story.

Northeast of Louisville, Kentucky, and southwest of Cincinnati, Ohio, there is a gentle bend in the Ohio River. On the river's south bank just below Sugar Bay reposes the city of Warsaw, Gallatin County,

Kentucky. First settled in 1794 the little village was at first called Ohio River Landing or Great Landing because of its ideal positioning at river's edge. Adolphus Frederick constructed a dockyard, began building boats and in due course the town was christened Fredericksburg in his honor. All too soon it was learned there was another Fredericksburg inside Kentucky's borders, one in Washington County. Postal authorities would not grant the river-front Fredericksburg a post office. At the suggestion of early settler Archibald Beall the name of the newest Fredericksburg was discarded, replaced by Warsaw. Warsaw blossomed into a busy river shipping port for the area. In 1837 the Gallatin County seat was moved from Port William to Warsaw. So vigorous was the business activity and population increase that by 1838 the county government was being housed in its third courthouse—down the street from the Warsaw Post Office.[2]

Carlotta J. Thompkins [also often written as Tompkins] was born at Warsaw on the 21st day of April 1844.[3] Carlotta was the older of two girls born to wealthy parents. They were so well-to-do that in addition to the huge plantation in their portfolio they also owned *hundreds of slaves* [author's emphasis] and a *string of race horses*, as well as one of the *finest race tracks* in the Blue Grass State. Carlotta's father was also a respected member of the Kentucky Legislature.[4] With such blue-blooded lineage Carlotta and her as yet unnamed younger sister did not attend a public school, but were educated in the area's finest Episcopal Convent.[5]

Carlotta's childhood was not spent on a vast cotton plantation; her father raised tobacco and hemp which he shipped upriver to Detroit, down river to New Orleans. Mr. Thompkins' passion for raising and racing top-quality Thoroughbreds prompted his appearance at tracks throughout the South, particularly at that nerve center for racehorse men, New Orleans. His breeding stock was in such demand that he bought and sold horses in England, indeed, throughout the whole of "continental Europe." From time to time Mr. Thompkins allowed the adolescent Carlotta to accompany him on these business excursions up and down the river.[6] During an extended trip abroad in the "great casinos of the World," Mr. Thompkins taught his daughter, the aspiring gambling princess, all the "tricks of the trade," a clever euphemism for cheating.[7] Carlotta was a good pupil. Under her father's expert tutelage Carlotta maintained her spirit, but became a skillful gambler:

> She told funny stories about her childhood; about how she'd traded the darkies out of their share of 'cherry bounce' though she was forbidden to have it as it was alcoholic; about how her father would take her with him on trips, and at least once had taken her to Europe

to buy horses. On the ship she loved watching the stylish ladies in their beautiful clothes, and was enchanted with their jeweled snuff boxes. She had begged her father for one, and although he indulged her most ways, he wouldn't allow her to have one. Her father liked to gamble and taught her to play cards. He owned race horses and she would slip off and play poker with the jockeys. This was, of course, forbidden, but she didn't often get caught.[8]

Carlotta, a social butterfly, was living the good life. She was a child of big money. She was a child of unbridled privilege. Presumably her little sister was too, although she wasn't mentioned as being in on any of the fun. Nor was she a vacationer on the extravagant trips to Detroit, New Orleans, or throughout continental Europe. Preservation of Carlotta's cultured status and perpetual elegance was but assured. Someday she would inherit an enormous tobacco plantation surrounding a palatial mansion, the hundreds of respectful black slaves tending manicured fields of tobacco, and a stable crowded with hot-blooded Thoroughbreds.

The wonderful life was not to be. Ravages of the Civil War destroyed Carlotta's promising future. Her loving father, a committed Southerner, enlisted in the Confederate Army and was killed during his first battlefield engagement, so says one writer.[9] Carlotta told a US Army officer that her father had been lost at sea when the *CSS Alabama* went down.[10] Somewhat later Carlotta advised a friend that she had been disowned by her family because of marriage to a gambling man [1880].[11] Carlotta's real story is plagued by these kind of subtle inconsistencies. Continuing, Carlotta was fatherless, homeless and penniless, the cherished plantation now in the hands of Unionists—those damnyankees! The brokenhearted and widowed Mrs. Thompkins was in ill-health, an invalid. Carlotta's beloved sister was but a helpless child in need of an expensive education. The weight of the world had fallen on Carlotta's shoulders. She was a true daughter of the Old South. As the oldest child Carlotta did not inherit the plantation in this instance, but was by tradition bequeathed responsibility. She would support her devastated mother and sister, though just how she acquired the cash would best be kept her little secret.[12]

Accompanied by an adoring black nanny, the six-foot plus Mary Poindexter, "the last of her father's slaves," Carlotta traveled to Detroit, Michigan. Although the Yankee controlled destination does seem bizarre for a diehard Southern aristocrat, she had a plan: Carlotta would reluctantly turn "to the only lucrative profession she knew— gambling."[13] A card playing option had won out over the two other choices; getting a job which would wreck her elitist standing or getting a man just for convenience's sake—which would stifle her free-spirited independence.[14] Circulating through the luxurious betting clubs and sitting in on high-stakes private games the seventeen year old Kentucky girl "soon found herself in the midst of a social whirl that classed her as the belle of the ball from the deep South."[15] In next to no time Carlotta was a regular gambler at one of Detroit's private clubs. Without delay the teen prodigy was winning enough money to pay for her sister's education and provide necessities for her ailing mother.[16] The societal flurry created by such an ornately attired natural beauty, one of tender years with lithe fingers and card playing skills tweaked to perfection was overlooked by Detroit's social scene editors, however. Their collective silence is deafening.

Carlotta soon grew weary "of smoke filled rooms and the tireless activity of the gambling halls."[17] Doubtless she had overheard that betting establishments in the Lone Star State were not near so smoky, nor near so noisy. Carlotta decided to move her card playing talents to Texas. There were not any thoughts of shirking responsibility. She would still provide for her sibling's costly education in post war Kentucky. The gambling girl just wouldn't tell her were the money came from. Carlotta told her sister that she had married a rich fellow, one who was a "wonderful provider." Out of the goodness of his heart he was furnishing the funds. Carlotta was waltzing around the truth about being wed, but not about relocating to Texas.[18]

Such a trip required a marvelous paddle-wheel steamer ride down the Mississippi River to New Orleans. Although it dilutes the stereotypical idea, by the time Carlotta had decided to relocate technology had overtaken the demand for riverboat captains; railroad travel was the rage.[19] Nonetheless Carlotta would travel the waterways, not concerning herself about money. She would gamble her way downstream emptying pockets as surely as the muddy current emptied into the capricious Gulf of Mexico. Apparently times had changed. Earlier, Robert Fulton had launched his second magnificent steamboat named the *New Orleans*, the maiden vessel having gone under during unfortunate circumstances. The craft was 140 feet long, 28 wide, and could register 10 miles an hour moving downstream carrying 200 tons of freight and 50 passengers, "who were separated by sex."[20] Gentlemanly riverboat gamblers "had nothing against women—far from it—but they believed that the proper place for the fair sex was out of the way."[21]

Even in the few lavishly furnished steamer's social halls or main saloons nice gals and games of chance were oddities: "Women, although not excluded by any law or regulation, customarily left the tables to the men"[22] Perhaps Carlotta defied convention. By at least one account

Carlotta "soon became a fabulous name on the river boats and in the gambling halls on her route west."[23] If it were true, it would seem Carlotta was an aberration:

> Women, of course, never were admitted to dramshops, nor did they wish to enter. The rule held on the Mississippi. On river steamboats there was a ladies' lounge at the stern end of the main cabin; the bar usually was at the other end in deference to the custom of separating women and liquor as widely as possible.[24]

A Russian traveler touring America, Aleksandr Borisovich Lakier, made firsthand observations about 19th-Century steamboat travel and the sporting gentry, on the whole noting that nearly all passengers gambled: "Except for the ladies...."[25] A disheartening inference may be found in Lakier's remark: Carlotta was either a lady or a gambler.

For the southbound riverboat trip Carlotta's sole protection was "the negress, Mary Poindexter."[26] "Mary was a giant, and so black that the palms of her hands and the soles of her feet were a deep mahogany."[27] Mary might have shuddered had she known a few of the ugly truths about an easygoing trip down the Mississippi. Inveterate riverboat gambler Tom Ellison recalled:

> Many a time I've seen a game player just skin off his watch and ring and studs and play them in. Men often lost their goods playing in their way bills. I've seen them betting a bale of cotton at a crack, and it wasn't at all uncommon to hear an old planter betting off his Negroes on a good hand. Every man who ever ran on the river knows that these old planters used to play in their lady servants, valuing them all the way from $300 to $1,500. I saw a little colored boy stand up at $300 to back his master's faith in a little flush that wasn't any good on earth.[28]

Stereotypical folklore suggests pleasant amenities of riverboat passage were ubiquitous. However, the elegantly furnished "main cabin" or "saloon" was not exclusively reserved for everyone's enjoyment. A majority of people booked passage where accommodations "remained crude at best, and not all vessels included a richly appointed main cabin."[29]

Whether Carlotta and Mary purchased first-class tickets or were relegated to second-class travel below the main deck is unanswerable. Gambling was not limited to the upper decks: "Entrepreneurs with limited means and dirty cards went down to the second deck where the immigrants were, and there tried to take away from the poor whatever extra they might happen to have."[30] Discarding any misplaced fantasy another former riverboat gambler cautioned:

> It's very pretty to read about, but the real thing was not so nice. The black-eyed, black-mustached hero gambler that you read about was anything but a hero. There was no chivalry in his nature, and he was ready for any dark deed that would profit him. Of course I am speaking of the professional gambler, for everyone gambled; if they had not done so the professional's occupation would have been gone. The chivalrous ones were the young Southern planters, reckless, but not mean, who would play the full limit and get fleeced.[31]

Fleecing "pigeons" was expected from the Mississippi River's sporting fraternity: "All riverboat gamblers were expert at cheating, and perhaps 99 per cent of them, either occasionally or all the time, did cheat."[32]

Prevailing images of riverboat travel are somewhat askew. The passenger was not a prisoner of the vessel from departure to destination. While it is probable that Carlotta spent most of her onboard time in the "women's parlor astern," such did not necessarily prohibit the girl from gambling her way to New Orleans.[33] At scheduled intervals the boat docked to refurbish storerooms and take on fuel for boilers. There was as much, if not more, money changing hands in the onshore clubrooms as in the floating staterooms. Carlotta and Mary would have for the interim disembarked at such delightful Old South river towns as Memphis, Vicksburg, Natchez, and Baton Rouge, as well as the smaller landings, before docking at New Orleans. A gambler unable to find a card game in those towns should have had a real job. And it does seem, at one spot or the other, Carlotta reaffirmed that separating soldiers from their specie was easy work.

Whether the unlucky fellow was a US Army man or was a discharged Johnny Reb may be left to the reader's choice; there are two competing versions.[34] While docked at an unnamed port Carlotta and Mary were enjoying sunshine on an outside deck prior to the steamer getting underway. Two of the boarding passengers were soldiers. A flirtatious white girl and an oversized black girl are conspicuous. The gals caught the eye of one solider, who at once recognized Carlotta. He was not smitten, but was mad. Upriver Carlotta had parted him from his paycheck. In his mind the poker game had not been fair; Carlotta had dealt dirty from the bottom of the deck. Why the sorehead had not cried foul upriver, at the time of the injustice, is a question best not asked. It would muddy the traditionalized tale. Carlotta had whipped him at the card table, chauvinistically the soldier was going to whip her across his knee—or worse. In a fit of rage he lunged at Carlotta. Mary Poindexter jumped just in the nick of time. Squarely she stood between the clinched-fist accuser and Carlotta, daring him to finish what he had started. The soldier hesitated, Mary didn't. She grabbed the maddened soldier, picked him up over her head and tossed him overboard. Any eagerness for settling scores had been washed away when he hit the water. They never saw him again. Mary Poindexter must have been a brawny and powerful superwoman![35] Both Carlotta's and Mary's lives would be marked by more violence.

Before they arrived at New Orleans, Mary had another occasion to rescue Carlotta. While docked the pair were strolling on the Mississippi River's bank. The eerie sound of buzzing rattles stopped both in their tracks. Reactively, Mary pushed Carlotta aside and fell on the gigantic rattlesnake, just as it needled poison into her finger. To forestall the onset of gangrene Mary's index finger was amputated, but she had saved Carlotta's life.[36]

The steamer finally docked at New Orleans. Carlotta's and Mary's stern-wheeler ride was an adventure but to remember. Creatively it's mentioned that Carlotta, because of her card playing skill, earned a wonderful name on the Mississippi steamers and in the port's gambling halls.[37] Once more contemporary newspapermen in rough and tumble river-front towns let pass the compelling story of a twenty year-old poker playing princess and her attendant Amazon protector.

For a gambler, or someone that wanted to be, New Orleans was Mecca. By the end of the 19th-Century's first decade New Orleans had a population of only 17,000, but "that small city may have had more gambling houses than Philadelphia, Baltimore, Boston and New York combined."[38] Less than ten years later 40,000 called New Orleans home. A New England lawyer on holiday noted that New Orleans was "wicked" and the populace was indulging in "unlimited" amusements. The shocked vacationer observed that New Orleans' women were beautiful with "fine features, symmetry of form, and elegance of manners," but many were of loose morals, and that there were countless gambling halls operating around the clock.[39] He also mentioned the New Orleans menfolk: "Here men may be vicious without incurring the ill opinion of those around them...."[40] Not only had New Orleans served as marketplace for Mr. Thompkins' tobacco crops and a ready outlet for his Thoroughbreds, but the Crescent City had also timelessly beckoned riffraff and the "operators of dens of iniquity, grog shops, gambling joints, and vulgar ball rooms."[41] Most New Orleans gambling—and other forms of vice—took place in "the Swamp," a section bordered by Julia, Girod, South Liberty, and South Robertson

Streets. "It was there that one could find liquor, gambling, and prostitutes."[42]

New Orleans had a reputation as a raw river-front town: a modern Sodom, the Babylon of the South.[43] She was epicenter for American gambling. New Orleans served as the "nation's port of entry for such European games as poker, craps, and faro, and for the Mexican game of three-card monte."[44] Although the following specifics were taken from a newspaper ad prior to the onset of Carlotta's New Orleans gambling sojourn, the come-on is remarkable—and chilling. If one were so inclined to take his son or daughter along and was willing to part with an admission fee [adults $1.00, children $.50], an afternoon could be spent at the New Orleans circus. While a military band played background music spectators could watch and bet on the outcome of an array of contests: six of the strongest dogs in the country vs. an Attakapas bull, a Canadian bear vs. six bulldogs, a tiger vs. a Black bear, and twelve dogs vs. a "strong and furious" Opelousas bull. Assuring that customers got their money's worth, the promoter made a guarantee. If the tiger wasn't done in by the bear it would be pitted against the Opelousas bull, but should the bull triumph the show wasn't over: "....several pieces of fireworks will be placed on his back, which will produce a very entertaining amusement."[45] By the time Carlotta had made her Grand Entry into New Orleans the city was, indeed, known as the nation's horse-racing capital, "with no less than five tracks open every winter season."[46]

Any inference that New Orleans was but a pit of debauchery would be erroneous. Many urbanized residents were zealous with efforts designed at bettering the city and improving its atmosphere. As early as 1812 New Orleans had establishments like the Exchange, a drinking emporium claiming rarity, a sanded floor. Numerous New Orleans businessmen, bankers, and newspapermen stood before the Exchange's polished bar, resting a shined shoe on the brass rail, intermittently expectorating nasty brown streams into ornately carved spittoons, as they visited, bargained, and gossiped.[47] Elegance could be found in New Orleans. A visiting Frenchman, Lagarde de Montiézant, invited to a Grand Ball found that

> The hall was lighted with 200 candles, and sixty young demoiselles, dressed in white were the ornaments....They were simply but elegantly dressed, nearly all had white roses adorning their hair which was artistically cured and plaited with taste and dropped with grace in floating elastic spirals on a virginal forehead around an alabaster neck and upon rosy cheeks....[48]

Considerately it's been written that Carlotta rekindled her remembrances of those earlier trips with her father to New Orleans, a city of "southern grandeur." Fond memories of gambling palaces she had seen as a "sight-seer" were vivid. "The splendor of the halls and magnificent ladies and gentlemen, dressed in the prevailing styles of the period, furnished a setting of unbelievable elegance which she never forgot."[49] Carlotta's trip to New Orleans this time was for business, not pleasure. She had not come to New Orleans to find her fortune at the end of a rainbow, but in poker chips piled high. Carlotta would stay in New Orleans long enough to finance her sister's education and save enough for the trip to Texas.[50] Carlotta's gaming talents were honed to perfection. Not only did she win enough for her baby sister's continued welfare, but Carlotta began filling her own trunks with "the finest in Parisian fashions...."[51] Cigar smoking sufferers of her poker prowess watched in horror as their bankrolls shriveled. The New Orleans press corps was busy elsewhere. They missed the story.

Hypothetical images of the Old South have been ingrained. Drawing from such fallacious impressions is but customary. Stale as the characterization may be, it is often yet written, and perhaps believed, that 19th-Century Southerners

> dwelt in large and stately mansions, preferably white and with columns and Grecian entablature....in a world of social harmony and ease devoid of inward strife and conflict. Their estates were feudal baronies, their slaves quite too numerous to be counted and their social life a thing of Old World splendor and delicacy.[52]

In some respects that world may have really existed. But not for most people.[53] That there was "....no room for poor or middling sorts: no Crackers, yeomen, rednecks, lintheads, businessmen, or merchants..." is a classic but misguided caricature of the Old South.[54] Even in regions where there was a Southern planter culture the vast majority of citizens were by station of birth forced to eke out a living on the middle ground. Their spot was preset somewhere between the impoverished black slaves and the decadently affluent aristocrats. It is not unwarranted to think that tenant farmers' or wheelwrights' or bricklayers' daughters daydreamed about doting black mammies pulling corset strings tight, donning elegant gowns, and descending down the winding staircase for a lavish coming-out party. Poor girls could have fancy aspirations, too! A few could fabricate a nice story if such was thought necessary; just as a bad rich girl could invent a benign past. Carlotta Thompkins had a story.

Origins for customary adaptations of that story may be traced to someone who actually knew Carlotta—as Lottie Deno—Edgar Rye, author of the 1909 Western classic *The Quirt and the Spur: Vanishing Shadows of The Texas Frontier*. Although she had been fictionalized twelve years earlier in *Wolfville*, it was Edgar Rye who identified Lottie Deno as an authentic frontier personality. He was in a position to know. Mr. Rye had served as a Shackelford County Justice of the Peace during a time Lottie Deno resided in the county.[55] With three sentences Edgar Rye sprouted the angelic seed:

> Lottie exhibited all the traits of a refined, educated woman, who had been nurtured in high society and was a gentlewoman by birth....Strange stories were told about Lottie by those who knew the least, but some credence attached to the report that this strange woman lived a dual life of a saint in the East and desperate character in the West. It was said that money was sent to an invalid mother in her New England home and to pay the tuition of a sister at a fashionable boarding school, who never dreamed that it was tainted.[56]

Mr. Rye fails to particularize the town back East from which the fashionable debutante came from. Could Lottie Deno have stretched the truth? Had a tale of woe been convenient? Those questions are of significance in light of another writer's discoveries. John Warren Hunter, a newspaperman, was not personally acquainted with Lottie Deno, but he was surely interested. While employed by the *San Angelo Standard* Mr. Hunter interviewed persons who claimed to have known Miss Deno or knew someone who had.[57] For a 1910 human interest piece Mr. Hunter wrote that a military man previously stationed at Fort Concho had updated his unnamed historical informant by mentioning that Lottie

> was a woman leading a dual life—a saintly philanthropist in New Orleans, which it was claimed was her home city....that her father, a gallant knight of the Old South and an inveterate gambler, went down on the Alabama off Cherbourg, France and that the money she won at cards went to an invalid mother at Montgomery, Alabama, and to defray the expenses of an only sister at a fashionable boarding school in Virginia, while neither the mother nor sister dreamed that the money for their support bore the taint of iniquity. [58]

That an army officer was privy to her satchel of personal secrets is not surprising. Lottie's tromps from town to town may be tracked. Presumably Miss Lottie Deno had a patriotic affinity for the boys in blue; she followed them from camp to camp. There was no necessity to tell them the truth, though. Inconsistency and mystery would add to the allure. Lottie had a story, and knew how to tell it—selectively.

Nor should it be a great revelation that working-girls on the Western frontiers were practiced at engineering nice background stories. Charles L. "Doc" Sonnichsen learned: "Good-time girls used made-up names to conceal their true identities and they kept no records."[59] Lottie Deno's purported past seems to mesh perfectly. Dr. Sonnichsen also said that "concocted stories about their origins and the circumstances which forced them into a life of sin, and legend always provided a daughter [or sister] in an eastern finishing school who did not know, and would never know, where her mother's [sister's] money came from."[60] Striking even closer to home for the story at hand are the remarks of another writer: "Most Western sisters would invent any kind of story about themselves if it were good for business. A pathetic yarn about being a widow or an orphan might mean extra dollars. If a girl wanted to be superior in a veiled sort of way, she'd drop hints about having been a famous actress. Putting on the Southern drawl always went over with Texans. She might claim to be the daughter of some plantation family ruined by the damnyankees during the Civil War."[61] Gambling girls made up melancholy stories, too! "Since a woman who gambled professionally was considered by conventional nineteenth-century American society to be unfeminine, perhaps even unnatural, most such women chose to conceal their identities or to disseminate contradictory stories regarding their origins and prior lives."[62] Lottie was a conformist.

Purportedly Lottie Deno was interviewed about her past during 1900. What she told or did not tell a twenty-one year old newspaperman is suspect. Also disconcerting is the fact that for 59 years information gleaned from that interview with Lottie about her remarkable childhood and adolescence lay dormant. During the intervening half-century the prolific journalist penned several articles mentioning Lottie Deno, but none make mention of her magnificent Kentucky upbringing or her pre-Texas gambling career. Those assertions were publicly revealed posthumously. In large part those disclosures are what have built the foundation for others choosing to put Lottie Deno's story to paper.

The swirling mist masking the real Lottie Deno is there. Trying to legitimize her every movement with certainty is as elusive as bottling the perfumed fragrance lingering in her absence. Lottie Deno's charming story may be picked up with credibility in Texas. The Old South plantation dreamscape and her acquisition of a "fabulous name on the river boats and in the gambling halls on her route west," is troubling. That part of the story is fascinating, but factually deficient.[63] Scarlett O'Hara is allowed that kind of life. Lottie Deno is not.

Acknowledging Billy the Kid as a real person is easy. The beardless New Mexico gunslinger is an iconic Old West character known throughout the world. Lottie Deno and Billy the Kid share similarities, too: Both have been dipped in the ink well of mythology, and adequate evidence regarding their childhoods is missing. Should that scarcity stop the search for truth, or hold back biography? Frederick Nolan, the preeminent expert on Billy the Kid thinks not. The first chapter in his authoritative *The West of Billy the Kid* is thoughtfully titled "The Kid from Nowhere" for a good reason.[64] Mr. Nolan says:

> Few Americans lives have more successfully resisted research than that of Billy the Kid. It is almost as if he decided at birth to leave behind as little documentary trace as he could of his entry into, and passage through the world. Thus, in spite of a century of effort by a legion of researchers to document his early life, little more is known about him now than was current at the time of his death at Fort Sumner in 1881....It might be pertinent to ask why any of this matters. It might be relevant to propose that even if we knew now exactly where Billy the Kid was born and raised, or indeed, his complete genealogy, it would not add a scintilla to our understanding of him. Yet doubtless the search will go on, and perhaps one day someone will find the answers.[65]

Perhaps too, one day someone will provide all the answers regarding Lottie Deno's mysterious life. Such would be a worthy contribution. Billy the Kid captures attention with his exploits after migrating to New Mexico, a story that may be repeated with certifiable credibility. Lottie Deno's life may be appropriately chronicled after she makes appearances in frontier Texas towns. Billy's and Lottie's charisma stems from deeds and misdeeds in the Wild West, not from where they came. That is sufficient for biography.

Twenty-one years old and anxious to leave New Orleans, Carlotta, yet realizing that someday she'd be called Lottie Deno, directed Mary to begin packing all the fine Parisian fashions for a trip. Carlotta and Mary would be leaving the classy metropolitan lifestyle behind; 1865 Texas was yet untamed. Carlotta donned a nice puffy bodice with a high collar, and a gored skirt. Old South refinements would soon be but a memory. Carlotta would sit before the photographer for a memento. Supposedly!

Endnotes Chapter I

[1] See citations number 2 & 3 in Preface for Carlotta Thompkins' reincarnations into fictional characters.

[2] John E. Kleber, ed., *The Kentucky Encyclopedia*. 934; Carolyn Marksberry, Clerk/Treasurer City of Warsaw, Kentucky, to author February 21, 2006; pamphlets courtesy the Gallatin County Historical Society, Warsaw, Kentucky.

[3] *Certificate of Death*. State of New Mexico—Bureau of Public Health. Number 1459372. New Mexico Vital Records and Health Statistic, Public Health Division, Department of Health. Santa Fe; *Deming Headlight*, February 16, 1934; *Deming Graphic*, February 16, 1934.

[4] The classic—and standard—work on Lottie Deno is J. Marvin Hunter's *The Story of Lottie Deno: Her Life and Times*. Hunter does not identify his subject by the name Carlotta J. Thompkins, and reiterates, "....though she never did tell me her maiden name...." 1; Rose, *Lottie Deno: Gambling Queen of Hearts*. "It was here [Warsaw, Kentucky] that Lottie Deno, christened Carlotta J. Thompkins, was born on April 21, 1844. 13. Rose does have a reasonably sound basis for accepting Thompkins as the family name, although it is far from conclusive. A check with the Public Affairs Office of the Kentucky Legislature produced negative results for establishing Carlotta Thompkin's father as a state lawmaker. Mr. Allan Carter, Historian, National Museum of Racing and Hall of Fame, Saratoga Springs, New York, advised on December 14, 2007, that he could find no evidence of a "Thompkins or Tompkins" being a prominent race horse man for the pre-Civil War time period. Similarly an inquiry to the Jockey Club, Lexington, Kentucky, produced no result to indicate a "Thompkins or Tompkins" as a pre-war racing personality.

[5] Rose, *Lottie Deno: Gambling Queen of Hearts*. "Lottie's father saw to it that his daughters attended one of the area's finest Episcopal convent schools, which was located near the family farm." 13; Ellen Clifford, Archives Assistant, Sisters of Charity of Nazareth, Nazareth, Kentucky, to author February 21, 2006. "I'm sorry, but we don't have Carlotta as a student at Nazareth Academy. Actually, we have no students recorded from Warsaw. And our records for that are very good. I'd be guessing that, if Carlotta was at an academy anywhere, the years likely would be 1854 (age 10) to 1861 (age 17) with the most likely to be at her age of 15 or 16." The letter is not conclusive. There were other academies, but the Sisters of Charity of Nazareth Academy at Bardstown, Kentucky, was the area's "finest." The [Catholic] Academy was founded in 1814.

[6] Rose, *Lottie Deno: Gambling Queen of Hearts*. 13-14.

[7] Ibid; Hunter, *The Story of Lottie Deno*. 2.

[8] Roberta Tidmore Wilcox, "Aunt Lottie." *Password*. Volume XXVII. No. 2 [Summer 1982]

[9] Rose, *Lottie Deno: Gambling Queen of Hearts*. 19.

[10] Hunter, "The Mystery Woman at Fort Concho." *Frontier Times*. January 1927. 1.

[11] Wilcox, "Aunt Lottie." "She told Mother [Susie Tidmore] that she had been wealthy and influential, but that her family had disowned her because they disapproved of her marriage to Mr. Thurmond." 87; Hunter, *The Story of Lottie Deno* asserts "(Lottie told me that she was married in 1866 and that her husband soon after left to make his fortune in the west, promising to send for her.)" 7; Rose, *Lottie Deno: Gambling Queen of Hearts* says that Lottie was disowned by her parents due to a romantic entanglement with a Jewish gambler. 23-24; Hunter's mention of a marriage in 1866 is not supported by citation. Lottie's 1880 marriage to Frank Thurmond is

sustainable through Grant County, New Mexico, marriage records. Lottie's first-person remarks to Mrs. Tidmore, if true, would place the father/daughter discord after the Civil War.

[12] Hunter, *The Story of Lottie Deno.* "After the death of Lottie's father and the loss of the vast plantation with its palatial home during the Civil War, Lottie, being the eldest child of the family was left with the task of making a living for her mother and younger sister." 2.

[13] Ibid; Rose, *Lottie Deno: Gambling Queen of Hearts*, says Carlotta was sent to Detroit, where she could stay with family friends—and find a husband. 20.

[14] Rose, *Lottie Deno: Gambling Queen of Hearts.* 20.

[15] Hunter, *The Story of Lottie Deno*, 2; Rose, *Lottie Deno: Gambling Queen of Hearts.* "Lottie at seventeen was old enough to become head of the household when her mother's health began to fail....Lottie, it was decided, would be sent to Detroit....The two arrived in Detroit sometime during the year 1861...." 19-20.

[16] Ibid. 2.

[17] Ibid.

[18] Ibid. "....she supported the young sister, all the while letting the girl think she was married to a rich man who was a wonderful provider, and was giving her money to keep the sister in school." 3.

[19] Paul O'Neil, *The Rivermen*, 7; John M. Findley, *People Of Chance: Gambling In American Society From Jamestown To Las Vegas.* "In the late 1850s and the 1860s, the emergence of railroads in the Mississippi Valley and the outbreak of the Civil War began to erase many such vestiges of a bygone frontier as river gambling....Railroads started to supplant steamboats as the favored vehicle of transport....They also prompted the construction of bridges spanning the waterways...." 76.

[20] Jim Hicks, ed., *The Gamblers.* "The women's quarters consisted of a 30-foot cabin belowdecks; the men slept in what one early traveler called 'an elegant roundhouse' abovedecks." 51.

[21] Ibid. 52.

[22] Ibid. 60.

[23] Hunter, *The Story of Lottie Deno.* 4.

[24] Jim Marshall, *Swinging Doors.* 43-44.

[25] Findlay, *People of Chance.* 73.

[26] Hunter, *The Story of Lottie Deno.* 3.

[27] Ibid; Rose, *Lottie Deno: The Gambling Queen of Hearts.* "Lottie's father owned slaves, and each of his daughters was assigned a nanny. Lottie's was a seven-foot-tall woman by the name of Mary Poindexter." 14.

[28] Hicks, *The Gamblers.* 61.

[29] Findlay, *People Of Chance.* 72.

[30] Ibid. 73.

[31] Hicks, *The Gamblers.* "The appearance of the professional riverboat gambler was sometimes as crude as his morals." 54.

[32] Ibid. 61.

[33] Robert L. Brown, *Saloons Of The American West.* "On stern-wheeled riverboats, there was usually a ladies' drinking lounge near the back end of one of the decks." 99; Findlay, *People of Chance.* "....women's parlor astern...." 72.

[34] Hunter, *The Story of Lottie Deno.* "....Confederate soldiers, lately of General Lee's army...." 4; Rose, *Lottie Deno: Gambling Queen of Hearts.* "Two Union soldiers...." 28.

[35] This highly unlikely drama is reported by Rose, *Lottie Deno: Gambling Queen of Hearts.* "With her strong arms she picked up the solder, lifted him over her head, and tossed him into the muddy water below." 28; and Hunter, *The Story of Lottie Deno.*

"Mary met him as he rushed in to injure her mistress and gathered him in her powerful arms, with one heave, left him floundering in the muddy waters of the river." 4.

[36] Ibid; Likewise the anecdotal tale is preserved by Hunter in *The Story of Lottie Deno*. 4; Rattlesnake adventures are common in Texas literature, fiction and nonfiction alike. Reportedly the infamous frontier gambler "Rowdy Joe" Lowe killed a "monster" rattlesnake while riding a stagecoach from Luling, Texas, to San Antonio, Texas, see, Lewis Ginger, "Rowdy Joe Lowe, A Character." *Frontier Times*, December 1926. 9; J. Frank Dobie, one of the Southwest's most respected folklorist and historians devoted an entire book to the serpent, *Rattlesnakes;* James A. Michener in his epic novel *Texas* incorporates a rattler "eight feet three inches long from the tip of his rattle and as big around as a small tree" into the story, coming close to making the snake an actual character in the book. 230; N. H. Kincaid in "Saved By A Rattlesnake," *Frontier Times*, February 1948, asserts that a Diamondback inadvertently saved the lives of Oliver Loving and William L. "Bill" Wilson when they were under siege by Comanches on the banks of the Pecos River near present day Carlsbad, New Mexico. "A big rattlesnake, scared up by the Indian, came out rattling, looking back at the redskin. He coiled up near the two men but facing his back trail The Indian, still not having seen his quarry, decided not to force the issue with this new enemy and turned back." 125.

[37] Hunter, *The Story Of Lottie Deno*. "Lottie Deno soon became a fabulous name on the river boats and in the gambling halls on her route west." 4; Rose, *Lottie Deno: Gambling Queen of Hearts*, correctly acknowledges: "Not much is known about Lottie's days on the river." 26.

[38] Hicks, *The Gamblers*. 51.

[39] David Dary, *Seeking Pleasure In The Old West*. 50.

[40] Ibid.

[41] Ibid. 52.

[42] Ibid; Findlay, *People Of Chance*. "The Crescent City had its own waterfront district, the 'Swamp,' located in the Old Quarter of the metropolis...." 59.

[43] Findlay, *People Of Chance*. 59-60.

[44] Ibid.

[45] Dary, *Seeking Pleasure In The Old West*. 53.

[46] Findlay, *People Of Chance*. 60.

[47] Marshall, *Swinging Doors*. 42.

[48] Dary, *Seeking Pleasure In The Old West*, quoting Estwick Evans' "A Pedestrious Tour, of Four Thousand Miles, Through the Western States and Territories, During the Winter and Spring of 1818," as found in Reuben Gold Thwaites' 1904 *Early Western Travels 1784-1846*. 11.

[49] Hunter, *The Story of Lottie Deno*. 4.

[50] Ibid.

[51] Rose, *Lottie Deno: Gambling Queen Of Hearts*. 28.

[52] W. J. Cash, *The Mind of the South*. ix.

[53] For a discussion of false impression regarding the Old South, see, Darden Asbury Pyron, *Southern Daughter: The Life of Margaret Mitchell*. 308-336.

[54] Ibid. 312.

[55] Edgar Rye, *The Quirt and the Spur: Vanishing Shadows Of The Texas Frontier*. From the *Afterword* by Charles Linck: "As soon as a rancher sited the new Shackelford County seat at Albany to counter the troubled Fort Griffin area, Rye in 1877 wangled and appointment as Justice of the Peace, probably exploiting his legal experience back in Cincinnati." 336.

[56] Ibid. 70-71; Interestingly in light of the modern era mythology, in Don Hampton Biggers' *Shackelford County Sketches* there is no mention of Lottie Deno.

[57] John Warren Hunter [J. Marvin Hunter, ed.], "The Mystery Woman at Ft. Concho." *Frontier Times* January 1927. 1-3; Reprinted in the 1947 *West Texas Historical Association Yearbook.* "In the issue of *Frontier Times* for January, 1927, I published a short article about 'The Mystery Woman of Fort Concho,' written by my father, John Warren Hunter, in 1910. Father was at that time on the editorial staff of the San Angelo Standard, and gathered his information about the 'mystery woman' from old timers who were living there at the time the incidents mentioned took place." 30.

[58] Ibid. "….and some credence attached to the statement of one of the officers at the post [Fort Concho] to the effect that she [Lottie Deno] was a woman leading a dual life…."

[59] H. Gordon Frost, *The Gentlemen's Club: The Story of Prostitution In El Paso.* From the *Introduction* by C. L. Sonnichsen. 9.

[60] Ibid.

[61] Philip Rainman, "The Legend Of Lottie Deno." *The West.* December. 1965. 19 and 58.

[62] Robert K. DeArment, *Knights Of The Green Cloth: She Saga of the Frontier Gamblers.* "Many used assumed names. Some, like Belle Siddons, to confound the curious even more, adopted different names in different towns." 257.

[63] The basis for assigning Lottie Deno a birthplace of Warsaw, Kentucky, derives from her *Certificate of Death* on file in New Mexico. That Lottie had rather colorfully invented her past is probable. Notoriously inexact US Census records tender more than one alluring possibility for identifying Carlotta Thompkins—if indeed that was her real name—but in each and every case roadblocks stand in the way of any unconditional findings. Also see endnotes 4 and 5 this text.

[64] Frederick Nolan, *The West of Billy the Kid.* 3-6.

[65] Ibid.

Chapter 2

"What's in a Name—or Photograph?"

Housekeeping chores are drudgery, but necessary. At the moment digressing from Carlotta's chronological story is disagreeable, but must be done. Earlier it was mentioned that Carlotta Thompkins was a girl of many names. It is important to explore this phenomena; girls of the Old West having more than one name. Also, many enthusiasts of nonfiction Western literature believe they more-or-less know Lottie Deno. This is a result of several previously published photographs. These may be delightful images, but connecting them to Carlotta Thompkins, aka Lottie Deno, requires an impartial study. Provenance for the photographs is uncertain.

An alias is an assumed name. It is a fraudulent *nom de plume* taken upon one's self purposefully, forsaking the Christian name bestowed by parents. The alias is worn with consent. Rationales for donning an assumed name are countless; running from the law, sidestepping humiliation or shame, hiding from a spouse or ex-spouse, protecting the family's good name; avoiding payment of debts, or even an overdose of pure vanity. Wrapping themselves in veils of anonymity many young ladies reinvented themselves and ventured west during the 19th-Century. It would have been commonplace for Martha Osborne, carrying a valise packed with frilly unmentionables, to timidly buy a ticket at St. Louis and self-assuredly step out of stagecoach at Denver, Deadwood or Dallas as Maggie O'Riley. Burying the past in secrecy were shared threads for women's adoption

> of pseudonyms, a habit not unuseful, as it was a period when your right name, the region you came from and the reason you were not there now were all distinctly your affair.[1]

Even as this story is being written an article about a 21st-Century crime and its female participants is illustrative. A southwestern New Mexican, a lady herself, told an inquiring newsman writing for the *Albuquerque Journal*: "In these parts, we don't ask questions. You can be an outlaw here and do your own thing."[2]

Many silver screen stars have forsaken their real names. Bronco Billy Anderson who debuted in the first Western, *The Great Train Robbery*, was in fact Max Aronson. The Western hero of heroes, John Wayne, was actually Marion Michael Morrison. Name transitions were not limited to men. In real life she was Greta Lovisa Gustafson, but the movie-going public knew her as Greta Garbo.[3] Needless to say when Alfred Henry Lewis' *Wolfville* novels appeared on the market and the fictionalized Western heroine Faro Nell was born, the central character of this story, using her own name, was not in search of notoriety's spotlight.

An alias served a purpose. A nickname, unlike an alias, was not meant to disguise but to describe. Nicknames are awarded without permission. They are, however, often accepted without protest or too much objection.

Old West history flaunts numerous examples of men's colorful nicknames.[4] The American Southwest was flooded with fellows known best by their inherited handles. Men such as 'Mormon Bill', 'Two-Belt Johnny', 'Shoot-Em-Up-Dick', 'Slap-Jack Jim', 'Johnny-Behind-the-Deuce', 'Hair-Trigger Johnnie', 'Sore-Eyed-Kid', 'Dutch Joe', 'Jim the Banty', 'Sammy Behind the Gun', and Jimmy 'Sweetheart of the San Simon' Hughes, just to name a few—a very few.

The feminine gender wasn't overshadowed.[5] Mentioning but a meager sampling would include such *ladies* as 'Squirrel Tooth Alice', 'Sorrel Mike', 'Silver Heels', 'Russian Rose', 'Irish Kate', 'No Nose Maggie', 'Dirty Neck Nell', 'Snuff Box Annie', 'Yellowstone Nell', Minnie 'Dirty Alice' Smith, and Lucy 'Legs' Coronne, "a tall, stylish, good looking dame of French extraction."

Carlotta Thompkins also had a nickname, Lottie Deno. It was not a name she picked out. So far there is no reason to think she passed herself off as Lottie Deno. If Lottie Deno didn't create or even use the name herself, and if frontier newspaper editors were stingy with its use, where did the nickname come from?

"Lottie" would not be an uncommon and everyday used derivative for the first names of Charlotte, Charlotta or Carlotta; all of which our Miss Deno has been referred to in both primary and secondary writings; and by necessity such will be the case for this text. Where did the nickname stem from?

> Lottie was successful in her profession, so successful, in fact, that other gamblers took to calling her 'Lotta Deniro'.[6]

On the surface such an apocryphal origin does seem quite farfetched. The Spanish word *dinero* does translate into the word "money" for English usage.[7] The frequent intermixing and amalgamation of Mexican words into the everyday vocabulary of Southwesterners is routine. *Amigo, bandido, fandango, hombre, pronto*, and *siesta* are words that do not need translation.

Was "Lottie Deno" a bastardization of "Lotta Dinero?" The intriguing question cannot be answered. There is a clue that sparks the possibility. In exaggerated writings about Lottie Deno it is often downplayed or sometimes even omitted, but the "Gambling Queen of Hearts" did have an arrest record in Texas. For some of those criminal filings she is not identified as "Lottie Deno," but "Lotta Deno."[8] "Lotta Deno" appears more than once in the court's docket book. The suggestion that Lottie Deno might have been an abridgment from the suggestive characterization "Lotta Dinero" is fascinating.

Carlotta did not refer to herself as Lottie Deno.[9] It was an ingenious appellation that others applied to her, even in those legal documents. It seems that Carlotta did not object to the nickname. Southwestern history knows the gambling girl as Lottie Deno, for that there's no argument. And for this story, so, too, will she be known.

More troubling than a nickname is the much publicized photograph depicting a young Lottie Deno. A lesser circulated photo which is claimed to be the image of an even younger Lottie Deno is also suspect. According to experts neither of the photographs are of Lottie Deno. A third picture is represented to be a color photo of a quite young Lottie Deno. To this writer's knowledge that photograph has yet to be published. Despite an artful touchup the image, now hanging in a Texas Hill Country museum, will not pass muster. It is not Lottie Deno either.

Normally witnesses may testify to what they observed, heard, or did, but their personal opinions are generally inadmissible. Such is not the case for testimony rendered by a person the judge has qualified and recognized as an "expert."

> If scientific, technical, or other specialized knowledge will assist the trier of fact to understand the evidence or to determine a fact in issue, a witness qualified as an expert by knowledge, skill, experience, training, or education, may testify thereto in the form of an opinion or otherwise.[10]

Experts have made impartial examinations regarding the supposed photographic images of a young Lottie Deno. Their independent conclusions are in accord. The evidence is overwhelming. It rises well beyond any level of reasonable doubt. Certainly such is the case in this writer's mind. Readers may also evaluate credentials qualifying the experts, weigh their objective opinions, and reach their own conclusions about those findings.

The first mentioned photograph of an appealingly youthful Lottie Deno appeared in Mr. J. Marvin Hunter's *The Story of Lottie Deno: Her Life and Times* published posthumously in 1959 by The 4

Hunters, the children of Mr. Hunter.[11] The photograph portrays the alleged Lottie Deno sitting on the edge of an ornate wooden chair, coifed hair peeking from a flower adorned hat, and wearing a fashionable dress. Correlating the age of the person depicted with the clothing is revealing. Miss Lottie Deno was a teenager at the outbreak of the Civil War and is photographically depicted in Mr. Hunter's book wearing clothing that did not come into vogue until the subsequent century. Nineteenth-century and early 20th-Century fashion expert Ms Robin Gilliam-Crawford, Curator, National Ranching Heritage Center, Texas Tech University, Lubbock, Texas, and a working historic consultant for the Public Broadcasting System was interviewed. She declared that "absolutely" and "positively" the young woman in the photograph could not possibly be Lottie Deno if she indeed were a Civil War era teen. Clothing in the photograph is irrefutably classic after the turn of the century formal wear.[12] Lottie would have had to be well passed her middle-aged years, well into her late fifties or early sixties when she posed for the photographer. The person in the photo is not of that age bracket.

The professional opinion of specialist Robin Gilliam-Crawford is buttressed by another authority on frontier-period fashion, Evelyn Lemons, Historian, Fort Concho National Historic Landmark, San Angelo, Texas. Based on the same formula—probing the connection between age and fashion—expert Lemons' deduction is identical to that of Ms Gilliam-Crawford; the Lottie Deno of historical note is not the person depicted in the frequently used photograph, the one on the cover of Mr. Hunter's book and on the front cover of another volume, *Lottie Deno: Gambling Queen of Hearts* by Cynthia Rose.[13]

A third knowledgeable historic consultant, Susan Berry, Director, Silver City Museum, Silver City, New Mexico, confirms: "The clothing worn by the person typically identified as Lottie Deno on the covers of Hunter's and Rose's books is not time appropriate."[14]

Mr. J. Marvin Hunter's book on Lottie Deno has no provenance or authentication regarding the questionable photograph. The charming image of a beautiful young girl was straightforwardly captioned "Lottie Deno" and, as such, it has time and time again been reproduced and so identified. Though not a bona fide image of the actual Lottie Deno, the photo has gained universal acceptance. Subsequent nonfiction writers have used but not questioned the photograph. From the best evidence at hand it appears that the simple misidentification was inadvertent, and not an intentional act of duplicity—knowingly passing off a photograph of someone who J. Marvin Hunter knew it really was not. There is not a scintilla of evidence to sustain any assertion of deception. It must be remembered that Mr. Hunter passed away on June 29, 1957, and *The Story of Lottie Deno: Her Life and Times* was not published until

1959. The publishers, Hunter's four children, by their own admission did themselves not do the painstaking research, but amassed their father's voluminous reams of written material and photographs into a publishable manuscript; one "with the exception of a few coordinating passages" which were already completed by their father before "death stilled the hand that had written so many authoritative accounts of frontier history."[15]

Equally noteworthy is the other photograph purporting to be a studio portrait of Lottie Deno, a strikingly good-looking young girl wearing a rather large and elaborately plumed hat. As far as this author knows the photograph first appeared in Robert Thomas' article "Lady Luck" for a 1983 edition of *Ranch Magazine*. Thomas' skillfully composed caption for the photo is imprecise, purposefully, but adding to that, historically flawed. His footer for the replicated image was: "Is this the woman Lottie Deno? This photo, from the Ragsdale Collection at Fort Concho, was taken about the time Lottie was gambling in the San Angelo area."[16] Mr. Thomas—absent a shred of provenance—wisely steered around an absolute declaration that the photograph was of our mysterious Lottie Deno. His remark that the photograph was of a time when Lottie was partaking of the area's games of chance is faulty.

Eleven years later another writer did not even try to skirt the issue. Rose's volume *Lottie Deno: Gambling Queen of Hearts* published in 1994, carried the same photograph with an unadulterated declaration: "Lottie Deno as she looked at Fort Griffin, Texas, in the 1870s."[17] The source citation for the charming photograph is "Fort Concho National Historic Landmark, San Angelo, Texas."[18] The aforementioned Ms Evelyn Lemons, the Fort Concho National Historic Landmark's full-time professional historian was interviewed at San Angelo regarding the photograph's provenance. Ms Lemons reported that the photograph in question was most certainly one from their archival collection, but that for years it had been marked "unknown female." Sometime during the early 1990s an unidentified person visiting the Fort Concho National Historic Landmark asked to see the museum's old photographs. Upon finding this particular image it was declared, "That's Lottie Deno!" As far as Ms Lemons knows, there was not then—nor is there now a link guaranteeing the veracity of a claim, "That's Lottie Deno!"[19] In fact, it is not Lottie Deno! Not according to Curator Robin Gilliam-Crawford, at Texas Tech University, and Director Susan Berry at Silver City's eminent museum. Using the technique of trying to reconcile Lottie Deno's known age with the clothing, hat and hairdo depicted in the photograph leaves but one conclusion. Since the representative fashion statements were most likely—according to the experts—post 1910 creations, the young girl in the photograph could have been born in the 1840s, sixty plus years earlier.

The search for an authentic early photograph of Lottie Deno goes on. The fashion experts have also scrutinized another alleged youthful image of our biographic subject. This photograph is prominently hanging in the Frontier Times Museum at Bandera, Texas. Noticed by its absence is provenance for this photograph. It, too, is not a picture of Lottie Deno.

Painstaking examination of period clothing is a dependably effective method for dating photographs. Such methodology is exemplified in the dazzlingly researched 592 page volume *Dressed for the Photographer: Ordinary Americans And Fashions, 1840-1900* by one of the renowned authorities on 19th-Century apparel, Joan L. Severa:

> Over the last thirty years, some historians have expanded the definition of historical evidence, going beyond written documents to include material culture—objects and images—including photographs. With these new types of evidence being considered, historians have developed new methodologies to deal with them. As a rule, most objects seem to be best understood when placed in a historical context. For example, we can speculate most confidently about a photographic portrait when we know its date, the identities of the sitter and the photographer, the circumstances under which it was taken, and the expectation of the audience for whom it was made. When these facts are known, portraits may reveal a great deal. However, this leaves a very large mass of anonymous photographic portraits of unknown sitters by unknown makers under unknown circumstances and at unknown times. Considering the dearth of context, can these images, which account for the vast majority of those extant, ever be made meaningful? There is, in fact, one element in these images that can be identified; the clothing the sitter is wearing.[20]

Maureen A. Taylor, author of *Uncovering Your Ancestry Through Family Photographs*, an active member of the American Society of Picture Professionals, the former Librarian of the New England Historic Genealogical Society and the Rhode Island Historical Society, and *the* 'Photo Detective' for *Family Tree Magazine* graciously made an impartial analysis of the suspect Lottie Deno photographs.

According to Ms Taylor the girl's photo taken from Hunter's *The Story of Lottie Deno: Her Life and Times* depicts a person attired in clothing reminiscent of a turn-of-the-century era. That is not consistent with what Lottie Deno would have been wearing, had she been sitting for the photographer at an early age.[21] Unequivocally the photograph is not Lottie Deno.

The photograph of a gorgeous young girl captioned "Lottie Deno as she looked at Fort Griffin, Texas in the 1870s" reproduced in Mrs. Rose's *Lottie Deno: Gambling Queen of Hearts* is even more worrisome. The subject of that darling depiction is making a fashion statement suggestive of 1910 [or later], and, too, it is unconditionally not a photographic image of the real Lottie Deno, not according to Ms Taylor. When that particular photo was made, according to the clothing, Lottie Deno would have been in her mid-seventies, exhibiting her gray hair and flabby jowls as she appears in later pictures of unassailable provenance.[22] The supposed Lottie Deno image displayed at Frontier Times Museum may be discarded by use of the same methodology.

Distinguished fashion/photograph expert, Leslie A. Bellais, Curator of Costume and Textiles, Wisconsin Historical Society, made an examination of the dubious Lottie Deno photographs. She reported her findings:

> Those who have looked at these images before are correct—all of them date between 1900 and 1912.
>
> Image # 1: 1906-1908 [Hunter, *Story of Lottie Deno: Her Life and Times*]
> Image # 2: 1910-1912 [Rose, *Lottie Deno: Gambling Queen of Hearts*]
> Image # 3: 1903-1905 ["Lottie Deno," Frontier Times Museum]
>
> Just in case you want to know what dates each image, here is what I'm seeing.
>
> Image #1: The puffy bodice with high collar, the gored skirt (tight at the hips, full at the hem), and the lightweight, lacy fabric put this dress between 1898-1908. However the puffy sleeves were only worn with this style between 1906 and 1908. Earlier the puffiness would have been at the wrist. By 1909 the puff had almost completely disappeared. I did notice in the 1907 Sears we have that pleated skirts are available. They are out of style by 1909.

Image #2: This is the style that immediately follows the fashion of image #1. The look is columnar topped by an extra large hat. This style was introduced in 1908-1909 and was worn to about 1912-1913. It is unlikely to be the early years because the suit coat has no puff at the sleeve.

Image #3: This is essentially the same style as in image #1, except note the top of the sleeves. There is no puff and the bodice's yoke continues onto the top of the sleeve. This widened yoke was worn from 1903-1905.

An overall comment: All 3 women are wearing stand-up collars about 3" tall. This collar is not worn before 1898.[23]

These authorities' expert conclusions are consistent: These photographs are not images of a youthful Lottie Deno. Even more reason for questioning the two images' authenticity is found when comparing them together, one against the other.

Several years ago in a piece written for *Trails End Magazine*, much to the author's credit, origin of the two photographs mistakenly tendered as a youthful Lottie Deno were questioned; and appropriately so. That the photos were of Lottie Deno was improbable because of the "1890s and early teens" clothing, and dissimilarity of the subjects' physical features: "Examination by a police facial expert suggests they may not even be the same person." For this article the "police facial expert" was not identified.

The questionable photographs of an alleged Lottie Deno were presented to an alternative expert, an individual with impressive credentials in another discipline. Shirley Timmons is that expert. Though now recently retired after twenty-six years service with the Texas Department of Public Safety, Ms Timmons honored this author—and the reader—with her expert opinions. As a forensic artist assigned to the famed Texas Rangers, the state's investigative arm for major criminal investigations, Ms Timmons is a person well-qualified to turn to for such matters. Shirley Timmons is a court certified expert in her chosen field. Therefore she is permitted under the state's Rules of Criminal Procedure to offer opinions of her findings. In a nutshell Shirley Timmons' scientific specialties are these; postmortem reconstruction of facial features; forensic age progression analysis [how facial features change as a person ages]; and development of the sketch of a suspect through interpretive questioning of victims and/or witnesses. In other words, drawing an identifiable portrait of the unknown bad guy—or girl, so that an arrest may be made.

Ms Timmons' unequivocally stated that the photograph on the front cover of Hunter's *The Story of Lottie Deno: Her Life and Times* and the representation utilized by Rose, allegedly depicting "Lottie Deno as she looked at Fort Griffin, Texas, in the 1870s," in the book *Lottie Deno: Gambling Queen of Hearts*, are absolutely and positively not photographic images of the same person. Ms Timmons' conclusions are decisive. We now know who the two popularized photographs are not. They are certainly not Lottie Deno.

Rhetorically the same essayist who penned the *Trails End Magazine* article ponders: "Where did J. Marvin Hunter get the photos? Probably not from Lottie in her lifetime. Then who identified them as Lottie?"[24]

Asserting J. Marvin Hunter did not come into possession of the misidentified photograph through the auspices of Lottie Deno is too categorical. That same writer said: "A young writer named J. Marvin Hunter contacted Lottie around 1900. He gathered information from her about the old days...."[25] The source for J. Marvin Hunter's acquisition of the popularized photograph has not been determined, and likely never will be. It is conceivable that the disputed image was furnished to Mr. Hunter by Lottie, it just was not a photograph of her. Is it also feasible that someone else furnished Mr. Hunter the photograph? Was Mr. Hunter told it was a photo of Lottie Deno? Regardless, the photograph first appearing in *Ranch Magazine* and then subsequently used by Ms Rose for *Lottie Deno: Gambling Queen of Hearts* has also been misidentified. There is an unyielding bottom line: There are to date no known published photographs of the so-called Gambling Queen of Hearts, Miss Lottie Deno, not at a time while she was a young lady in her poker playing prime. Later in life Lottie Deno willingly stood before the camera on numerous occasions. Several of those photographs have been previously published, a few more are herein included for the first time.

From *The Story of Lottie Deno: Her Life and Times* by J. Marvin Hunter. Identified in this chapter as image #1. This photograph is typically reproduced and identified as Miss Lottie Deno. Unfortunately it is not. *Courtesy Hunter Family.*

Note the striking fashion similarities with image #1. This properly identified photograph is of the 1901 female graduates at Deming, New Mexico Territory. *Courtesy Sylvia Ligocky and the Deming/Luna Mimbres Museum.*

For this chapter the image is catalogued as image #2. This photograph was used by Cynthia Rose in *Lottie Deno: Gambling Queen of Hearts* and captioned: "Lottie Deno as she looked at Fort Griffin, Texas, in the 1870s." Unfortunately it, too, is not a photograph of Miss Lottie Deno. *Courtesy Fort Concho National Historic Landmark.*

Note the remarkable comparison with image #2. This properly identified photograph is of Isabel Lopez Lucero and was made during 1918. The clothing and hat are near identical to the misidentified image #2. *Courtesy Augustin V. Lopez.*

Identified in this chapter as image #3. This color retouched photograph is hanging in the Frontier Times Museum, Bandera, Texas, and is identified as Miss Lottie Deno. Once again—unfortunately—it is not a photograph of Miss Deno. *Author's photo, courtesy Frontier Times Museum.*

Endnotes Chapter 2

[1] J. Marvin Hunter, ed., "Picturesque Characters Among Women of Wild West." *Frontier Times.* Volume 9. No. 12 [September 1932]. 559. Reprint of an article carried in the *Kansas City Star,* January 20, 1932.
[2] *Albuquerque Journal,* January 28, 2007.
[3] Jay Hyams, *The Life And Times Of The Western Movie.* 20, 40; Mario DeMarco, "Bronco Billy Anderson." *Real West.* September 1973. "Anderson's real name was Max Aronson and he was born in Pine Bluff, Arkansas in 1883…He decided that westerns were for him and adopted the name 'Broncho Billy' as a continuing character. Later he dropped the 'h', making the name Bronco Billy." 32.
[4] Robert K. DeArment, "Western Lore—Badmen of the Wild and Woolly West had a handle on some of the more colorful nicknames." *Wild West.* June 2003. 10, 72-73. Another insightful article which highlights many Old West characters' colorful nicknames may be found in Mr. DeArment's "The Outlaws of Clifton, Arizona Territory." *National Association For Outlaw and Lawman History* [NOLA] *Quarterly.* Volume XXVII. No. 1. January-March 2003. 35-38.
[5] The nicknames herein cited were principally taken from four sources; Anne M. Butler's *Daughters of Joy, Sisters of Misery: Prostitutes in the American West, 1865-90;* Jay Moynahan's *Talkin' About Sportin' Women: A Dictionary of Terms Related to Prostitution on the American Frontier,* the same author's series of books, *Fifty Years of Prostitute Photos, 1870-1920* [Vols. I, II, III] and Anne Seagraves' *Soiled Doves: Prostitution In The Early West;* Michael Rutter, *Upstairs Girls: Prostitution in the American West,* takes a position that the working girls nicknamed themselves as a means of advertisement and so their customers would remember them: "Like most red light girls, a nickname was more than a nickname; it helped her maintain anonymity and protect her family. It was also an important advertising tool…but prostitutes often chose nicknames that their male customers would remember." 148, 150. Many of the *nymphs du pave* had less than complementary nicknames, and it's more than just a little difficult to imagine a girl—even a working-girl—naming herself 'Nellie the Pig', 'Sadie Sow', 'Galloping Cow', or 'Sloppy Sue', whores specifically identified from Rutter's listing on page 202. Common sense would seem to dictate that derogatory nicknames were passed out by the customers and saloon crowd, rather than self-selected.
[6] Preston Lewis, "Lottie Deno, Gambler." *True West.* September 1987. 19; Robert K. DeArment, "John Shanssey: From Prize Ring To Politics." *True West.* March 1999. "They began calling her 'Lotta Dinero' in [Fort] Griffin." 27.
[7] Peter Watts, *A Dictionary of the Old West.* 114; *Webster's Spanish-English/English-Spanish Dictionary.* 85, 190; J. Frank Dobie, *Coronado's Children.* Glossary of Mexican and Other Localisms of the Southwest: "*dinero:* money." 325.
[8] *The State of Texas vs. Lotta Deno.* Criminal Case Number 26: "Keeping a disorderly house." Shackelford County Criminal Docket Book—November 5th, 1877. Shackelford County Courthouse, Albany, Texas. Additional examination of courthouse documents again reveals usage of the first name "Lotta," indicating it was not haphazardly penned—nor are the handwritten entries difficult to read. Certain subsequent filings utilize "Lottie's" real name, or at least the one commonly accepted as being her maiden name.
[9] Though there's no down-to-earth evidence that Carlotta Thompkins ever referred to herself as Lottie Deno, there was a piece written in 1946 that said: "Pausing only long enough to see about her baggage, she walked into the hotel. The lobby was empty

except for the sleeping clerk. She stood looking at her surroundings for a moment; then rousing the clerk, she registered. After she had gone to her room, the curious clerk glanced at the register book. In a neat hand was written Lottie Deno. She gave no address." See, *The Junior Historian*, Volume VII, Number 3, December 1946, "The Saga Of Lottie Deno" by Millie Gene Lipscomb, Albany [Texas] High School. 1.

[10] State of Texas, *Rules of Criminal Evidence*, "Opinions and Expert Testimony" Article VII, Rule 702; Sue Titus Reid *Criminal Law*: "Expert Testimony—Opinion evidence given at a trial by a person who possesses technical knowledge or skill that is both relevant to the case and not possessed by the average person." 431.

[11] James A. Browning and Janice B. McCravy *A Complete Guide To Hunter's Frontier Times*. "His [J. Marvin Hunter, Sr.] last book, *The Story of Lottie Deno*, was published after his death by my brother and sisters and me. I [J. Marvin Hunter, Jr.] printed it in my print shop at Grand Prairie [Texas]." x. Fascinatingly, Ty Cashion wrote a 1995 [October] article for *Journal of the West* titled "Rewriting the Wild West for a New History." Mr. Cashion, in referring to Hunter's *The Story of Lottie Deno: Her Life and Times* said: "Over the years, the legend of this so-called mystery lady grew with the speculation attending her life at Fort Griffin. In 1959, *Frontier Times* editor J. Marvin Hunter gathered the accumulated litany of heresay and lore into a biography. His readiness to pass off obvious tall tales as fact cost him the respect of fellow historian Don Biggers, who accused Hunter of 'garbling' some Deno-related information to which he appended 'a whole bunch of wild fiction.'" 57. Unfortunately Mr. Cashion's remarks are only partly true. Indeed it was J. Marvin Hunter that published *The Story of Lottie Deno: Her Life and Times*," but it was Jr. rather than Sr. The implication that Mr. Biggers disapproved of the senior Mr. Hunter's treatment of Lottie Deno may be traced to a 1941 letter, not the 1959 release of the purported biography of Lottie. When that book was released both Mr. Don Hampton Biggers and Mr. J. Marvin Hunter, Sr. were long dead. Insight about the 1938 tiff between Mr. Biggers and Mr. Hunter may be found in *Buffalo Guns & Barbed Wire: Two Frontier Accounts by Don Hampton Biggers*. 216. Interestingly, from the same title a biography of Biggers is included, written by Seymour V. Connor. Of the disagreement between Biggers and Hunter, Mr. Connor writes: "In Hunter's behalf it should be noted that he had known a Mrs. Charlotte Thurmond who he believed was the famed Lottie Deno. His posthumously published *The Story of Lottie Deno* (Bandera, 1959) is sufficient evidence that he did not rely wholly on Biggers' article for his information about the woman." 237, n. 67. Two other salient facts are noteworthy. First, from the Introduction of *Buffalo Guns & Barbed Wire* prominent writer A. C. Greene points out: "Sometimes these editors were unfair. Biggers certainly was, especially in his later, political writings, frequently going back and forth across the boundaries of fairness and balance. Even friends suffered. Biggers had no use for tact if called on for an opinion." Secondly, and most interestingly, Biggers makes no mention whatsoever of Lottie Deno in his frequently cited tome, *Shackelford County Sketches* [Edited & Annotated by Joan Farmer]. The obvious omission would imply that Miss Deno may not have actually achieved status as the Southwest's greatest poker playing princess, certainly not the gambling gal characterized in the 20th-Century mythology.

[12] Interview by author with Robin Gillam-Crawford, Curator, National Ranching Heritage Center, Texas Tech University, Lubbock, Texas, on May 5th, 2006, at Lubbock, Texas.

[13] Interview by author with Evelyn Lemons, Historian, Fort Concho National Historic Landmark, San Angelo, Texas, on May 4th, 2006, at San Angelo, Texas.

[14] Interview by author with Susan Berry, Director, Silver City Museum, Silver City, New Mexico, on May 6th, 2006, at Silver City, New Mexico.

[15] J. Marvin Hunter, *The Story of Lottie Deno: Her Life and Times*. iii.

[16] Robert Thomas, "Lady Luck." *Ranch Magazine*. August 1983. 22.

[17] Rose, *Lottie Deno: Gambling Queen of Hearts*. 61.

[18] Ibid.

[19] Interview with Evelyn Lemons, as cited.

[20] Joan L. Severa, *Dressed for the Photographer: Ordinary Americans And Fashion, 1840-1900*. From the *Forward* by Claudia Brush Kidwell, with Nancy Rexford. ix. The interested reader might also find helpful *How the West Was Worn: Bustles and Buckskins on the Wild Frontier* by Chris Enss. This popular type book "explores how changes in fashion ran alongside the changing western United States." 3.

[21] Maureen A. Taylor, Boston, Massachusetts, to David Fryxell, Publisher, Gila Books, Silver City, New Mexico, May 20, 2006.

[22] Ibid.

[23] Leslie Bellais, Curator of Costume & Textiles, Wisconsin Historical Society, Madison, Wisconsin to author, Maypearl, Texas, May 23, 2006.

[24] Bergdale, "Lottie Deno: Queen of the Pasteboards." 75

[25] Ibid. 29.

Chapter 3

"She Took Her Place as Queen"

Making the final leg of the trip by stagecoach Carlotta Thompkins and Mary Poindexter rolled into San Antonio on the first day of June 1865.[1] For the enchanted story it is alleged, just as she had done in New Orleans, that Carlotta Thompkins' arrival in San Antonio "caused a furor," because of her "beautiful dark red hair and sparkling brown eyes were enough to turn any man's head...."[2] To suggest that Miss Carlotta Thompkins didn't turn heads would be petty—actually catty—but adorning her with a crown of sentimentality is inappropriate. Of the lady's stay at San Antonio it has been written:

> She soon became an elite member of the social set, and was a frequent patron of the theater and attended many fine entertainments in Casino Hall where she enjoyed the rich theatrical performances of that time. These were brilliant affairs in which she took her place as queen.[3]

There is a chronological point where the biographical haze circling Carlotta Thompkins can be shooed away with exactness, but it is not at San Antonio during the 1860s. There is worth associated with carrying the frequently repeated tale forward. It provides salient insight into how repetitive storytelling may sometimes distort history. Regardless of the paucity of solid primary evidence or even an employment of sound logic, Carlotta Thompkins' stopover at San Antonio—if it took place at all— makes for an enjoyable first-rate story. It also underscores the plight so common to single women finding themselves alone and utterly destitute on America's western frontiers.

Carlotta was ensconcing herself in the finest social circles that Reconstruction era San Antonio had to offer. Mary Poindexter was availing herself of the pains, pleasures, and publicity of the city's sordid-sided economy. Mary began associating with known police characters such as Sarah Porter, Nelly Stanley, Annie Holland, Sally Randall, Caroline Lee, Susan Runnels, Mary Cochran, Mary Wall and most tellingly for Carlotta Thompkins' profile, Jenny Thurmond.[4] Mary became "increasingly involved with the local community of freed slaves." Several of those girls were actually "gang leaders" who trained orphaned or wayward children in the knack of thievery.[5] Carlotta Thompkins as the biographical model for such a delightful Texas saga would not lower herself to that rung of commonality; socializing with San Antonio's working-girls or their pimps. Much less would Carlotta involve herself in the "street fights" like her one-time friend and confidant Mary Poindexter.[6] Carlotta and Mary parted company.[7] One a darling of the city's privileged elite, the other but a shameful example of decadence and despair. The "Angel of San Antonio," as Carlotta was now being known, was on a mission.[8] It was not to roll on the cobble stone streets in a hair-pulling brawl; nor was it to roll in the hay with some lowly enlisted man far from home or a lonely cowboy come to town riding a whirlwind of self-indulgence. Sinking to that level would be counterproductive. Carlotta had dreams and aspirations. But a girl did what she had to do! Was Carlotta Thompkins pushed down the road to San Antonio because of unhappy circumstances beyond her management? Was she a disobedient daughter, a near penniless waif running away from home? Was she just a free spirited girl with a devil-may-care touch of wanderlust? Or, did she saunter into San Antonio seeking what so many of her contemporaries were looking for, the good life with its appended trimmings? Evidence reveals that Carlotta Thompkins, at least during her several years on the Texas frontier, was many things. She was sassy, stubborn and self-reliant. Regardless of any uncontrollable or unfortunate situation, Carlotta Thompkins was chasing dollars.

There is not confirmation to substantiate it [to this author's knowledge], but often it is written that Carlotta underwent her name change and became Lottie Deno while eking out a livelihood at San Antonio.[9] The gist of this part of the story is not to belabor the point about what to call her, but to examine the legend, which sprouted its Texas roots in 1865 San Antonio. Quite eloquently it has been written:

> After several months in San Antonio, Lottie's first appearance in a gambling hall was on October 25, 1865, at the Cosmopolitan Saloon. She created a never-to-be-forgotten picture when she arrived, dressed in the finest style of that day, followed by Mary Poindexter [prior to them irrevocably separating]. Mary, being a negro, was allowed to sit behind Lottie's chair during the evening, much to the chagrin of Lottie's gambling companions. Lottie's dexterity in handling the cards soon won her the respect of the biggest gamblers in San Antonio and she was welcome companion at many tables. Her grace and beauty soon opened the doors for her everywhere, and her refinement and good breeding brought her fame and untold success.[10]

Another decidedly skilled writer picks up J. Marvin Hunter's drumbeat:

By then her well-honed dexterity with the cards, not to mention her alluring looks and stylish dress, was bringing men to her table and money to the satchel she carried solely to hold her winnings. Winning not only the money but also the respect of local professionals, Lottie progressed through a series of San Antonio gambling houses, including the Cosmopolitan Saloon, Comanche Club, Jockey Club, and Vaudeville Saloon, until she had a regular table at the University Club. Owned and operated by the Thurmond brothers, the University Club was San Antonio's most prestigious gambling house, attracting bankers, businessmen and cattlemen, many of them as interested in winning her heart as her money.[11]

A remark that the twenty-something gambling queen's success at the gaming tables went "untold" is true. Contemporary newspapermen and social column writers failed to take notice.[12] For Lottie's San Antonio venture old-timers' remembrances—the typescripts and oral histories—remain silent, too. Such a beautiful and stylish poker playing princess raking in the greenbacks and gold coins while spurning dreamy overtures and breaking hearts was overlooked. Later, after she had moved on down the line to other frontier gambling centers, the claims of first-hand acquaintanceship will be abundant. Likewise, an assertion that this female card-plying prodigy never allowed smoking, drinking, or profanity at her layouts is more romantic than realistic.[13] This was frontier Texas where most men were not sissies, wore six-shooters, and occasionally used them. Gamblers and good-timing girls were not saints. And for whatever may be said of Carlotta, good or bad, for the next several years her life was spent in the barrooms and back rooms, not Sunday school. Furnishing date specifics for Carlotta's arrival in San Antonio [June 1, 1865] and her debut as the Alamo City's most fashionable gambling queen [October 25, 1865], raises an understandable question: How was this attractive young single woman financially supporting herself and providing money for her sister's costly education during the intervening time-period?

A brief sketch of San Antonio post the Civil War is not out of place. An examination of the Alamo City's vibrant nighttime goings on is also fitting. To be sure, historic San Antonio was inhabited by "a locally colorful cast of characters. San Antonio was a hodgepodge of cultural diversity. Silk parasols, French-plumes, and dainty high-buttoned shoes, intermingling with Stetsons, sombreros, scuffed boots and sandals contributed to the ever-changing human kaleidoscope."[14] As a burgeoning trade center, military quartermaster depot, and staging point for cattle drives bound for the Kansas cow towns, San Antonio was the right place to be for a man or woman looking to make a living in lieu of holding down a legitimate job. Respectable employment opportunities for the feminine gender were scarce to nonexistent. It has been written and, perhaps it's even true, sometimes when wealthy Texas cattle barons hit town the "champagne flowed like water."[15] During the post Civil War period San Antonio suffered not unforeseeable economic hiccups, but within a short time caught her pecuniary breath and bounced back. While Carlotta Thompkins was there plying her high-stakes gambling trade, San Antonio was basking in one of its zenith periods.[16] "Many fortunes were won and lost. The winnings were principally by gamblers conducting the games and not by the players, but there were some few exceptions, and several of the players won and in some instances broke the game."[17] San Antonio was considered a wide-awake town. "Not only the men, but the women, gambled openly and, as a rule, the games were fair."[18] As it was throughout the frontier Southwest, there was no dearth of violence taking place near the gambling tables: "All gambling resorts had saloons in connection," at San Antonio. "Some had variety shows and dance halls operating in combination. All were money makers for the owners and separators for the players, customers and patrons, although most of the gambling establishments were conducted fairly."[19] Fair or not, it was a place and time out West where, as one esteemed historian dryly noted, "nearly all men drank nearly all the time, which made nearly all men more or less drunk most of the time."[20] "Numerous shoot-outs took place in the gambling halls and saloons of Main and Military plazas" at San Antonio.[21] The lifeblood of whiskey emporiums and gambling halls is rudimentary; money must change hands. "The principal ways to relieve a man of his liquid assets were the old standbys of gambling, liquor, and women, all of which were available in plenty."[22] San Antonio was awash with bulging-pocket high-rollers and, the guys and gals that wished they were.

> Here as in all the other establishments of early days, money was displayed so profusely and abundantly that it can best be described by a phrase used by one of the old-time gamblers who said: "It was in heaps and heaps—in piles and stacks. It towered high on the tops of the tables and was often handled with shovel-like scoops…The money of the players was not only carried in "morals," or bags, to the tables by the players or their servants, but sometimes it was hauled to the gambling houses in Mexican oxcarts or "carretas" or in other

vehicles. But money was not the only thing wagered. Many of the old stockmen played not only their small numbers of cattle or staked single steers but sometimes whole herds of hoofed animals, both cattle and horses, goats and sheep, oxen or mules, and wagons... [23]

That a certain big-time West Texas cattleman, while on a holiday spree at San Antonio, washed in a claw-foot bathtub filled with bubbling champagne may actually be a distention of the truth—or not?[24] There is an undeniable truism about bare bodies and the city. San Antonio had plenty of them. They were nakedly available for a peek or to play, for a price. Prevailing public attitudes about prostitution, as voiced by the communities' newspaper editors, would occasionally vary from settlement to settlement, and could often fluctuate from time to time within a given town.[25] Such was the case with early day San Antonio.

Frontier editors took the high-ground setting a moralizing tone of denunciation for the frail sisters who had fortuitously fallen into or willingly sought the licentious way of life. Depravity and debauchery were condemned passionately—from afar. San Antonio's newspapermen were vocal antagonists when it came to bad girls prostituting themselves elsewhere. A scholarly study specific to frontier San Antonio and this phenomenon is extant:

> The intensity of the moral indignation and the length of the newspaper accounts appear to be in direct ratio to the geographical location of the news dispatch. The greater the distance from San Antonio of the fallen one, the longer and sadder the articles. The most scathing criticisms were reserved for that pit of debauchery, Paris. Those prostitutes had no redeeming features in San Antonio.[26]

Closer to home ambiguity and hypocrisy crept to the forefront. There was, deferential to the era and area, a prevailing excuse—at least in some quarters:

> The contradiction of expecting chasteness among women, while promoting promiscuity among men, encouraged the rationalization that a group of "fallen" women was required to preserve the chastity of "respectable" females. The prostitute became the personification of corruption as she assumed the burden of absorbing the illicit lust of a community. Social anathema has been her reward.[27]

San Antonio was not exempted from editors railing against the inherent evils of prostitution in foreign lands or distant cities and then but winking with indifference about brothels down the street. Another factor played well to apathy—cash. While Carlotta Thompkins was busily engaged making money by whatever means in 19th-Century San Antonio the systematic collection of license fees for gambling establishments, brothels and bagnios, supplemented by monetary fines assessed working-girls, were bulging the city' coffers.[28]

During expansion of America's frontiers the local governments, as soon as wives joined their husbands and the institutional foundations for a town's permanency were laid, enacted misdemeanor ordinances prohibiting prostitution. Passage of such regulations somewhat pacified indignant spouses and church builders, but actually had but negligible effect on the flesh selling business, other than the production of revenue. Local lawmen routinely arrested the girls, the local magistrate quickly assessed a minimal fine, the *nymphs du pave* paid up, and the court distributed the municipality's money. The symphony of sin resumed scarcely missing a beat. For the city of San Antonio, as was typical throughout the West, the applicable criminal charge was "Keeping A Disorderly House." It was distinctly an accusation which was applied to madams operating the bordellos, to the working-level prostitutes, as well as the pimps and procurers cannibalizing on their powerlessness.

Money generated by prostitution in most cases was not set aside for a rainy day or sympathetically sent home. It was spent locally, a noteworthy boost to the economy which most merchants recognized and welcomed. It might have been denied for public consumption but most towns' business communities "welcomed the bordello women."[29] Unlike the majority of housewives who were caught in the hectic swirl of running day to day operations of a home, one constrained by a tight budget, as well as raising and clothing children, the *demimonde* girls unhampered by responsibility spent money on themselves. Collectively they lavishly purchased "fancy clothing, expensive wines and ornamental jewelry."[30] Contemporarily it was underplayed and almost certainly refuted, but on the frontier many of the upper-end prostitutes were style setters for ladies' fashion during the nineteenth-century. "Red-light ladies often were at the fashion forefront during non-working hours, and even respectable residents took note of the latest trends."[31] Regarding Carlotta's fashion statement it is customarily recorded that she outfitted herself in the "finest Parisian fashions," clothing befitting royalty for the "brilliant affairs in which she took her place as queen."[32] Stunning notions on just how Miss Thompkins attired herself may be traced to the photographs cited in the second chapter, delightful images we now know are not Carlotta. There is no definitive method of robing Carlotta during those days she spent in the Texas gambling halls and barrooms.

Episodes of working-gals trading sexual favors for money near military posts is a timeless phenomenon. It was/is a practice predictable and permitted; easily documented, though for the 21st-Century seldom admitted. A well-reasoned sociological study from the historic viewpoint reflects a dissimilarity regarding prostitution outside the garrison's gate, and the flesh peddling business as it was conducted in the boomtowns. Traffic in the silver and gold mining camps, constantly moving cattle shipping centers, or temporary tent cities dotting day's end at a railroad line's terminus, was but temporary.[33] The boomtowns were basically just that, boom today, bust tomorrow. Although there were no tangible guarantees, military installations were more permanent. The US Army was in large part dependent on civilian contractors to supply construction, commissary, livestock and forage needs. It was uncommon for a frontier military post not to have an adjacent civilian community.[34] Profitable economic interaction between enterprising capitalists and bureaucracy's armed services was not a facet missed by certain females eyeing improved financial prospects. San Antonio had its military men, and its girls-of-the-night.

> Here was a practical demonstration of the double standard in operation. Tacit acknowledgment that soldiers, single or far from wives, were entitled to the opportunity for regular sexual contacts demanded that prostitution be tolerated in San Antonio, but the individual prostitute censured. These concepts help to explain the ineffectual conduct of the reform campaign, the spotty execution of the law, and the almost total silence from the press about the moral conduct of soldiers stationed in and around San Antonio.[35]

Pinching a tinge of sardonic humor out of gloomy reality regarding 19th-Century soldiers' $13 a month paychecks and their predilection for entertainment has been typified: "While room and board were provided, which at best was subsistence, there wasn't much left over for extras. Sadly, with the little they did have left, most soldiers weren't investing in retirement plans or sending back spare change to help their mothers. They invested in the local economy—specifically gambling, liquor, and women…"[36] The Army's officers, banking considerable more than enlisted privates, could elevate their sights, and pay for the personal services of a higher caliber female friend.[37] After the paymaster had made his distribution the boys in blue were ripe for a plucking—and? Committed to siphoning soldiers' pockets dry, San Antonio's racially mixed cluster of working-girls, be they cardsharps or courtesans—and some were both—or low on the ladder crib-girls, stuffed full their sequin studded purses.

Time and again it is written that San Antonio is the place where Carlotta Thompkins was introduced to the man that would in due course take up the central role in her life, Mr. Frank J. Thurmond. Born near Atlanta, Jackson County, Georgia, during 1840 [November 21st], Mr. Thurmond, with a degree of Cherokee Indian ancestry, was in certain quarters thought to be the absolute epitome of a true "Southern Gentlemen." Frank Thurmond was a man's man.[38] He was a fellow with good manners, undaunted courage, and an unbreakable spirit. Attesting to his strength of mind one oldtimer simply said of Mr. Thurmond, "he wasn't the kind of guy you could cry in front of."[39] At age twenty-one Frank had enlisted as a private in the Confederate Army and served until the Civil War's end. During that conflict Frank Thurmond had been wounded in the leg during the Battle of Murfreesboro, and also had been made a prisoner of war. Mr. Thurmond, during the same month Miss Carlotta Thompkins made her initial appearance at San Antonio [June 1865], was no doubt overjoyed. He was released from Union incarceration, as reflected by the U. S. Army's General Order:

> *In pursuance of General Orders No. 109, A. G. O., dated Washington, D. C. June 6, 1865, the Quartermaster's Department will furnish transportation from Chicago, Illinois, to Social Circle, Ga. for the following named released Prisoner of War: Frank J. Thurmond.*[40]

Thereafter along with his brothers, Frank crossed the burned out South finally ending up in the Lone Star State at San Antonio. Gradually working their way upward, the tenacious Thurmonds found themselves very near the top echelon in sporting circles. Eventually the gambling Thurmond boys, by most accounts, either acquired or opened the University Club, one of San Antonio's luxurious casinos. As a nightspot superb the University Club attracted many of the city's most affluent gamblers, not only because it was upscale, but because the proprietors were honest, as were the games they oversaw.[41]

Though it has been written—and more or less accepted—that the Thurmond brothers operated the University Club "for about thirty-five years," such a claim may not be sustainable.[42] One writer asserts—and maybe rightly so—that the sons were accompanied by their father, J. C. Thurmond and the boys' sister, Jenny Thurmond, to start a "new life" in Texas.[43] Coincidentally it will be recalled that another author in reeling off a list of female "police characters" working the San Antonio neighborhood enumerated a girl named Jenny Thurmond.[44] Along with

Miss Carlotta Thompkins' story unwinding into the realm of particulars, it will also be confirmed that the Thurmond brother's close association with shady ladies was no anomaly. For aficionados of Old West lore the cozy affiliations and shared living arrangements by frontier gamblers and working-girls will come as no revelation. Not just a few of the now well-known and legendary characters of the Wild West were cohabiting with prostitutes as census and arrest records reveal, or with "actresses," the often worn-thin euphemism designed for politely veiling a Fair Cyprian.[45] A smattering of those frontier gamblers were even pimping their way to prosperity.

At San Antonio the decidedly sexy and exceptionally well turned-out Carlotta Thompkins took up residence at Mrs. Adam's boarding house, before "she secured a place of her own, a small but respectable adobe house on San Pedro Street, near the business section of the city."[46] Because of Carlotta's later verifiable brushes with Texas' legal system, where she stayed is more than a little interesting—maybe revealing—since the idiom "Boarding House" was "a term used by Western madams to infer that their brothels were respectable." Furthermore, if the place was actually listed or advertised as a "Female Boarding House," even the meticulously drawn Sanborn Insurance Maps of the time would designate the building as a house of prostitution.[47]

The reason for christening Madam Blanche Dearwood's parlor house at 110 Elm Street with a military sounding sobriquet, Fort Allen, remains a mystery. The two story pleasure palace built of adobe with a stylish French-style mansard roof, just three short blocks east of the Alamo, was a landmark institution in San Antonio, architecturally and scandalously.[48] At the time Fort Allen was probably San Antonio's most upscale bordello; home to the city's upper-tier bevy of Fallen Angels. For working whores, they were San Antonio's elite.[49] Lottie Deno's familiarity with Fort Allen is indefinite.

Resuming the frequently repeated but less than adequately documented tale about Miss Carlotta Thompkins is uncomplicated. It is taken as gospel that she, as a fashionably dressed darling of the city's finest, landed herself a spot dealing faro and poker at the Thurmond's posh University Club. Capitalizing on the deep well of experience gained gambling in Detroit's deluxe establishments, in the drifting riverboat's sumptuous staterooms, and at New Orleans' classiest nightspots, Carlotta soon was the cat's meow at San Antonio's University Club. Miss Thompkins had at long last arrived, financially and publicly, regaining the social status stripped from her by the cruel and indifferent ravages of war—and heartless damnyankees. It was at the University Club that many men fell head-over-heels in love with Carlotta, but "her pride and unaltered purpose to take care of her loved ones and her unapproachable attitude kept them at a distance during the years of her gambling career."[50] If it is true that Carlotta Thompkins was the poker playing princess of San Antonio, she was atop the pinnacle of her dominance at the betting tables. She gambled about "three years" at the University Club. Then somewhat surprisingly, for such a superlative poker player riding a high-rolling crest of popularity and preeminence, "fortune began to elude" the angelic champion of the pasteboards. Now and then romantically disposed writers add a previous paramour—one from her distant past—into the muddle leading to Carlotta's downfall as San Antonio's paramount poker player. One author promises to "eat the felt off a poker table" if such was true. Because, to him, this ingredient of Miss Carlotta's biography "sounds like dime novel romance."[51]

A mention that Carlotta began her San Antonio gambling career during 1865 and at the University Club "spent about three years," which would be 1868, is worthy of note and quite germane to the story at hand. That date specific dovetails with another happening taking place that very same year at San Antonio, one in particular involving the play-for-pay girls. A predictable and periodic reform movement was underway. The 1868 pressure to rigidly enforce the laws dealing with those infractions classified as "traditional vice" in one sense backfired, but not before much to their utter horror the prostitutes of San Antonio were literally driven from the city. Suffering "without food or shelter, exposed to the elements and battered by a terrible storm," San Antonio's working-girls were literally up the creek without a paddle—or anything else.[52] New ordinances outlawing prostitution had been put into effect within San Antonio's municipal limits.

"The ordinances opened Pandora's Box for the city of San Antonio. Suddenly the official policy had shifted from one of mild control through periodic fines to total elimination through exile. The resulting chaos made the authorities look ludicrous and inhumane. No less awkward was the position of the *San Antonio Daily Express*. Having maintained that Galveston should adopt a firmer line with prostitutes, the *Daily Express* was faced in San Antonio with the horrors such a tough law enforcement policy could produce. No thought had been given to just what was supposed to become of these 'fallen women.' These females, devoid of any kind of occupational skill other than promiscuity, depended totally on their day to day earnings to maintain a marginal existence in San Antonio. Driven to the fringes of the frontier without housing or economic means, their condition deteriorated immediately. In an unprecedented move the *Daily Express* addressed in lengthy detail the subject of local prostitution."[53]

> Since the appearance of the ordinance against houses of
> ill fame, there has been considerable commotion among
> the 'nymphes du pave.' The ordinance took effect

Tuesday last, and a number of the poor wretches inhabiting the O'Det House started from there Monday without prospect of home or shelter. They camped on the prairie west of the city limits, and that night a fearful storm that flooded everything came up and continued through the night; their condition the next morning was indescribable—drowned rats were no comparison. As soon as their condition became known, they were provided with temporary comforts.[54]

Carlotta Thompkins could well read the city's ceaselessly vacillating public stance about games of chance and ladies of easy virtue. Melodramatic assertions that one of Carlotta's former lovers made a surprise appearance in San Antonio are not subject to any verifiability. Or is demonstrable an allegation that during some inter-fraternity fracas over just who was entitled to the gaming pot's healthy proceeds, Mr. Frank Thurmond mortally skewered his competitor with a razor-sharp Bowie knife and gutlessly fled San Antonio. The innuendo and subplots do, nonetheless, make for a dandy script; how and why the lead characters all hurriedly departed San Antonio. Fanciful melodrama does help explain the circumstances of their reuniting a few years later. At that time evidence will more than sustain an exceptional Western story.[55] For whatever reason or reasons, Miss Carlotta Thompkins preferred to make San Antonio a city to visit, but not one to call home.

Early day photograph of Alamo Plaza, San Antonio, Texas. *Courtesy San Antonio Public Library, Texana/Genealogy.*

The Alamo City's famous Military Plaza. Foot and wheeled-vehicle traffic was brisk. *Courtesy San Antonio Public Library, Texana/Genealogy.*

Early day San Antonio street scene. It may have been a tough gambling town, but even then it had a book store. *Courtesy San Antonio Public Library, Texana/Genealogy.*

Interior image of the posh University Club's reception room, San Antonio, Texas. From *The Art Work of San Antonio* [W. H. Parish Publishing, 1894]. *If* Miss Lottie Deno ever gambled here it was a far cry from where she usually could be found—the sin spots dotting Texas' crude frontier. *Courtesy San Antonio Public Library, Texana/Genealogy.*

Though many upright and upstanding ladies may not have wanted to admit it, because prostitutes were unencumbered with outside responsibilities like husbands and children they were frequently style setters. They could lavishly spend money on themselves, as exhibited in this photograph. *Courtesy Robert G. McCubbin.*

During the early days bicycles were reasonably expensive and, correspondingly, an authentic status symbol. Working girls took note and often posed with bicycles. Here are two from Madam Alice Abbott's scrapbook; captioned by Alice as "Bitches of the Road." *Courtesy Robert G. McCubbin.*

Early day photographers were quick to pickup on an interminable fact: Sex sells. Risqué images were not a 20th-Century creation. Nineteenth-century *Nymphes de Pave* shed their clothes and inhibitions for the dollar, sensually enticing the menfolk with their revealing charms. *Courtesy Robert G. McCubbin.*

An old fashioned mud-wagon. This is the type vehicle frequently used in the Old West for crossing rough country, the type conveyance Miss Lottie Deno would no doubt have traveled in from time to time. Dusty and dirty; not a terrific mode of transportation. *Courtesy, Robert Mullin Collection, Nita Stewart Haley Memorial Library.*

Endnotes Chapter 3

[1] Hunter, *The Story of Lottie Deno*. 4.

[2] Ibid. 5.

[3] Ibid.

[4] Ibid.

[5] Rose, *Lottie Deno: Gambling Queen of Hearts*. 34-35.

[6] Hunter, *The Story of Lottie Deno*. 7.

[7] Ibid. "After several brawls Mary became so obstreperous that Lottie could not manage her. One evening as Lottie was dressing to go to her nightly game of chance, she called Mary to assist her and received no answer. Mary had completely disappeared, taking along her meager possessions and was never seen again." 7-8.

[8] Ibid. "Lottie was a frequent visitor in these places [gambling establishments] and was given the name of the 'Angel of San Antonio!'" 7.

[9] Lewis, "Lottie Deno, Gambler." "Plying her skills on Mississippi River steamboats, Lottie worked her way to New Orleans and eventually to San Antonio where she took up the name 'Lottie Deno.'" 17.

[10] Hunter, *The Story of Lottie Deno*. 6.

[11] Lewis, "Lottie Deno, Gambler." 17.

[12] Deborah Countess, San Antonio Public Library, Texana/Genealogy Department, San Antonio, Texas. Understandably an absolute declaration that Carlotta was not ever mentioned in San Antonio's newspapers cannot be proffered. However, Ms Countess conducted an exhaustive search under the names "Lottie Deno" as well as "Carlotta and Charlotte Thompkins [Tompkins] with negative results.

[13] Rose, *Lottie Deno: Gambling Queen of Hearts*. 32.

[14] Jan Devereaux, "Gentle Woman, Tough Medicine." *National Association For Outlaw And Lawman History* [NOLA] *Quarterly*. April-June 2003. 21-22.

[15] Donald E. Everett, *San Antonio Legacy*. 17.

[16] Ibid. 35.

[17] Ibid. 35-36

[18] Ibid. 34; *San Antonio Daily Express*, December 9, 1867. "The professional cardists were present in force."; March 6, 1868.

[19] Ibid. 36.

[20] Robert M. Utley, *High Noon in Lincoln, Violence on the Western Frontier*. 176. Also see Bob Alexander's *Desert Desperadoes: The Banditti of Southwestern New Mexico*. "Therein, then, were the handy ingredients for disastrous six-shooter dustups; the flowing amber current that sometimes washed away sound judgment and firearms that could be brought into play upon a split-second's notice. Mix in a dash of youthful exuberance, salted with *machismo*, and the toxic recipe for calamity is well seasoned. Festooned with a 'stand your ground' mindset developed during formative years, Westerners, young and old were too frequently loathe to ignore or overlook an affront to their masculinity, real or imagined." 24.

[21] David Bowser, *West of the Creek: Murder, Mayhem and Vice in Old San Antonio*. vii.

[22] Richard Selcer, [Compiler and Editor], *Legendary Watering Holes: The Saloons That Made Texas Famous*. For San Antonio particular attention is drawn to Chapter Two, "Jack Harris's Vaudeville and San Antonio's 'Fatal Corner'," a contribution of David Bowser. 53-121.

[23] Everett, *San Antonio Legacy*. 36-37.

[24] Ibid. 15-18.

[25] Anne M. Butler, *The Frontier Press And Prostitution: A Study of San Antonio, Tombstone, Cheyenne.* Master of Arts Thesis, Untiversity of Maryland, 1975. 5-6.

[26] Ibid. 19.

[27] Ibid. 4.

[28] Ibid. "[San Antonio] City officials by this time may have quietly developed the policy of low keyed harassment of on-going social ills as a means of increasing the city's coffers." 23; *San Antonio Daily Express*, December 9, 1867, January 11, 1868, February 21, 1868, March 18, 1868, March 26, 1868, March 28, 1868, and April 9, 1868..

[29] Jay Moynahan, *Soiled Doves, Sportin' Women and Other Fallen Flowers— Prostitution on the American Frontier.* "The town's business communities welcomed the bordello women. They usually had a good deal of money to spend and they bought expensive and lavish clothes as well as other items." 58.

[30] Seagraves, *Soiled Doves: Prostitution In The Early West.* viii.

[31] Sherry Monahan, *The Wicked West: Boozers, Cruisers, Gamblers, and more.* 110.

[32] First quotation from Rose, *Lottie Deno: Gambling Queen of Hearts.* 28. Second quotation from Hunter, *The Story of Lottie Deno: Her Life and Times.* 5.

[33] Rutter, *Upstairs Girls: Prostitution in the American West.* "While it was normal for prostitutes to relocate periodically, working girls who catered to railroad workers and miners were more mobile than those who pursued a military clientele." 25.

[34] Butler, *Daughters of Joy, Sisters of Misery: Prostitutes in the American West, 1865-90.* "All persons close to the forts contributed to the dynamics of human sexuality certain to be explosive among communities of isolated men and women. Prostitution within and around garrisons represented the visible acknowledgment of that sexuality." 126.

[35] Butler, *The Frontier Press and Prostitution: San Antonio, Tombstone, Cheyenne.* 32.

[36] Rutter, *Upstairs Girls: Prostitution in the American West.* 35.

[37] Ibid. The author clarifies: "Consorting with women of questionable virtue violated the officers' 'code.' What is more likely is that officers spent just as much time with prostitutes, but that their behavior was simply off the record—as were the consequences (venereal disease)." 36.

[38] *Deming Headlight*, June 11, 1908. Mathews, *The History of Luna County* inadvertently confuses Frank Thurmond's date of birth with that of his father, but does offer conformation that Frank served in the Confederate Army during the Civil War. 103.

[39] Bob Alexander, *Sheriff Harvey Whitehill: Silver City Stalwart.* 86; *Southwesterner.* May 1962.

[40] Julie Coley [Comp.], *J. K Street Civil War Letters: Ninth Texas Infantry.* J. K. Street to Melinda Elizabeth Pace "Ninnie" Street, December 31, 1863. "....Frank Thurmond slightly [wounded] in the leg." 90. J. K. Street's original letters may be found at the Southern Historical Collection, Wilson Library, University of North Carolina, Chapel Hill, North Carolina; Frank J. Thurmond's military record, courtesy Steve Engerrand, Asst. Director, Georgia State Archives, Morrow Georgia.

[41] Hunter, *The Story of Lottie Deno: Her Life and Times.* "The three [the Thurmond brothers] were honest gamblers and their club was visited by some of the nation's most flamboyant characters." 7.

[42] Ibid. As the chronological story of Carlotta Thompkins unfolds, census records will place the Thurmond brothers at locations other than San Antonio. If they did, indeed, maintain a financial interest in the University Club for thirty-five years as Hunter asserts, it was from afar—though not likely, possible.

[43] Rose, *Lottie Deno: Gambling Queen of Hearts*. "The three [Thurmond] brothers were Confederate veterans who, along with their father J. C. Thurmond and their younger sister Jenny, had come to San Antonio from Georgia to start a new life." 32.

[44] Hunter, *The Story of Lottie Deno: Her Life and Times*. 5.

[45] Moynahan, *Talkin' About Sportin' Women: A Dictionary of Terms Related to Prostitution on the American Frontier*. "**Actress.** Some prostitutes claimed this was their profession. The term was used by some census takers to denote a prostitute." 11.

[46] Hunter, *The Story of Lottie Deno: Her Life and Times*. 5. Rose, *Lottie Deno: Gambling Queen of Hearts*. "They [Carlotta Thompkins and Mary Poindexter] found lodging at Mrs. Adams's Boarding House." 31.

[47] Seagraves, *Soiled Doves: Prostitution In The Early West*. 167; Moynahan, *Talkin' About Sportin' Women: A Dictionary of Terms Related to Prostitution on the American Frontier*. "**Female Boarding House.** The Sanborn Insurance Maps used this designation on buildings to denote places where prostitution took place. This was used on both cribs and houses. There are some instances where saloons with rooms and prostitutes above were also labeled Female Boarding. Later, instead of writing female boarding on the maps, it was shortened to F. B." 21.

[48] Bowser, *West of the Creek: Murder, Mayhem and Vice in Old San Antonio*. 29; *San Antonio Daily Express*, April 11, 1868. "The elite prostitutes came en masse on Thursday morning to the Mayor's office, from 'Fort Allen,' but finding they had made a mistake, were directed to Justice Briggs...."

[49] Ibid.

[50] Hunter, *The Story of Lottie Deno: Her Life and Times*. 6.

[51] J. Lee Butts, *Bad Girls: Hussies, Harlots and Horse Thieves*. 132.

[52] Butler, *Daughters of Joy, Sisters of Misery*. 117, n. 17.

[53] Butler, *The Frontier Press and Prostitution: A Study of San Antonio, Tombstone, Cheyenne*. 25-26; *San Antonio Daily Express*, March 6, 1868.

[54] *San Antonio Daily Express*, March 13, 1868.

[55] Of Carlotta's departure from San Antonio, Hunter in *The Story of Lottie Deno: Her Life and Times* writes: "Fortune continued to elude Lottie, and she began to be restless and think about a change of location." 7; Rose, *Lottie Deno: Gambling Queen of Hearts* reports: "Frank Thurmond, who would give ground to no one, got into an altercation during a game and killed a man with his bowie knife. He fled San Antonio and stayed on the run for the next ten years." 34. The author does candidly admit: "Strangely, there is no record of his [Frank Thurmond] having been wanted by the authorities." 34.

Chapter 4

"The Law Was Your Pistol"

Carlotta Thompkins stepped into a stagecoach at San Antonio. Good-naturedly, she waited for the tobacco spitting driver to crack the whip and shake the leather ribbons, unleashing her stay at the Alamo City. It would be a dusty, dirty and dangerous trip. Did she have a particular destination in mind? Was she simply riding the west bound coach until funds were depleted? Had San Antonio's reformers run her out of town, or was she just searching for a new place to trade on her femininity and card dealing talents? Between San Antonio and San Diego, California, all 1475.76 miles, the roadway was dotted with stations that might ignite profitability for a person with an adventuresome spirit and elastic ethics.[1] Carrying money and memories with her, Carlotta had hopped aboard the four horse stagecoach on a Monday, Wednesday or Friday at 8 A. M. and clamored out of town.[2] She did not have to read Tarot Cards. She had cards of her own to play. Lonely men liked gambling with girls. Seducing soldiers was easy. In Texas, army boys were stationed on the state's western frontier. Carlotta wanted to see the West. During her trip Miss Thompkins enthusiastically took in the countryside's splendor while the coach interchangeably lurched between the horses' ambling walk, marching trot, and a jostling gallop. She quickly left behind such pleasant Texas Hill Country places as Leon Springs, Boerne, Fredericksburg, Mason, Menardville, and McKavett.[3] Carlotta ended her expedition near an isolated and under construction U. S. Army base, Fort Concho.

With the status of an errant stepchild the military base had first been named Camp Hatch, then Camp Kelly, and finally on February 6, 1868, officially designated as a full-fledged grownup, Fort Concho. Located in West Texas at the junction of the Main and North Concho Rivers, Fort Concho was perched on the Lone Star State's frontier.[4] West and north of Fort Concho was for the most part an unexplored and uninhabited no man's land. It was occupied by nomadic bands of Indians and the occasional wanderings of profiteering Comancheros. Fort Concho was positioned to interdict raiding plans of warriors from the Llano Estacado, as well as the Trans-Pecos region.[5] Birthing the fort was not easy, the labor pains had been intense. Supplies and building materials had to be freighted "by ox-cart over a route hundreds of miles in length."[6] Due to Fort Concho's sheer isolation construction of permanent buildings was agonizingly slow. Belatedly it had been learned that "stone was the best construction material, but only after lengthy experimentation using adobe."[7] All too soon the troops assigned to Fort

Concho meandered across the river and came into contact and sometimes conflict with "a rough lot of civilians."[8] Dancing into the Fort Concho picture, Carlotta Thompkins stepped off the stagecoach and into stardom. Maintaining the mythology it is necessary to repeat:

> If the arrival of Lottie in San Antonio was hailed with sensationalism, her arrival in Fort Concho was as if an angel from heaven had suddenly dropped into their midst. She arrived on the San Antonio stage coach one day in the early seventies. Except for the absence of the customary wings and halo, she might well have been an angel. Her dark red hair and brown sparkling eyes in a pleasant face portrayed a perfect picture of innocence, refinement and gentility. Ladies were scarce in the wicked frontier town of Fort Concho and all eyes turned to follow her as she alighted from the stagecoach that day. Dressed in elegant fashion she brought beauty into a drab frontier fort. All wondered who she was and from where she had come.[9]

There is not any justification in questioning whether or not Miss Carlotta Thompkins made an appearance near Fort Concho. Absent a finitely documented starting point, which there is not, mentioning she arrived "along about 1870" certainly grants leeway for a year or two.[10] Remembering that a newspaperman asserted he had interviewed folks who had known an Army officer previously stationed at Fort Concho, one who had personally known Carlotta while so posted, should be quite sufficient. Outlining her activities while there is a bit more complicated. Taking a look at the neighborhood will prove insightful. The examination will serve as a common sense platform for shattering myths and asking pertinent questions.

Even more telling than the writer had wished for might be found in his specificity; saying that Carlotta rented adobe quarters "Over the River."[11] Or, was it a tantalizingly implied hint? "Over the River" or "Across the River" was not generic terminology broadly meaning somewhere across the Concho River opposite the fort. Across the River was an identifiable part of the 320 acre survey which in an 1870 real estate transaction transferred land title from Granville Sherwood to Bart DeWitt. Across the River was a real place. The tract being in close proximity to Fort Concho made it a pulsating nerve center for the skin trade—buffalo robes and fair maidens. Over time the tiny settlement would evolve from Across the River to Saint Angela [or, San Angela], and later acquire the name she is currently known by, San Angelo. The little hamlet would reach maturity with refinement and good manners, becoming a West Texas pacesetter. That would come later though. When Carlotta Thompkins stepped off the stagecoach the town was anything but saintly.[12] During the time Carlotta was sashaying up and down Concho Avenue it was a smutty "community composed primarily of buffalo hunters, dismissed post traders, saloon keepers, gamblers and prostitutes."[13]

The civilian settlement was no bona fide city. There was no assortment of frontier folks living life with a sophisticated and metropolitan flair. Pleasingly furnished and attractively painted hotels, tastefully outfitted gambling halls and elegantly appointed saloons were at once noticed—by their absence. Across the River was primitive and rude. It was but a dirty village haphazardly and hastily thrown together. The small number of buildings were made of green planks and crooked pickets, a few of crudely fashioned adobe bricks. An illustrative description underscores reality regarding Miss Carlotta's chosen destination. It was "a horridly wicked portion of the universe."[14] Across the River was model for a rip-roaring Wild West helltown; "a collection of hovels, grog shops, gambling dens, and bawdy houses and offered neither amenities nor wholesome recreation."[15] The first fatal shooting of record erupted during June of 1870. A drunken enlisted man named Stuart from Fort Concho began assaulting a local civilian named Wiley. He paid for the nonsense with his life. There may have been law in Texas, but there were not lawmen at Across the River. Wiley turned himself over to the military commander, who after hearing the man's justification, bid the much relieved civilian adieu. It had been a clear-cut case of self defense.[16] "With the homicidal ice broken the deaths mounted at an alarming rate, or what would have been an alarming rate if anyone had been concerned."[17] Not all of the West Texas riffraff was concentrated in the "two dozen hovels, each one a whiskey shop or something worse."[18] Outside town limits the countryside was swarming with "the greatest set of scoundrels that ever lived on the face of the earth."[19]

Although he would rise to one of the region's foremost businessmen and most respected citizens William Smith Veck would in due course become known as the "The Father of San Angelo." Mr. Veck was a true pioneer hewn from the roughest cut. Preceding his 1867 arrival in the area, New Jersey born Veck had seen military service during the Mexican War. After sailing around the horn of South America he had sought a mining fortune in California during the Gold Rush. Somewhere along life's journey W. S. Veck had acquired the aptitudes of a seasoned freighter. That is the role that led to him settling at Across the River.[20] Mr. Veck had realized that more real money could be made gratifying the ravenous cravings of cowboys, buffalo hunters, soldiers and town builders, than could be made laboriously freighting the merchandise.[21] Whiskey was a big seller at Across the River. Mr. Veck opened a store and saloon.

At the time it happened a few eyebrows were no doubt raised, but the furor about Mr. Veck eloping with and then marrying at Fredericksburg a beautiful fourteen year old girl—thirty years his junior—Catalina [Katalina] "Kate" Wuertemburg, quickly died down.[22] Dying of another type wasn't diminishing at violent Across the River, nor around William Veck's jam-packed emporium of frolic and fun. It is a sad fact confirmed by listening to contemporary voices, people in the know—two males and a pair of ladies.

William M. Notson, Post Surgeon, Fort Concho, for an extensive 1871 monthly report penned about the infectious reality plaguing civilian congestion so very close to the military post. Dr. Nostson opined about the epidemic of senseless shootings and wasted lives:

> St. Angela, the village across the North Concho river, is attaining an unenviable distinction, from the numerous murders committed there. This condition of society seems to be almost necessarily a concommitant [sic] with the advances of American civilization, but it is certainly fostered by the residents themselves and the shortsightedness of the State authorities...While the Military, tied hand and foot, through the jealously of civil powers, dares not assume any control, lest like Sheridan at Chicago it be charged with ursupation [sic]. The result of the last six weeks there have been seven murders in a population of less than a hundred, men, women and children all told, and during the residence of the Post Surgeon over one hundred murders have taken place within a radius of ten miles from the Adjutants office, in a population which has never at any time exceeded two hundred and fifty...[23]

Another medical practitioner, Dr. S. L. S. Smith, an Army contract surgeon, offered his plainspoken appraisal of the conglomerate of San Angela businesses catering to carnal pleasure and card playing:

> [San Angela] is full of human sharks, and as every inducement is held out there to soldiers to spend money, the nights succeeding pay day are hideous. There are so many gamblers, cutthroats, murderers, horse thieves living and finding harbor at San Angela it is never considered safe to pass through there at night,

and no officer even thinks of leaving the garrison after dark.[24]

For this story about a remarkably fascinating woman, the ladies, too, may be heard from. The first, Mrs. Kate Veck, was the person responsible for instigating the name change for Across the River. It was her suggestion that the village be renamed after the deceased wife of Bart DeWitt, Carolina Angela de la Garza. The settlement shed its undignified name and emerged as Saint Angela.[25] Aside from Kate Veck mothering ten children and becoming a prominent force in the community's betterment, she was Mr. William Veck's better half. As such she was in a perfect position to make first-hand observations about their business venture, the combination store and saloon. For better understanding of Carlotta's story, listening to Kate Veck is but a worthwhile treatment. It paints a picture of the world—or underworld—that Miss Thompkins was circulating in. Not mincing words or draping herself in contrived social niceties Mrs. Kate Veck says:

> We lived in a picket house near the store. The building was a store, saloon, and bank…I have heard men come out of the saloon and stop near my home to discuss who they will kill and when they would kill him. And soon enough in a few minutes you would hear the shot. There was no law here, no town, just a few saloons, gambling houses and adobe or picket residences. The law was your pistol and you could carry as many as you wanted to.[26]

Forrestine "Birdie" Hooker, the daughter of First Lieutenant Charles Lawrence Cooper, accompanied her father and mother throughout the American West, living at several military posts. Though she was but a child at the time, Forrestine's recollections about the family's 1873 Fort Concho assignment is applicable to grasping Carlotta Thompkins' story in an overall context. Otherwise, disregarding the facts and fictionally inventing a naïve dreamscape about everyday life at San Angela but fosters the folklore. Forrestine Hooker remembered:

> Shooting affrays were common occurrences at Veck's, where Mexicans, outlaws, and unruly characters came to buy tobacco, ammunition, arms, and principally to get whiskey and gamble where there was no law to restrain them.[27]

Putting aside references to San Angela's folks killing themselves with guns, from an aesthetic viewpoint the place was a burrow of squalor and nastiness. During the mid 1870s one journalist described the settlement: "San Angela, or Concho City, is a little town across the river, built chiefly of mud-brick baked in the sun. It presents a miserable aspect, and looks like a fitting abode for wretchedness and poverty."[28] In those days San Angela was so defined by physical appearance and sociological demographics it was not monetarily worth much. Bart DeWitt, the man holding title to much of the land, borrowed $1500 from a thriving San Antonio entrepreneur, Marcus Koenigheim. The collateral had been some of the town lots upon which San Angela was located. After DeWitt's financial inability or failed inclination to settle the outstanding debt, Mr. Koenigheim tried to unload his newly acquired real estate hurriedly. Marcus Koenigheim was so uninspired and unimpressed with San Angela that he offered to trade the whole parcel of town lots to anybody—for a wagon load of whiskey. Koenigheim had no takers.[29] There was more demand for the liquor than the land.

In the neighborhood, however, was a community where more reputable folks gathered. It was absent the gambling dens, dance halls, barrooms and, by default, Miss Carlotta Thompkins. Tucked safely away three and a half miles south of Fort Concho and in the opposite direction from San Angela was the pert little Concho River village of Ben Ficklin [or, Benficklin], "a respectable town frequented by officers and wives from the fort and farming and ranching families."[30] Named after the recently deceased [1871] Benjamin Franklin "Ben" Ficklin, an esteemed tycoon in the then competitive stagecoach business, the little town attracted investment and uprightness. Indulgence and indecency were relegated to San Angela.[31] San Angela was still wicked: "Wise men and good men avoided the place."[32] Though the maneuverings between Ben Ficklin's and San Angela's folks for political dominance in that quarter is interesting, Mother Nature awarded the prize.[33] Ben Ficklin would be destroyed by raging floodwaters and San Angela would be the beneficiary. Ben Ficklin's demise would be well after Miss Carlotta Thompkins had moved to greener pastures and an altogether different set of greenhorns.

Mrs. Veck's mentioning the only arbiter of the law was a pistol, followed by an implication that carrying but one was foolhardy, is not exaggeration. Forrestine Hooker's contention that there was no law is correct. There was not a town marshal. There was not a county sheriff. The famed Frontier Battalion of state commissioned lawmen, the Texas Rangers, were yet to be birthed. San Angela and Ben Ficklin could not even lay claim to being within boundaries of a lawfully drawn county. That distinction—a sign of encroaching civilization—would not come

about until 1875 when Tom Green County was organized and a slate of
county officers elected.[34]

The closest village of real significance was Fredericksburg, the
charming German enclave on the Perdnales River's bank some 160 miles
southeast.[35] San Angela was not an easy location to get to. Any person
safely making the trip was fortunate, especially a woman supposedly
traveling alone. For that Carlotta Thompkins deserves credit. This West
Texas locale lay in the Bexar Land District. Almost incomprehensible by
modern standards, after the original twenty-three counties were
organized during 1836, the remaining land in Texas sculpted the
gargantuan Bexar Land District. In the end Texas would be carved into
254 separate counties. The transition would take years. At the time San
Angela and Ben Ficklin were floundering into existence they lay in a
region of the Bexar Land District that would later be developed into 67
individual counties.[36] They, too, lay within a vast region that was already
heavily populated—with buffalo and, correspondingly, Comanches.
Those two factors were what prompted Carlotta's 1870s stopover at
San Angela. Buffalo beckoned the hide-hunters. Indians brought the
soldiers.

One of the principal buyers of buffalo hides in the San Angela/Fort
Concho section was the aforementioned William Veck. Selling needed
supplies to the buffalo hunters and offering an outlet for disposing of
their work product, merchant Veck maneuvered himself into a most
lucrative position. Almost monopolizing on the Concho River area hide
market, it was not unusual for Mr. Veck to deal in as many as 40,000
units annually. Mrs. Kate Veck remembered that William "often had as
many as 10,000 of them [buffalo hides] at the store awaiting shipment
east." Of the whole Concho region's harvest of buffalo hides, Mr. Veck
brokered roughly half.[37] William Veck's and others' participation in the
hide buying business affected San Angela in two distinct ways. The
overall ambiance of San Angela was appreciably enhanced by the
perfume emitting from green-hides piled high. With the town built of
either pickets vertically implanted in the ground or drab sun-dried
bricks, and considering the stench from buffalo hides stacked about, San
Angela had no eye appeal but did have an arresting aroma. The traffic in
buffalo hides was also good for the local economy, as were the
spendthrift soldiers from Fort Concho. Hide-hunters and lonely army
fellows had funds to spend—and lose. Money in constant circulation
was not a detail missed by Miss Thompkins:

> The impact of the buffalo business on the Concho
> region was enhanced because much of the income
> generated by the sale of the products was immediately
> returned to the local economy. For one thing, crew

owners invested considerable sums at local stores in order to buy supplies for their outfits. Purchases included sugar, flour, and coffee, but the major expenditure was for the lead and powder hunters used in loading their ammunition. James Keaton, an early San Angelo resident, once saw a party of hunters leave Veck's store with a ton of lead, and the common practice was to buy several kegs of powder at one time. Moreover, the owners paid their crews in San Angelo [San Angela], and consequently the men spent a good percentage of their wages in the saloons and gambling houses that had sprung up in the town.[38]

There are numerous citations regarding the Concho River region's buffalo hunters and skinners making a "stand," then freighting the stretched hides and most desirous cuts of fly-drawing meat to San Angela.[39] Later, burdened ox-teams pushed north carrying thousands of hides destined for railhead markets, leaving behind cash paying customers for whatever tempting treats San Angela and Carlotta Thompkins had to offer. There may have been tea parties and serene social get-togethers at Ben Ficklin, but San Angela was no teasippin' town. There the whiskey was poured straight-up, the cards placed face-down, and the frilly petticoats lasciviously peeled back.

Adding to the mix making up Carlotta's clientele were the free-spending soldiers. It has been insightfully written: "Like a domineering parent and an unruly stepchild, for more than a decade the post and the community had maintained an uneasy equilibrium, occasionally punctuated by violence."[40] That "uneasy equilibrium" may have awakened to fruition, but only after a tussle. It was a truth speedily revealed to Reverend Norman Badger, the earliest Post Chaplain assigned to Fort Concho. He crossed the river and tried his mightiest to bring the word of God to San Angela and it was "probably the first time that the name of the Diety, was ever publicly used in reverence in that place."[41] Minister Badger sermonized to a pitiably diminutive and deaf congregation. Nearly ten years later another preacher, Andrew J. Potter, was forced to do his sermonizing in a San Angela saloon, there yet was no church.[42] San Angela was, in those earliest days "a rough-and-tumble cattle country equivalent of a 'hell-on-wheels' railroad town…"[43] There the business houses, among other things, "sold supplies to buffalo hunters and poured drinks for parched cowboys."[44] There was no shortage of cowboys at San Angela. The town lay in West Texas ranching country. It was the last semi-civilized settlement on the legendary Goodnight-Loving Trail.[45] Before cattle herds were pushed further west on a march across desolate country to military markets in

New Mexico Territory, a last stop at untamed San Angela was mandatory. The conscientious foreman restocked his chuck-wagon. The drovers, taking turns, also raced into San Angela for that last round of liquid fortification, faro and fornication. It was a long way to Fort Sumner.

Whether or not Miss Carlotta Thompkins had intended on making San Angela her destination or found herself the unwilling victim of an empty purse does not alter the tale. Perhaps for a single girl not put off by the sporting way of life Carlotta was right at home in San Angela. Single men, lonesome and harboring an obsessive mindset could provide just the ticket for an ingenious girl with a plan. Part of that plan, aside from making money hand over fist, was to muddy the water about her previous life; to make those persnickety details but mysterious questions.

John Warren Hunter was the first journalist to publish an account of Carlotta Thompkins and her subsequent visit to San Angela's gambling halls and saloons. According to Mr. Hunter, while there Carlotta "assumed different names as occasion might demand." Among San Angela's odd assortment of permanent residents and the much larger transient crowd rambling into and out of town, the secretive Carlotta was by "those who knew her least," dubbed the "Mystic Maude,"[46] Later, J. Marvin Hunter asserted that it was his father who had awarded the nickname to Carlotta: "In those days people did not ask who you were or where you were from, so my father, John Warren Hunter, early day Newspaper Man, gave her the moniker of 'Mystic Maud,' which she carried during her stay at Fort Concho, seemingly content to be so called."[47] For the elder Mr. Hunter to measure Carlotta's contentment with being labeled Mystic Maude is problematical in light of the fact that he didn't even know the girl. He had "gathered his information about the 'mystery woman' from old timers who were living there at the time the incidents mentioned took place."[48] That point is most helpful in rendering fact from fiction. To believe that Carlotta Thompkins even made an appearance at San Angela, which she likely did, Mr. Hunter's visits with people who did know the anonymous Army officer must be accepted. For a primary source that's the sum of it. In looking back recalling his earlier days and personal acquaintance with Carlotta the soldier may have felt comfort wrapped in the blanket of anonymity. The talkative old warrior might very well have deliberated—with good reason—what had happened in San Angela had best stay in San Angela. There is relevance in once again reviewing what the military man said— or didn't say:

> ....that she was a woman leading a dual life—a saintly philanthropist in New Orleans, which it was claimed was her home city; in Fort Concho a desperate character

of the booming West.....that her father, a gallant knight of the Old South and an inveterate gambler, went down on the Alabama off Cherbourg, France, and that the money she won at cards went to an invalid mother at Montgomery, Alabama, and to defray the expenses of an only sister at a fashionable boarding school in Virginia, while neither the mother nor sister dreamed that the money for their support bore the taint of iniquity.[49]

Denying Carlotta Thompkins and an unnamed U. S. Army officer ever engaged in a soul-searching tell-all private conversation—or possibly more—is pointless. Impugning Mr. John Warren Hunter's claim that he conducted such interviews would be unjust. Absent documentation to the contrary, it is but equitable to presume that the editorial writer got it right; the soldier's words telling of bygone days. Questioning the validity of Carlotta once being the Belle of the Ball and one of New Orleans' "saintly philanthropists" is more than just a little logical however. That query is not rude. Too, it should not go unnoticed, though it interferes with timeworn mythology, the military man said naught of Carlotta's gambling expertise, only that "the money she won at cards" she sent back East. The same could be said of any number of gambling queens, barroom maidens or cat-house courtesans chiseling subsistence along Texas' frontiers. Most all of them were sending money back East—to hear them tell it.

To acknowledge that Miss Carlotta was for a time at San Angela is not troubling. To accept as fact that she sat in on high-stakes or low-down card games and from time to time actually won is believable. To think, since she was also "a desperate character of the booming West," that she sometimes resorted to other pecuniary pastimes is also probable and, somewhat later, certifiable.

There are disturbing unanswered questions. It is recurrently alleged that Miss Carlotta Thompkins was an aristocrat by right of birth. Some claim she was an unconquerable Mississippi Riverboat gambling queen. Others profess that Carlotta was the near perfect princess of San Antonio's tastefully furnished saloons and clubrooms. If Carlotta was all that, why was she residing at scandalously shabby San Angela? It is suggested, minus any solid foundation, that Carlotta was somehow hiding from an ex-boyfriend or even an estranged husband. Could that be true? If so, considering her successful talents at the gaming tables, her upscale standard of living with stylish Parisian fashions tucked into an overstuffed trunk and her smartly coifed red hair never mussed, did not the big city make more sense? A mouse can hide better in a mansion than in a child's doll house. Tiny San Angela was not a good place to avoid notice, especially if she was drawing attention to herself by poker playing; raking in piles of cash and coin from a mixture of West Texas' hardest and hardiest. Nor was San Angela a marvelous place to guarantee an affluent living at gambling. The cities and booming mining towns—where business deals were made and closed—was where the big money changed hands, not the hide-buying settlements, cow camps, or the army's scabtowns. A degree of naïveté would have to creep into one's psyche to believe that the Gambling Queen of Hearts, the girl who was an angel but for the absence of the customary wings and a halo and the very real Carlotta J. Thompkins were one and the same person. The first was a fanciful creation. The other is prime example of a girl cast into the frontier's seedy underworld. Miss Carlotta Thompkins was no angel. In the beginnings, angels bypassed San Angela. Though he wasn't any angel either, John Henry "Doc" Holliday found San Angela was a little too tough, even for him. Or, maybe it was just a town too unrefined and unattractive. Moreover: "It was not a place apt to hold Doc Holliday."[50]

There is merit in brining up the errant dentist's name. Though the actual depth of the personal relationship between Mr. Holliday and Miss Thompkins is shadowy, nevertheless there was one. Tracing their cozy affiliation will run the gamut; anecdotal gossip, circumstantial common sense, secondary source allegations, and finally in New Mexico Territory, a primary resource notation that to a very real extent buttresses acceptance of the others.

Faint though her footprints may be at San Angela there is room for a touch of supposition. Soon Carlotta's tracks may be followed with a growing number of citations to primary source materials. The particular social and business activities taking up Miss Carlotta's time in the very near future, presumably are reflective of the same dynamics mirroring her recent past. People may be reborn philosophically and undergo a reformation of the heart—or mind. But, at this point in Carlotta's story, reforming or mending her naughty ways was not on the sporting girl's agenda. What was progressively consuming her thoughts revolved around making another move. San Angela certainly was not growing dull. The rampant misbehavior, fist fights and shooting scrapes, the sin and sensuality and seductiveness of an anything-goes town had not subsided. The buffalo hunters, soldiers, cowboys, and wayward husbands still moved freely and, sometimes recklessly, through the town's beer halls and bawdy houses. San Angela was yet an exciting town, it had not lost its edge. For an unknown reason Carlotta Thompkins had decided to decamp San Angela. Working-girls and wagering-men habitually pulling up stakes and prospecting pockets at ever changing locations was but traditional business for those caught up in the games of adult amusement. Carlotta Thompkins was a player.

Near Fort Concho the mail and stagecoach line that came in from San Antonio forked. Westbound the semi-weekly coaches struck out for distant El Paso and beyond. A traveler desiring a link in the other direction would board the stagecoach and gallop along a northeasterly route through Camp Colorado, Fort Griffin and Jacksboro to the Sherman/Denison area where railway connections broadened one's choices.[51]

It was time to move on! Why she went is yet mysterious. Where she went is not. Carlotta Thompkins stuffed all of those fine Parisian fashions in the trunk and once again boarded a stagecoach, this one heading northeast. When she stepped out of the coach it was not at the roadway's end, but at Jacksboro, Texas. At Jacksboro she became Miss Lottie Deno. There, too, unedited pages of a primary source documented biography opens.

Reasonably early view of early "Over the River" [present day San Angelo]. Fort Concho in the background. *Courtesy Fort Concho National Historic Landmark.*

Post Hospital, Fort Concho. *Courtesy Fort Concho National Historic Landmark.*

Quartermaster Headquarters, Fort Concho. *Courtesy Fort Concho National Historic Landmark.*

The crudeness of early day San Angelo, better known as Over the River, is illustrated in this photograph of the jail. *Courtesy Fort Concho National Historic Landmark.*

A photograph of the Concho Hotel at Over the River. Certainly not the prototypical image of where the Southwest's premier gambling princess would be staying, but elegance was a scarcity in West Texas, despite the myth. *Courtesy Fort Concho National Historic Landmark.*

W. S. Veck, is generally characterized now as the Father of San Angelo, Texas. In the beginnings Mr. Veck was proprietor of an irrefutably unsavory hangout for West Texas troublemakers, ne'er-do-wells, and a bevy of enterprising "ladies." *Courtesy West Texas Collection, Angelo State University.*

W. S. Veck's store and saloon. As with the image of Over the River's hotel, this spot does not seem appropriately attractive for the so-called Gambling Queen of Hearts. This is the location where Mrs. Kate Veck [see residence to left of store] overheard toughs hatch their murder plots and "where the law was your pistol and you could carry as many as you wanted to." *Courtesy Fort Concho National Historic Landmark.*

West Texas cowboys ready for action—or a studio photographer. *Courtesy Fort Concho National Historic Landmark.*

Endnotes Chapter 4

[1] R. C. Crane, "Stage-Coaching In The Concho Country." *West Texas Historical Association Yearbook*. Volume X [October 1934]. "But at any rate, in June, 1857, the Post Office Department awarded [a] contract to James E. Birch of California for the establishment of a mail stage line, from San Antonio, Texas, to San Diego, California, for twice a month service, on the basis of $140,000 per annum. The service was to run in four horse coaches; the distance was 1475.76 miles, and the time was to be 30 days." 59.

[2] Ibid. "At this time the stages left San Antonio on Mondays, Wednesdays and Fridays at 8 A. M...." 65.

[3] Ibid. 67; J. D. Fauntleroy, "Old Stage Routes of Texas." *Frontier Times*. July 1929. 420-423. The stagecoach trip made by Carlotta Thompkins from San Antonio to Fort Concho/San Angela is a travel experience paralleled by Emily Andrews, a soldier's wife. Andrews' irreplaceable perspective—that from a female's eye—is a treasure. See, Sandra L. Myres, Editor, "A Woman's View of the Texas Frontier, 1874: The Diary of Emily K. Andrews." *Southwestern Historical Quarterly*. Volume LXXXVI, No. 1. [July 1982]. 49-80.

[4] Thomas T. Smith, *The Old Army In Texas: A Research Guide to the U. S. Army in Nineteenth-Century Texas*. 60; J. N. Gregory, *Fort Concho: Its Why And Wherefore*. 19.

[5] Loyd M. Uglow, *Standing In The Gap: Army Outposts, Pickets Stations, And The Pacification Of The Texas Frontier, 1866-1886*. 131. For an interesting sidebar regarding the Comanchero traffic attention is drawn to Bob Alexander's article "Comanchero Nightmare: John N. Hittson," *National Association For Outlaw And Lawman History, Inc.* [NOLA] *Quarterly*, Volume XXVIII, No. 2. [April-June 2004]. 24-36.

[6] Ibid. 132.

[7] Ibid.

[8] Ibid.

[9] Hunter, *The Story of Lottie Deno: Her Life and Times*. 8.

[10] Hunter [John Warren], "The Mystery Woman at Fort Concho." 1; J. Marvin Hunter, "The Lottie Deno I Knew." *West Texas Historical Association Yearbook* 1947; Rose, *Lottie Deno: Gambling Queen of Hearts* disregards Hunter's somewhat ambiguous "along about 1870," and absent any citation confidently declares: "Lottie arrived at Fort Concho, Texas, on the stage from San Antonio early in 1870." 37.

[11] Ibid. "She [Carlotta] came in on the overland stage from San Antonio, secured and furnished a room in an adobe 'Over the River' and during her stay exhibited all the traits of a refined, educated woman who had been brought up in the best society and was by birth and training a typical gentlewoman." 1.

[12] William M. Notson, Post Surgeon, *Fort Concho Medical History, 1869 to 1872*. From Dr. Notson's monthly report of February 1870: "An effort is being made to establish a town or village on the north side of the North Concho river. The pioneer in the venture is Mr. B. de Witt, one of the traders of the Post. Two hackel [*sic*] or picket houses are in process of erection." 24.

[13] Suzanne Campbell, [Contributor], *Tom Green County: Chronicles of Our Heritage*. Volume I. 1; Tanya Lynn Lee, *The Avenue: A Social and Economic History of Concho Avenue*. Master of Arts Thesis. Angelo State University, San Angelo, Texas. 1998. "For a long time the settlement had no name, it was merely designated as 'Over the River.'" 1.

[14] Shirley Anne Leckie, Editor, *The Colonel's Lady on the Western Frontier: The Correspondence of Alice Kirk Grierson.* 72.

[15] Ibid; Susan Miles, *Fort Concho In 1877.* "Directly opposite the post on the north bank of the North Concho river sprawled the miserable hovels which made up the village of Saint Angela…" 6.

[16] Notson, *Fort Concho Medical History, 1869 to 1872.* 28.

[17] J. Evetts Haley, *Fort Concho and the Texas Frontier.* 317-318.

[18] William H. Leckie & Shirley A. Leckie, *Unlikely Warriors: General Benjamin Grierson and His Family.* Quoting letters from General Grierson to his wife Alice, May 1st and May 8th, 1875. 225.

[19] Ibid.

[20] Robert F. Bluthardt, Director, Fort Concho National Historic Landmark, San Angelo, Texas. Presentation paper, "William Veck, Forgotten Father of San Angelo," for the Tom Green County Historical Society. 1. Courtesy, Fort Concho National Historic Landmark.

[21] Ibid. 2.

[22] Ibid.

[23] Notson, *Fort Concho Medical History, 1869 to 1872.* 50.

[24] Gus Clemens, *The Concho Country.* Quoting Dr. S. L. S. Smith. 69.

[25] Campbell, *Tom Greene County: Chronicles Of Our Heritage.* Volume I. 1.

[26] Clemens, *The Concho Country.* Quoting Kate Veck. 88.

[27] Forrestine C. Hooker [Steve Wilson, ed.], *Child of the Fighting Tenth: On The Frontier With The Buffalo Soldiers.* 104.

[28] Gary L. Roberts, *Doc Holliday: The Life and Legend.* Quoting A. M. Hobby. 432, n. 73.

[29] Campbell, *Tom Green County: Chronicles Of Our Heritage.* Volume I. 1. Clemens, *The Concho Country.* 88.

[30] Ibid.

[31] Clemens, *The Concho Country.* "It [Ben Ficklin] was owned by the most respected gentlemen in the area, most of them connected to either the stage line or the ranching interests. Officers and wives from Fort Concho frequented Ben Ficklin stores and defended the town in bureaucratic intrigues with Washington. Santa Angela, on the other hand, had earned a lurid reputation as a place to which soldiers, cowboys, and buffalo hunters went to drink, gamble, satisfy sexual lust, and murder each other." 86.

[32] Ibid.

[33] Wayne R. Austerman, *Sharps Rifles and Spanish Mules: The San Antonio-El Paso Mail, 1851-1881.* The author concisely explains the political tug-of-war between Ben Ficklin and San Angela. 274-276. The November 1928 issue of *Frontier Times* carries a first-person narrative about the demise of Ben Ficklin: "[F. A.]Karger Tells of Flood Loss At Ben Ficklin." 83-84.

[34] Luke Gournay, *Texas Boundaries: Evolution of the State's Counties.* Tom Green County was created March 13, 1874, and officially organized January 5, 1875, with Ben Ficklin as county seat. Later, after a 1882 flood destroyed Ben Ficklin, the county seat was moved to San Angelo. 92; Sammy Tise, *Texas County Sheriffs.* "Frank Lamotte was elected the first sheriff on January 5, 1875…." 493.

[35] W. M. Notson, "Fort Concho in 1870." *Frontier Times.* May 1926. 6.

[36] Gournay, *Texas Boundaries: Evolution of the State's Counties.* 31; William Roberts Gardner, [Contributor], *Tom Green County: Chronicles Of Our Heritage.* Volume I. 21.

[37] *Tom Green County: Chronicles of Our Heritage.* Volume I. Extract from "Hunters Frontier: Exterminating the American Bison in the Concho River Region," by Marvin Schultz, *Fort Concho Report.* Spring. 1998. 20.

[38] Ibid.

[39] Miles Gilbert, Leo Remiger & Sharon Cunningham, *Encyclopedia Of Buffalo Hunters and Skinners.* Two Volumes. Citations to Fort Concho, Concho River and San Angela [San Angelo] throughout.

[40] Bruce J. Dinges, "The San Angelo Riot of 1881: The Army, Race Relations, and Settlement on the Texas Frontier." *Journal of the West.* Vol. 41, No. 3. [Summer 2002] 35-45.

[41] Bill Green, *The Dancing Was Lively, Fort Concho, Texas: A Social History, 1867-1882.* 75.

[42] Barbara Barton, *Pistol Packin' Preachers.* "Potter's first sermon in a saloon in San Angelo is well documented..." 45.

[43] Frank N. Schubert, "Gunfire at San Angela: When 10th Cavalry troopers from Fort Concho retaliated against Texas civilians." *Wild West.* February 2004. 14.

[44] Ibid.

[45] Gary and Margaret Kraisinger, *The Western: The Greatest Texas Cattle Trail, 1874-1886.* 23.

[46] Hunter [John Warren], "The Mystery Woman at Ft. Concho." "She was a mystery to nearly all, good and bad, who chanced to know her and hence she was called the 'Mystic Maude.'" I.

[47] Hunter [J. Marvin], *The Story of Lottie Deno: Her Life and Times.* 8.

[48] Hunter [J. Marvin], "The Lottie Deno I Knew." 30.

[49] Hunter, [John Warren], "The Mystery Woman at Fort Concho." I.

[50] Roberts, *Doc Holliday: The Life And Legend.* 432, n. 73.

[51] Crane, "Stage-Coaching In The Concho Country." 67.

Chapter 5

"A Red-Hot Town"

Carlotta Thompkins had not changed her game plan. She had merely moved her nucleus for action—and Jacksboro was action-packed. Like San Angela, Jacksboro was within but a stone's throw of an army base, Fort Richardson.[1] Dissimilar to San Angela, Jacksboro lay within the boundaries of an established county. Originally stamped out of Cooke County during 1856, Jack County was officially organized on July 1st the following year. In 1858 Jacksboro was awarded county seat honors.[2] Lying on the rolling plains cut by the West Fork of the Trinity River southwest of Sherman/Denison and northwest of Fort Worth, Jacksboro was at the frontier's brink. It was the jumping off place for the U. S. Army's military campaigns and a supply point for hide-hunters venturing further west in search of buffalo. Since it was ranching country too, many were the Longhorns rounded up and shaped into northbound trail herds destined for Kansas.[3] Demographically Jacksboro was much the same as San Angela, excepting for the fact its roots were deeper, resulting in a heavier and more concentrated civilian population. For a particular class of humanity at Jacksboro the coming and goings of Uncle Sam's fighting men, buffalo hunters and cowboys was measured not by harmonious poundings of hoof beats or the squeaking wheels of teamsters' busy freight wagons, but by the melody of rattling change in their pockets. Carlotta Thompkins had a good ear—she liked the sound of jingling coins.

Fort Richardson, established in 1866, was the northernmost link in the chain of army bases tasked with covering the northwestern frontier of Texas. Trailing off to the southwest some seventy odd miles was Fort Griffin, then below there well over a hundred miles Fort Concho, next Fort McKavett near Menardville, and close to the border with Old Mexico, Fort Clark. The northwestern frontier of Texas was a hotbed of Comanche and Kiowa incursion. Diverse raiding parties struck from camps hidden somewhere on the Llano Estacado. Others simply slipped off the reservation in Indian Territory, just across the Red River, launching lighting strike raids, marauding and murdering as they went. The Indians "considered the northwestern half of Texas their rightful domain and the Texan inhabitants of that region their perpetual enemies."[4] Having split into subgroups for hit-and-run attacks on isolated ranches, lumbering ox-teams, and unfortunate victims cutoff from reinforcement, the Indians speedily reunited, meeting at some designated place, "and escaped back to the reservation during the waning moon."[5]

The ambiance at Fort Richardson was much like at San Angela, totally lacking. A comparative extrapolation may be made by drawing from the frontier fort's architectural blueprint; the layout was simple, the construction rudimentary:

> The plan of barracks consisted of buildings constructed of pickets, as the timber was too small to cut up into boards. The large timber for rafters was hauled from the Big Sandy, thirty-eight miles east. The pickets were eleven feet long, sunk two feet in the ground. They were chinkd [*sic*] with adobe and roofed with shingles. Three barracks were 85x20 feet; four were 85x20 feet with a wing 73x27; one was 100x27 feet, and another 114x27 feet. The quartermaster storehouse and commissary were of sandstone and were 86x29 feet, with a space of 20 feet between them. There were four stables, each 200x35 feet.[6]

An onsite voice, U. S. Cavalryman H. H. McConnell, differs only slightly with the above outline of Fort Richardson's design, saying, "a 'Plate' was spiked on the top, a roof, slightly inclined was made by laying poles side by side, the interstices filled with twigs, and the whole covered thickly with dirt. The spaces in the walls were 'chinked' with chips and plastered with mud; doors made of boxes from the Quartermaster's department were hung, and with a rude chimney and capacious fireplace, a house was finished in no time. The weak point about the mud roof was that it continued to rain for forty-eight hours *inside* after the rain had ceased to fall outdoors."[7]

The admitted overemphasis on the fort's construction is indispensable in setting the stage that Miss Carlotta Thompkins walked onto. The town, like Fort Richardson, was undergoing its growing pains. It was not an attractive picture. Overtime the good citizens of Jacksboro would nurture her with care, replacing her initial ugliness with structures more pleasing to the eye. In the whole of Jack County, before the Civil War, there had been but a single building built of stone, the Masonic Lodge. At one time "an old 'rawhide' building served as the courthouse. These 'rawhide' cabins built with green sawed lumber warped out of shape as the lumber dried leaving gaping cracks in the walls."[8] Jacksboro's folklore offers the citizens' solution to a problem. Worrying that their crudely built county jail was so insecure it couldn't be counted on to hold a prisoner, the townsmen acted: They hanged a Negro prisoner to keep him from escaping.[9]

For several years Jacksboro, as county seat for Jack County, would serve as the jurisdictional headquarters for much of West Texas in regards to court proceedings. During the earliest days prisoners were actually housed in the Wise County jail at Decatur, a neighboring town forty miles east.[10]

Rediscovering the analogous relationship between soldiers and the so-called sporting crowd is not required: Honey attracts flies, as does rotting meat. As close to Fort Richardson's outside edge as they could possibly get, the "saloons" and "groceries" sprang up. Other shady businesses blossomed as well. Not surprisingly the primitive little town of Jacksboro began to flourish. Again H. H. McConnell gifts the reader with his colorful eyewitness impression:

> The erst-quiet—desolation in fact—of Jacksboro began to blossom, if not "like the rose," at least like a sunflower and gorgeous and euphonious names graced the board or picket shanties that dotted the hillside and invited the thirsty and unwary to enter.[11]

The intervening half mile between Fort Richardson and Jacksboro's town square was but an unwrapped invitation to bathe in the waters of wickedness. Looking after unbridled wants of the masses twenty-seven saloons of varying caliber were strewn along the short roadway. Some were in tents with a wide board resting on beer kegs for a bar, others were but crudely built picket hideaways or more traditional log houses, while a few could boast of a more substantial and an eye-appealing erection. In name each held its very own distinctiveness, although the shenanigans taking place in one but echoed the naughtiness of all. Just to name a few, there were the Union Headquarters, the Gem, the Little Shamrock, the Emerald, the Sunflower, the Island Home, the First National, the Last Chance, and Mollie McCabe's Palace of Beautiful Sin.[12] At the Wichita Saloon a shot of straight whiskey was $.25 and it took three bartenders to work any given shift. Still the customers had to wait in line, at least so said Henry Strong, a U. S. Army guide.[13] After discharge from the military Mr. H. H. McConnel would become the city's mayor, but even he admitted that for awhile Jacksboro was a "red-hot town." It was a turbulent community "where the sound of the fiddle and the crack of the six-shooter was heard the livelong night."[14]

A third voice, that of young Thomas F. Horton, spoke of the "payday orgy." He begged for believability: "I am not exaggerating when I say I have seen the time when I could have walked on soldier[s] lying drunk along the road from the south side of the Square to the creek and not touch the ground.[15] Perhaps Tom Horton's recollection is somewhat spiced—a little windy—but the distance between town and fort wasn't that far. Even if there were not sufficient soldiers for steppingstones, a few of them were capable of participation in a "payday orgy." The following oldtimer's remarks may not have been site specific to Jacksboro, nevertheless:

> Sergeant T. E. Guy, First Cavalry, 1889-92, told of an incident he witnessed in which some of the soldier "sports" in his company conducted an orgy in an off-limits brothel and saloon. A nude prostitute postured to accommodate the "sports," standing in the center of the table around which the soldiers were drinking. Of his own low moral level and that of others in his company, another Indian Wars regular said, "I lived a disgraceful life as a kid in the army!"[16]

Just how much Carlotta Thompkins contributed to any disgraceful behavior on the part of young or old soldiers is measureless, though she did want to relieve them—if not of their virginity—their cash money. At Jacksboro, Carlotta Thompkins acquired her new name, Lottie Deno. That she herself instigated use of the new moniker is unknowable; that others now knew her as such is conclusively firm. Too, she managed another acquisition; identifiable primary source recognition.

Whether or not Miss Lottie Deno was the proprietor of one of those twenty-seven saloons scattered along the dirt roadway, or simply thought it best at her private place—whatever and wherever it was—to be in strict compliance with the letter of the law is elusive. At Jacksboro "she paid occupation tax as a retail liquor dealer..."[17] Literally, she may have had to pay a fiddler standing in her parlor, one sawing entertainment with strings of a resined bow; figuratively she would have to pay *the* fiddler, a gavel-tapping judge. Angelic or amoral, Lottie Deno was living the fast life; her wings fluttered at a high-speed.

Lottie Deno wasn't the only vivacious female of the sporting genus catching notice. Jacksboro had many. For most history has been kind, they have been forgotten. Others are much less fortunate, their names made the docket book or newspaper or both. Happy-go-lucky girlfriends like Polly Turnover, Molly Hipp, Maggie Truelove, Mollie McCabe, Louisa Welch, Rosa Lee, Long Kate, Jane Blackwell, Mollie Bowman, Catharine Lemely, Belle Little, Nettie McGuire and a notorious pay-for-pleasure girl, Sally Watson, have all had their names immorally immortalized.[18]

Accepting the fairy tale makes for a nice narrative, but certainly one historically flawed. Imagining Lottie Deno decked out in those fine Parisian fashions, sitting at the corner table in a gracefully furnished saloon, whipping the financial pants off of veterans of Indian campaigns, buffalo hunts, cattle drives, as well as neophyte tourists and thriving businessmen all with the turn of a card is a good read. In light of the dingy environment she was working in, an atmosphere reeking with an aroma of sour whiskey and cheap perfume inescapably trapped beneath the low hanging haze of stale smoke, any pristine claim that Lottie never tolerated profanity, tobacco usage, or whiskey drinking at her tables is naiveté stretched to the limit. Why would she buy an occupational liquor license? The truth reveals a picture of unpainted and unkempt buildings making up 1870s Jacksboro. It wasn't pretty. Indeed the next decade would see the city's improved physical appearance, but when Lottie Deno knew Jacksboro there was nothing in the way of housing— either at the town or fort—that could have been considered even remotely luxurious.[19]

Peeling back the paint of reality leaves bare the fact: "The fort and town had little to offer the men but drinking and bawdy houses."[20] Declaring this was the life Miss Lottie Deno had chosen, absent hard conformation, would be pettily impolite. An unforeseen state of affairs for her—unknown to history's trustees—may have encouraged her migration to Texas. Whatever the reason, good or bad, she was a member of the sporting community. Lottie was flexible, her survival instincts sharp. Acknowledging she gambled, playing poker and/or dealing faro is not troubling. First-hand witnesses have left their remembrances. There should be little doubt, sometimes Lottie Deno won—but not always. If that had been the case, surely G. W. Robson, owner and editor of Jacksboro's newspaper *The Frontier Echo* would have featured her in a human interest piece. Even then that would have made quite a story! He didn't mention Miss Deno's glamorous and glorious card playing career, but her name would grace the pages of his newspaper indicating another profession. When she sat down to deal a hand, according to more than one informant, her wagering rivals had best been eagle-eyed and double wary customers. Miss Lottie has been unsympathetically characterized as being a real person, but a gal "off-brand in her habits as well as her profession. Baffingly crooked at cards and disappointingly straight in more personal matters, she left everybody guessing as to where she had come from."[21] When the occasion either demanded it or when an opportunity presented itself, Lottie was not at all disinclined to cheat. That dexterous slight of hand might have put bread on her dinner table more easily than other options. At Jacksboro, yet still on an authentic western frontier, Lottie's career choices were limited. Miss Deno could lay out the cards, wish for the best or underhandedly guarantee an Ace. Or, she could just lay down for the dollar bills. Lottie Deno was a survivor!

Another of Jacksboro's survivors was William C. "Big Bill" Gilson. For part of the time Lottie Deno was earning a livelihood at Jacksboro the town had not been legitimately incorporated. When that officially changed on January 9th, 1875, the newly installed mayor, L. P.

Adamson, appointed Mr. Gilson to the hazardous position of Jacksboro's Town Marshal.[22] Big Bill Gilson usually carried two things with him into any battle; a hulking 225 pound frame and his "little gun," a sawed-off shotgun sans a regular stock, but outfitted with a pistol grip. Loaded with 00 buckshot, the short-barreled weapon was more than effective when precarious situations became too delicate and too dangerous.[23] H. H. McConnell, who personally knew Big Bill, remarked that he was a huge man of steel nerves; "cool, brave, quick and powerful, and possessing every element necessary to cope with the 'toughs' who sought to 'run the town.'. . . .Gilson took them all in alike, and they knew their man well enough to let him alone."[24] Miss Lottie Deno would all too soon come to know Big Bill Gilson—all too well!

Although Town Marshal Gilson's role is unverifiable, it is not too presumptuous to suggest he, in an almost immediate crackdown after assuming office, arrested Lottie Deno, charging her with Keeping A Disorderly House. At any rate Lottie was so charged in February of 1875.[25] Wording of the charge was consistent with that used in legally drawn *complaints* reserved for dealing with the problem of prostitution and the business of operating bordellos. There was no mention that indicated any violation of the state's gaming laws. Most likely filing of the criminal charge was but the defacto method of licensing the illicit business, rather than an attempt to eradicate Miss Lottie Deno's means of support. The city and/or county, less fees for the arresting officer and judge, received payment of the nominal fine, while the working-girl was gently reminded that she toiled, tawdry as it was, at the pleasure of a local government's rule. Society winked, the whores whored. On the raw frontier hypocrisy was often the handmaiden of government affairs.

One of the tough characters at Jacksboro was Mr. Joe Horner. He was whoring himself into a wicked life of outlawry. It would be credulous to think Lottie Deno didn't know him, either quite well, or merely as an acquaintance. Jacksboro like San Angela wasn't that big. And, Mr. Horner, like Miss Deno, was developing quite a curious "circle of carousing cronies," while he idled away time not on the ranch outside town, but "in the dives of Jacksboro." He even invested in one of them; the records show that during the years 1871 to 1875 he paid an 'occupation tax,' which authorized him to sell liquor at retail."[26] At Jacksboro Joe Horner and a pal, Bill Cotnam, more-or-less captained a gang of misfits known locally as the Horner/Cotnam Gang.[27]

During one Jacksboro saloon disturbance Horner assaulted Ed Harris. The Jack County indictment read:

> Joseph Horner in and upon the person of Ed Harris
> with a certain pistol which was then and there loaded
> and charged with gunpowder and leaden balls and was

then and there a deadly weapon, which said pistol he, the said Joseph Horner, in his hand then and there had and held at, to, against and upon the said Ed Harris, with the intent to injure unlawfully and violently, did make an aggravated assault and battery, for that he, the said Horner, did then and there, threateningly, unlawfully, and violently draw upon and present the said pistol at the said Harris and many other wrongs then and there did.[28]

Joe Horner was arrested by the Jack County Sheriff, L. L. "Lee" Crutchfield. Horner, also charged with two cases of cattle theft, made bail denoting he never saw interior walls of the jail. While awaiting trial on the felony matters at hand, Joe Horner put himself in another imbroglio when his racial insensitivity overrode common sense. Or, telling the story from his viewpoint, he was the victim of arrogant bigotry by black soldiers. Inside a Jacksboro saloon the confrontation between Horner and two troopers from Fort Richardson over just who should pay for a round of drinks, exploded. Private George Smith suffered Joe Horner's wrath, and a gunshot wound. One that was critically painful but not deadly. Smith's comrade ran from the saloon. On the barroom floor Smith bled. Out the barroom's swinging-door Joe Horner walked. Down the street and into another saloon he ducked, as if nothing at all had happened. After notification that their friend had been shot, moreover by a white man, other black soldiers decided to apprehend Joe Horner. It was not to be. A blazing gunbattle ensued on Jacksboro's streets, wherein one of Horner's rifle bullets connected, "hitting one Negro between the eyes, killing him instantly."[29] The now worked up Horner, by this time horseback, had his mount shot from underneath his legs, the bullet passing through "the sweat-leathers on each side just where Horner's knees apparently should have been, yet he was unhurt." Then, just as Hollywood would have scripted it, cowboy Frank Lake dashed out from behind Jacksboro's Island Home Saloon riding his horse and rescued Horner, "who jumped up behind him, and they galloped out of town."[30] The troopers gathered their mounts, chasing after Horner and Lake. Due to Lake's overburdened horse carrying double the soldiers overtook their targets and an exchange of gunfire erupted. It was Joe Horner's third gunbattle of the day. Mr. Lake took a bullet through the thigh, putting him out of action. Mr. Horner scooted into the saddle on Frank's horse and fled, leaving his pal and the irate troopers to work out details. The wounded Lake was taken to the army hospital at Fort Richardson where he was treated and released. After several days passed with no further news, Joe Horner sought legal advice from Moses Wiley, the then sitting U. S.

Commissioner. Having previous army service in his background, Mr. Wiley maintained working contacts with Fort Richardson's military hierarchy. Acting in Joe Horner's behalf Commissioner Wiley arranged a meeting with Colonel William Wood and an accord was reached.[31] Purportedly:

> Mr. Horner agreed not to kill any more Negroes if the Negroes would not kill any more of him.[32]

Joe Horner's battle with the black soldiers underscores post war posture in Jack County. The formality of Reconstruction might have been but recent history, but Jacksboro wasn't "reconstructed." A striking dichotomy raises its ugly head. Many of Jacksboro's and Jack County's citizens had little use for the U. S. Military in general, but even more particularly they despised regiments manned by black soldiers. At the time northwest Texas was a hothouse of obnoxious racial prejudice. Cruel acts of discrimination were commonplace. There was an unchecked double standard however. Soldiers of any color were more than welcomed—even encouraged—to spend payday proceeds with Jacksboro's businessmen. For those instances merchants were colorblind. Even more telling was the sporting community's duplicity; submerging racial hatred while outwardly enticing blacks to taste the wildly wicked pleasures of whiskey, wagering, and whoring. The commingling of profit and prejudice could prove risky. Joe Horner's dustup would be but one case. Two white troopers, Sergeant William Lawrence and Corporal Zachery Ringiron, during a fight at a Jacksboro dance house— predominately black—paid heavily. An affronted black man took issue with their maliciousness and shot them both, killing Lawrence. During another mêlée Joe Horner's partner in crime, Bill Cotnam, was fatally gunned down by three black troopers while enjoying his supper at a Jacksboro restaurant; at least so claimed Mr. Horner.[33] The potential for trouble was ever present.

Not all of Jacksboro's volatility can be traced to bigoted intolerance. Sometimes friction simply pitted civilian against soldier, no matter the color line. Following a white soldier named Burke being killed in a Jacksboro brothel, army buddies were not reticent. They burned the bordello to the ground. Their thirst for revenge yet sated, the soldiers threatened to torch the whole town of Jacksboro, at least so frightened citizens were led to believe. Skillfully maneuvering military commanders and even-tempered residents diffused the situation quashing the rumors and restoring peace.[34]

There is absolutely no doubt that Miss Lottie Deno and one of the Old West's iconic ne'er-do-wells became casual gambling associates or fast friends—maybe even something more fiery and titillating. John

Henry "Doc" Holliday's actual finesse as a frontier gambler and gunfighter has been somewhat overrated. Mr. Holliday's propensity for winding up in serious trouble has not. Acknowledging that the sporting fellow ended up in Texas for this narrative is all that's necessary; the sorted and sordid reasons that prompted his removal from a good Georgia home, his westward migration and Doc's wayward behavior are speculations best left to his biographers.[35] On a downhill slide from noble graces with the upright and reputable side of society, the tubercular Doc Holliday was wheezing and wandering throughout Northwest Texas, sometimes ahead of arrest warrants.

There is concurrence among his many chroniclers that Doc Holliday spent some time at Jacksboro. Finding the common ground as to just when that was, or exactly what he did while there is more difficult. That he spent a whole year at Jacksboro gambling his way to eminence seems not too probable.[36] His name is absent from the court's docket book as well as pages of Jacksboro's *The Frontier Echo*. Shrewdly avoiding publicity—usually bad—was uncharacteristic for Holliday. While not a conclusive methodology, Doc Holliday's misspent life is normally traced by mentions of his brushes with the law. So, during time spent at Jacksboro he was either walking the straight and narrow path—which does not seem probable—or he was not there for very long, which does seem likely.[37] Jacksboro, situated where she was, is geographically relative to Mr. Holliday's known movements. Considering the fact Jacksboro was, if not the destination, a stage stop on the heavily traveled roadway from Sherman/Denison down through the Fort Concho country adds to the probability of Doc's arrivals and departures from Jacksboro.

After stopovers at Dallas, Fort Worth, Denison, and Jacksboro, Doc Holliday had landed in Shackelford County, Texas. On an appealing hilltop stood the U. S. Army's sentinel, Fort Griffin. On the level ground below sprawled a rowdy civilian village. The immodest settlement would finally acquire legitimacy by an adoptive name, Fort Griffin, but commonly the tough little town was simply called The Flat. For a short time it would be Doc Holliday's new home. Not unexpectedly Doc Holliday fell in with a rough crowd. Not too soon thereafter he found himself running from the law. After considering his options, Holliday had decided to flee. For some reason he had chosen to run rather than pay a $10 to $15 fine for gambling at a house where "spiritous liquors" were sold and consumed.[38] Skipping one step ahead of the law, or trying to, would be one of the hallmarks of his life's story. Answering a court crier's call was an anathema for the wandering dentist. Whether Doc Holliday was dead broke—which may well speak to his veritable gambling genius—or he simply had not a friend in the world willing to make him a loan is immaterial. Maybe Doc Holliday was not wanting to undergo the indignity and humiliation of an arrest for such a small-time violation. The imposed fine no doubt would have been inconsequential to a successful gambler. During his June 1875 flight he bounced through San Angela just ahead of the *capias* warrant from Shackelford County which had been forwarded to Tom Green County Sheriff Frank Lamotte.[39] Where Holliday went from there is but tentative. Recently it has been written that from San Angela he *could have* gone to San Antonio or Austin, or Laredo or Fort Worth or Dallas or Denison.[40] *Perhaps* he showed himself in all six towns. *Maybe* not. Another biographer submitted that after warrants for Doc Holliday were issued, that "Jacksboro was Doc's next destination."[41] Another well regarded writer and researcher avows: "Even such legendary gamblers as Doc Holliday and Lottie Deno made regular visits to Jacksboro to help lighten the pockets of the suddenly affluent soldiers."[42] Therein is the central theme for this part of Lottie Deno's profile. Somewhere along the way—and Jacksboro is the most probable place—Doc Holliday and Lottie Deno were warmly introduced.

It does seem they met at Jacksboro; they were there at the same time, both were underworld habitués of barrooms and gambling halls, Jacksboro was small—everybody knew everybody—and the two independently-minded free spirits would in the future, at more than one juncture, find themselves thrown together again. Did Doc Holliday tout the possibilities of filling purses more easily at The Flat, where there too were soldiers, but a much larger population of hide-hunters, bullwhackers and cowboys? At The Flat money was flowing like honey running down an unruly child's chin. Did Holliday induce or seduce Lottie into abandoning Jacksboro? Did Doc take a shine to Lottie, or her to him? If so, was it mutual or but a one dimensional love—or lust? Were promises made? Or broken? Following either of their trails—day by day—is more than difficult. It may be said that Holliday had scooted out of San Angela before Sheriff Frank LaMotte executed service of Shackelford County's misdemeanor warrant and ran off to wherever before stopping in Denver. Lottie Deno had stayed behind at Jacksboro. Whether Lottie had met the hard-drinking traveler turned gambler while they were both living at Jacksboro, or while he was fleeing Texas through Jacksboro, or returning to The Flat by way of Jacksboro, is perplexing but extraneous. The outcome remains unchanged. Lottie Deno knew Doc Holliday. That is solid. The familiarity would endure well past their Texas adventures. Once again Lottie began thinking of folding those fancy Parisian gowns into the trunk.

She, too, mused about another matter. The legal noose was tightening for Lottie's colleague of the occupational tax paying crowd, Joe Horner. Perhaps tiring of his continued misbehavior one of the men standing good his bail-bond changed his mind and withdrew the pledge. Sheriff Lee Crutchfield ordered Horner's arrest, a task quickly but carefully accomplished by Jack County Deputy S. R. Hartley. With a spark of editorial glee *The Frontier Echo* dryly noted the "notorious" Joe Horner had been "gobbled up" and was "consigned to apartments in the Gilson House," a euphemism for the jail administered by Big Bill Gilson, the well-liked Town Marshal.[43]

Lottie Deno was planning to bid Jacksboro a friendly adieu. So, too, was Joseph Horner. His farewell would be at gunpoint. During the wee morning hours of September 13, 1875, a quartet of armed men disarmed the two guards at the Gilson House. After no little effort sawing through the chains anchoring him to the jail's floor, Joe Horner was a liberated man. Joe's highly-regarded biographer said of the daring escape: "When Joe Horner cut his shackles and walked out of the Gilson House, he also cut all ties to his former life."[44] Post his flight, a daring bank robbery at Comanche, Texas, and an escape from the state's penitentiary at Huntsville, Joe Horner reincarnated himself as Frank Canton. As such the one-time outlaw turned himself into a future sheriff of Johnson County, Wyoming, Livestock Detective, Deputy U. S. Marshal, and almost unbelievably, later, the politically powerful Adjutant General for the state of Oklahoma. Not even Lottie Deno, who was capable of fashioning a good story, could top that. Lottie had troubles of her own.

The Frontier Echo of March 10, 1876 carried stories about life on the wilder side at both The Flat and at Jacksboro. "More deviltry at Fort Griffin last Friday night a couple of our Uncle Samuel's dusky warriors got into a quarrel about a damsel of color, blows followed but hot words and cold led [lead] finished the fight and life of one of the combatants." Another soldier, Private Jacob Smith, had apparently been murdered by a culprit or culprits unknown or apprehended, much less convicted. There is even rhetorical innuendo implicating Mr. Doc Holliday in Smith's demise. Subsequent events more than reveal that the good-timing gambling dentist was capable of murder, but for this episode a paucity of any creditable evidence lets Doc off the hook.[45] Certainly 1870s peace officers in Shackelford County weren't hunting Doc Holliday for any unexplained killing. For them he was but an unexceptional misdemeanant.

Also in the newspaper was mention of the *State of Texas vs. Lottie Deno*. Charged with Keeping a Disorderly House the defendant was fined $100 and cost.[46] She without delay settled with the court. Admittedly records are somewhat jumbled but research does indicate Lottie Deno was charged with two other criminal cases of like value at the end of the year. By this time Lottie was growing weary with having to answer for her illicit behavior. She accepted imposition of a $100 fine in regards to one case, and entered a plea of *not guilty* for the other.[47]

Beginning the new year with legalistic style, on the 2nd day of January 1877, the court pronounced its judgment.

> *This day the cause came on for trial and now comes the county attorney representing the pleas of the State and the defendant Lottie Deno by counsel and both parties announce ready for trial and waiver a jury and submit the cause to the court and the defendant Lottie Deno plead not guilty to the indictment charging her with keeping a disorderly house and the court after hearing the evidence arranged by counsel as well as for the State as for the defendant is of the opinion that the defendant Lottie Deno is not guilty. It is there ordered, adjudged and decreed that the State take nothing and that the defendant Lottie Deno go home without delay.[48]*

Lottie Deno may have been legally vindicated and gone home without delay as instructed by the court, but her days as a participant on Jacksboro's rowdy nighttime stage were numbered. R. P. "Dick" Wheeler, a Knight-of-the-Road, pitched her little leather trunk stuffed full of stylish Parisian fashions atop, and Lottie Deno climbed aboard another stagecoach. This one was bound for that Shackelford County inferno of cavorting and card playing, The Flat.

H. H. McConnell came to Jacksboro, Texas, as a soldier and stayed, later writing of the time and place in *Five Years A Cavalryman*. He became this city's Mayor and a respected businessman. The photograph is of his drug store. *Courtesy G. J. Ritchie Library.*

Post Hospital, Fort Richardson, Texas. *Courtesy G. J. Ritchie Library, Jacksboro, Texas, and Texas Tech University, Lubbock—Southwest Collection.*

The old Jack County Jail at Jacksboro. Built during 1877. *Courtesy G. J. Ritchie Library, Jacksboro, Texas, and Texas Tech University, Lubbock— Southwest Collection.*

Outlaw Joe Horner, aka Frank Canton. Like Miss Lottie Deno the ever notorious Horner assumed an invented past, and eventually worked himself into a life of respectability. *Courtesy American Heritage Center, University of Wyoming.*

Mr. John Henry "Doc" Holliday. His true relationship with Miss Lottie Deno [of which there was one] is mysteriously shrouded between provable facts and glorified mythology. *Courtesy Craig Fouts.*

Endnotes Chapter 5

[1] Jack County Genealogical Society, *The History of Jack County*. "….Fort Richardson one half mile south of the town square." 19.

[2] Gourney, *Texas Boundaries: Evolution of the State's Counties*. The author asserts that Jacksboro was originally Jacksborough, the newer spelling taking hold in 1899. 69-70; The Jack County Genealogical Society's publication *The History of Jack County* disputes this theory: "Some local historians claim that the name was originally *Jacksborough;* however, the truth seems to be that the name was from the beginning *Jacksboro* and there was some confusion in the correct spelling. In all the early county and district court records the shorter spelling appears consistently; The *Frontier Echo* used the shorter spelling." 19. For this text Jacksboro will be utilized; the way the town's name is spelled today.

[3] Colonel Martin L. Crimmins, "Old Fort Richardson." *Frontier Times*. July 1940. "Nearly all the inhabitants were engaged in raising cattle." 421.

[4] Uglow, *Standing In The Gap: Army Outposts, Picket Stations, And The Pacification Of The Texas Frontier, 1866-1886.* 81.

[5] Crimmins, "Old Fort Richardson." 422.

[6] Ibid. 421.

[7] H. H. McConnell, *Five Years A Cavalryman: Or, Sketches Of Regular Army Life On The Texas Frontier, 1866-1871.* 54.

[8] Jack County Historical Society, *The History Of Jack County Texas*. 19.

[9] Ibid; McConnell, *Five Years A Cavalryman: Or, Sketches Of Regular Army Life On The Texas Frontier, 1866-1871.* "I believe this jail never had had but one occupant, a negro, confined for theft; but the terms of court were few and far between, and the jail not being a very secure building, the citizens had taken the precaution to hang him to prevent his escape from justice." 52.

[10] Ibid.

[11] McConnell, *Five Years A Cavalryman: Or, Sketches Of Regular Army Life On The Texas Frontier, 1866-1871.* 160.

[12] Allen Lee Hamilton, *Sentinel Of The Southern Plains: Fort Richardson and the Northwest Texas Frontier, 1866-1878.* 41.

[13] Ibid. 42.

[14] McConnell, *Five Years A Cavalryman: Or, Sketches Of Regular Army Life On The Texas Frontier, 1866-1871.* 160.

[15] Robert K. DeArment, *Alias Frank Canton*. Quoting Thomas F. Horton. 22.

[16] Don Rickey, Jr., *Forty Miles a Day on Beans and Hay: The Enlisted Soldier Fighting the Indian Wars*. 168.

[17] Ida Lasater Huckabay, *Ninety-Four Years In Jack County, 1854-1948*. "'She [Lottie Deno] seemingly departed from her 'quiet angelic ways' according to the court records of 1874. From 1871 to 1875 she paid occupation tax as a retail liquor dealer and more than once paid fines for maintaining a 'disorderly house.' She evidently departed about the time that Fort Richardson was abandoned. Court records show no cases against her after 1876. 'Old Jacksboro' had a dozen or more similar characters whose names adorn the court records." 155.

[18] Jack County Genealogical Society, *The History of Jack County*. 29. DeArment, *Alias Frank Canton*. 24, 39. Various issues of Jacksboro's *The Frontier Echo*.

[19] Ibid. "Housing in Jacksboro and at the fort was never luxurious in the frontier period. Jacksboro's finest houses were not built until the 1880s." 28.

[20] Ibid. 23.

[21] Rose, *Lottie Deno: Gambling Queen of Hearts*. The author offers the quotation but no citation. 38. Perhaps the actual quotation may be found in John Myers Myers 1955 publication, the book *Doc Holliday*. "One of a rarity—was a woman, Lottie Deno by name. A cultured and attractive red-head, she was off-brand in her habits as well as in her profession. Baffingly crooked at cards and disappointingly straight in more personal matters, she left everybody guessing as to where she had come from." 44.

[22] Huckabay, *Ninety-Four Years in Jack County, 1854-1948*. 109; DeArment, *Alias Frank Canton*. 33.

[23] Robert K. DeArment, *Bravo of the Barzos: John Larn of Fort Griffin, Texas*. 98. Rye, *The Quirt and the Spur*. "The marshal [Bill Gilson] was armed with a sawed-off shotgun mounted on a pistol handle. The gun was loaded with buckshot and capable of deadly execution at short range." 76.

[24] McConnell, *Five Years A Cavalryman: Or, Sketches Of Regular Army Life On The Texas Frontier, 1866-1871*. 296.

[25] *State of Texas vs. Lottie Deno*, No Cause Number, Jack County, Texas, February 26, 1875. Courtesy Joan Farmer, Albany, Texas.

[26] DeArment, *Alias Frank Canton*. 22; Huckabay, *Ninety-Four Years In Jack Count, 1854-1948*. 144.

[27] Ibid. 22-23.

[28] Ibid. Quoting from the indictment, *The State of Texas vs. Joe Horner*. 26.

[29] Ibid. 31.

[30] Ibid. Quoting Thomas Horton. 31; Huckabay, *Ninety-Four Years In Jack County, 1854-1948*. 149.

[31] Ibid.

[32] Ibid. Quoting Thomas Horton.

[33] Ibid. 32.

[34] William H. Leckie, *The Buffalo Soldiers: A Narrative of the Negro Cavalry in the West*. "Mackenzie's Fourth Cavalry had its troubles with [Fort] Richardson. Troop B had burned down a house of prostitution because one of their buddies had been killed there and threatened to burn the whole town." 73; Robert Wooster, *Soldiers, Sutlers, and Settlers: Garrison Life On The Texas Frontier*. 195.

[35] Roberts, *Doc Holliday: The Life And Legend*. Several other book-length biographies of Holliday are: Karen Holliday Tanner, *Doc Holliday: A Family Portrait*; Pat Jahns, *The Frontier World of Doc Holliday: Faro Dealer From Dallas to Deadwood*; the previously cited John Myers Myers, *Doc Holliday*; Bob Boze Bell, *The Illustrated Life and Times of Doc Holliday*; Ben T. Traywick, *John Henry: The Doc Holliday Story*; and Sylvia D. Lynch, *Aristocracy's Outlaw: The Doc Holliday Story*.

[36] Myers, *Doc Holliday*. "As he stayed in Jacksboro for about a year, his confidence in his ability to hold his own there was not misplaced." 45.

[37] Tanner, *Doc Holliday: A Family Portrait*. "Neither the Jack County court records not the *Frontier Echo* mention Holliday." 258-259, n. 38.

[38] Roberts, *Doc Holliday: The Life And Legend*. "Most of the fines were $10 to $15, but several of the men had more than one fine to pay." 76. Interestingly, a conformation of Roberts' statement may be found in Ty Cashion's *A Texas Frontier: The Clear Fork Country and Fort Griffin, 1849-1887*. "When the first session of the district court met in recently organized Shackelford County during June 1875, Judge J. P. Osterhout dealt severely with lawbreakers. In thirty-seven case during the five-day session he found a dozen men guilty of gambling and selling liquor illegally, and although the fines ranged from only $10 to $15, some of the accused faced multiple counts." 190. Shackelford County Court records do not indicate that John Henry "Doc" Holliday, or "Dock" as the case was legally styled, was one of the men that had more than one fine to pay. Author Ben Traywick in *John Henry: (The "Doc" Holliday*

Story) includes a photocopy of the Shackelford County docket book's page reflecting the charge lodged against "Dock Holliday." 60.

[39] Ibid. "On June 30, 1875, an *alias capias* was issued for Doc's arrest and forwarded to the sheriff of Tom Green County at San Angelo. Doc probably took the stage west along the military road to Fort Concho, but he does not appear to have lingered long there." 76; Tanner, *Doc Holliday: A Family Portrait.* "On June 30, 1875, an *alias capias* for John Henry's arrest was forwarded to the sheriff of Tom Green County at San Angelo, Texas, indicating that he had continued along the old stage route toward Fort Concho." 98; Tise, *Texas County Sheriffs.* 493. Jahns, *The Frontier World of Doc Holliday: Faro Dealer From Dallas to Deadwood.* "A *capais* was issued for his [Doc Holliday] arrest to Tom Green County by the sheriff of Shackelford County (Fort Griffin) on June 30, 1875." 57.

[40] Roberts, *Doc Holliday: The Life And Legend.* 78.

[41] Traywick, *John Henry: (The "Doc" Holliday Story).* 47.

[42] Hamilton, *Sentinel Of The Southern Plains: Fort Richardson and the Northwest Texas Frontier, 1866-1878.* 42; Roberts, *Doc Holliday: The Life And Legend* does suggest the likelihood of Doc Holliday visiting Jacksboro: "He may have paused briefly at Jacksboro, near Fort Richardson, but if he did, he did not tarry long, pushing on past Fort Belknap, and then southwest to Fort Griffin and the Flat." 74.

[43] DeArment, *Alias Frank Canton.* Quoting *The Frontier Echo* of September 11, 1875. 33.

[44] Ibid. 34.

[45] Roberts, *Doc Holliday: The Life And Legend.* 79. The rumor that Doc Holliday killed a soldier had its origin in Bat Masterson's *Human Life* series about some of the Old West's colorful characters. A compilation of these articles may be found in *Famous Gun Fighters of the Western Frontier* by W. B. (Bat) Masterson. Regarding an unnamed soldier's death, Masterson wrote: "He [Holliday] was not long in Jacksborro [*sic*] before he was in another scrape. This time it was with a soldier who was stationed at the Fort [Richardson], and who had been given permission to visit the town by his commanding officer. The trouble was over a card game in which the soldier claimed he had been given the worst of it by the man from Georgia. This of course, necessitated the fighting Georgian taking another trip on the road, for he knew it would never do to let the soldiers at the Fort capture him, which they would be sure to try to do as soon as word reached them about the killing of their comrade." 52; Roberts refutes the accuracy of Masterson's statement.

[46] *The Frontier Echo*, March 10, 1876.

[47] Ibid. January 5, 1877.

[48] Jack County, Texas, County Clerk Records. *State vs. Lottie Deno.* Cause Number 20. January 2, 1877. Courtesy Joan Farmer, Albany, Texas.

Chapter 6

"Within This Hive, We Are Alive"

When Lottie Deno stepped off the Jacksboro stage she was not surprised with the overall setting for her new home. In many regards The Flat was but a copycat of San Angela and Jacksboro. It was squalid and smelly. It was modest; a brisk five minute walk would traverse The Flat, east to west or north to south. Indeed the name seemed appropriate. Terrain where the town rested was pancake flat. On one end the smoothness did give way to an uplift that graduated into a prominent hill, one that supported the U. S. military base, Fort Griffin. On another side Collins Creek flowed nearby. The Flat was also bordered by an abrupt drop off angling downhill until it met the Clear Fork of the Brazos River. And there, at the north edge of town above the Clear Fork's southern bank, was where working-girls of The Flat kept house. There, too, was where Lottie Deno would make her home. "Lottie rented [or someone in her behalf] one of the shanties owned by George Mat[t]hews in the redlight district along the banks of the Brazos River."[1] Angelic penmanship that Miss Lottie Deno set herself apart from the lower class felines by occupying a quaint cottage in a separate neighborhood is whimsical and wishful thinking.[2] "...Lottie was a prostitute."[3]

Geographically appointing Lottie's stage would require a reminder that The Flat lay in Shackelford County. Notwithstanding impending danger at any moment of an Indian attack surveyors had staked out the county's boundary during February 1858, appropriating land formerly within Bosque County.[4] Sixteen years later, on the 12th day of September 1874, Shackelford County was organized. The budding civilian community heretofore called The Flat took on a new name, becoming Fort Griffin, the town, but only after a spat with the U. S. Government regarding lease agreements and clear title to township lots.[5] Colloquially the settlement was still referred to as The Flat. The new town of Fort Griffin was the first county seat of Shackelford County, but that distinction was short lived. The following year the town of Albany was selected to accept that honor.[6]

Between the time Shackelford County was created and then organized, the military garrison of Fort Griffin had been engineered. At the outset the army's four companies of Sixth U. S. Cavalry bivouacked on the "low soft ground" near the Clear Fork's banks during July, 1867. Originally the hilltop post was referred to as Camp Wilson in honor of a deceased lieutenant of the regiment. Sweltering summer heat along the Clear Fork, swarms of Texas size mosquitoes and nests of slithering

Cottonmouths had prompted military leadership to reposition troops on the nearby hill's crest, among the rocks and Diamondbacks. Even in death's quietness rank does have its privileges. Lieutenant Henry Hamilton Wilson's monument was pushed aside and the post renamed Fort Griffin in memory of General Charles Griffin who had succumbed to Yellow Fever two years earlier.[7]

Strategically, Fort Griffin may not have been any more relevant than Forts Richardson or Concho. It was a crucial link in the chain. Because of its position at an economic crossroads Fort Griffin did surpass its sister posts—for awhile. Such a dynamic was not due to Fort Griffin's military usefulness, but because of its crucial role in luring civilians. The end result would disclose that San Angela and Jacksboro, as municipalities, had a staying power alien to the town of Fort Griffin. During its brief heyday The Flat grabbed the spotlight. Aside from the expected economic linkage between city folks and citadel folks, the town of Fort Griffin was blessed with the dynamism familiar to San Angela and Jacksboro, but on a much grander scale. The Flat outshone both of them as a booming town catering to the outfitting of buffalo hunters and as a leading market center for buying hides. And similar to San Angela and Jacksboro, Fort Griffin businessmen could capitalize on the emergent cow business. The nationally known northbound Western Trail [sometimes referred to as the Dodge City Trail], the "Greatest Texas Cattle Trail," metaphorically stampeded right up The Flat's main street, Griffin Avenue.

With its origin at the southernmost tip of Texas, the Western Trail was *the* roadway for cattle driven to the railhead at Dodge City, Kansas. All along the route feeder trials merged into the Great Western's trunk line. After an angling elbow in the picturesque Hill Country's Kerr County northwest of San Antonio, the Western Trail made a straight line due north targeting Doan's Red River Crossing at the Texas border. Shackelford County lay squarely in its path. After closely skirting Albany the Western Trail followed the compass needle north, passing on the outskirts of Fort Griffin. The Western Trail then forded the Clear Fork of the Brazos at the old Butterfield-Military Road Crossing, before it entered Throckmorton County near the mouth of Tecumpsee Creek.[8]

Shackelford County's northern border was shared with Throckmorton County, formally mapped, yet not organized. Nor was Baylor County to its north, or Wilbarger County to its north; no local governments, no sheriffs, no stores.[9] After swimming a herd across the Clear Fork the next supply point was Doan's store, but it primarily served as base for filling emergency needs.[10] Fort Griffin reigned as top spot for supplies. The socioeconomic impact on tiny Fort Griffin was momentous. Fort Griffin was the very last stop where trail-worn cowboys could swig and swagger and swear and spend before climbing back into the saddle for a lengthy journey. Shooting off guns—especially in front of girls—was fun too! Sashaying around on a dance floor, savoring the sweet scent of perfume while listening to enticing whispers before stepping into a back room or a crib overlooking the river for a quick tryst were gratifying diversions.[11] All of the cowboys were not drovers. The entire region was settling up with stockmen intent on staying. Cowmen were carving massive empires out of the land wrested from nomadic Comanches during the pivotal Red River War of 1874-1875. Ranchers and their employees were welcomed at Fort Griffin. There they were embraced not only by the more or less respectable and upright merchants, but also by its energetic and insomniac sporting element; the saloon and dance house owners, gamblers, and calico queens.[12] Lottie Deno's crowd.

In certain quarters there is a propensity to try and downplay the violence taking place at The Flat. The technique of citing examples of violence to discredit the notion that there was violence is a peculiar methodology best left for the scholars and statisticians. When Lottie Deno made her early 1877 appearance at The Flat it was not too soon before or too soon after a notoriously publicized gunplay. On January 17, 1877, from Baylor County, Millett Ranch foreman Billy Bland, accompanied by cowhand J. C. "Charley" Reed, initiated their trip to The Flat. Knowing the boys' ranching headquarters speaks to their penchant for devilment. It has been written that when a cowboy was just too tough, too rambunctious and unable to "affiliate with civilization" he could always find a job at the Millett.[13] Billy Bland and Charley Reed were on a tear that evening. As the night wore down the blood alcohol content of Bland and Reed went up, their walking from saloon to saloon progressing into but a wobbling and drunken stagger. As stupified cowboys were sometimes inclined, Billy and Charley pulled out their revolvers and began shooting at the bottles, the polished glasses, and even the mirror behind the bar. Then they redirected their aim and started shooting at the coal-oil light fixtures. Rushing to the thunderous noise of gunfire were Shackelford County Deputy Sheriff [later sheriff] William R. "Bill" Cruger and Deputy John M. Bogart. Following close on their heels was the Shackelford County Attorney, Robert A. "Bob" Jeffress. Inside there was a pistol shooting commotion between the good guys and the not so good guys. Innocents were caught in the middle. Newlywed Dan Barrow was dead, shot between the eyes. J. W. Myers, an ex-U. S. Army officer was also fatally gunned down. Billy Bland, one of the instigators, took either Cruger's or Bogart's bullet just below his navel and died. The gutsy County Attorney had taken two bullets in the chest, vertically separated by his heart. Miraculously Mr. Jeffress lived to tell the tale. Sheriff Cruger had been wounded, but only slightly. Deputy

Bogart survived the shoot-out unscathed, as did Charley Reed who managed to run through the swinging doors and into the night.[14] Selling whiskey to cowboys was profitable business—but risky.

Lottie's rabble, indeed, all of Fort Griffin's businessmen [and women], were also propping up Shackelford County's economy by paying homage to the wants and needs of hide-hunters, who in turn were repaying the favor. Stereotypically the image of a buffalo hunter is a nasty picture. Normally his portrait is drawn as greasy, heartless, ugly and profane; an utterly immoral example of the human species. Often he is characterized as the Old West's model for despicable inhumanity, wantonly slaughtering harmless buffalo because killing anything on God's green earth was but his euphoric entertainment. The reality check spoken by a veteran buffalo hunter and, one who personally knew Miss Lottie Deno, is informative:

> Buffalo hunting was a business and not a sport; it required capital, management and work, lots of hard work, more work than anything else. Many magazine and newspaper articles claim the killing of the buffalo a national calamity and accomplished by vandals. I resent their ignorance.[15]

Professional hide-hunters were not all undesirables. As with any subgroup there were topnotch fellows and, too, a crosscut of genuine badmen pulled from dregs of the broader society. Buffalo hunting was a raw and dirty business, but it was business. America's demand, especially back East, for warm buffalo robes and durable belting leather was near insatiable. It was but an example of capitalism at work; supply and demand. There was not idle talk of ecology, no thought of extinction. For centuries Indians had trafficked surplus hides, but the 1870s onslaught of the Anglos with the better-quality weaponry, coupled with the improved mechanisms for transportation and marketing, brought forth a more efficient killing machine. The slaughter was a cogent reality that was not missed by military thinkers. They recognized the tactical advantage of depleting Plains Indians' walking storehouses. Too, killing buffalo was the gateway for a hard-working young adventurer to make his million. There were millions of buffalo west of The Flat.

Banner years for a buffalo hunt on the Southern Plains were 1876-1877.[16] "The buffalo kill those years was enormous. There was buffalo hunters, hide money, trail herd money, and soldier money and, too, it was provisioning point [Fort Griffin] for settlers going west and north settling up the country."[17] Joe S. McCombs, one of the better known hide-hunters, highlights his 1877 buffalo hunt:

On this hunt from September to May I made my biggest kill—same being 4,900, all of which I personally killed. [John William] Poe and [John C.] Jacobs had an outfit north of us that killed 6,300. There were several camps around us as the hunters were getting thick. Two outfits stacked hides at our camp and we had 9,700 stacked there. I account for our big kill that year by being favorably located at these springs [near present day Big Spring, Texas] where these animals could come for water...We decided to poison our hides this year, due to a low market and carry them through the summer. After doing this I struck out in advance of the wagon for Ft. Griffin, but met a hide buyer, W. H. Webb, of Dallas at Phantom Hill. He offered me $1.00 per hide, camp delivery, for the whole 9,700 hides and I sold, having authority to sell for the others, as well as my own. He and I returned to camp where he received the hides and our outfits returned to Griffin. That was the last year of the big kill and the biggest year for the buffalo hunters in Texas.[18]

The year before a youthful W. L. Evans impressively noted that at The Flat there were 50,000 sun-dried hides piled high and ready for transport further east.[19] The following year, 1877, there was a shortage of teamsters available to meet transportation needs:

Teams wanted to haul 200,000 pounds of buffalo hides to Dallas.
T. E. Jackson & Company
Fort Griffin, Texas[20]

Mr. F. E. Conrad, perhaps Fort Griffins' chief buyer, had "buffalo hides stacked higher than a man's head and covering about ten acres of ground."[21] The place was stinky. Unpleasant stench radiated from heaps of hides stacked hither and yon. Miss Lottie Deno wasn't bothered. With so much money changing hands daily it was another aroma that caught her notice, the sweet smell of greenery—greenbacks.

At Young County, almost bordering Shackelford County on the northeast, another 1877 happening took place, one that plays a part in Lottie Deno's story—the part about shattering myths. Cattle theft had become a major problem on the northwest Texas frontier. Thievery was running rampant, unchecked by local lawmen. An assembly of hopping-mad cattleman got together under an Oak tree at the little town of Graham and mapped their plans for dealing with a rising tide of rustlers. At that meeting The Stock-Raisers Association of Northwest Texas, parent of the present day Texas & Southwestern Cattle Raisers Association, was organized.[22] For the first time open range was divided into districts and inflexible rules for the roundup were adopted.[23] Trusted stockmen were assigned to oversee each district. A breach of the association's edicts? Consequences! A prominent enrollee with the newly fashioned alliance was Cornelius Kincheloe "C. K." Stribling, a powerful Shackelford County lawyer, land man and livestock owner. Stribling's name was recorded in the association's membership book:

> C. K. Stribling: P.O. Address, Fort Griffin, ranche located in Shackelford Co., mark, swallow in left and crop and two slits in right ear, branded CKS connected.[24]

Mr. C. K. Stribling—in due time—will play a key role in tracing Lottie Deno's footsteps. During the first half of the 20th-Century many enthusiastic and excited historians availed themselves of a resource pool that was fast evaporating—interviewing the so-called oldtimers. It was a methodology providing valuable insight into excavating the first-hand stories of fascinating bygone days. For all the obvious reasons these first-person chronicles must be reviewed with an appropriate level of skepticism, but not wholly devalued because of an inadvertent misstep on the part of the narrator, the interviewer, or even a well-intentioned stenographer's slip-up, a typo. Frequently modern era critics are all too quick to pounce; hypothesizing that if the raconteur is off the mark by a year or a month, his entire account must be faulty. Or even worse, intentionally deceptive. Such is not always the case. Taking a quick look at Fort Griffin through the pages of a distant newspaper, one contemporary to 1877, well before any turn-of-the-century fascination with the Old West might be beneficial. At Columbus, Colorado County, Texas, southwest of Houston and far removed from Shackelford County the local *Weekly Colorado Citizen* carried a human interest story about The Flat:

> The town of Griffin is composed of all the elements of man and woman kind. Sharpe's [*sic*] rifles and Colt's six-shooter is the supreme law of the land. Among the roughs, thieves and outlaws there is a class of good men here that are endeavoring to check the lawlessness, and at their own expenses have employed a marshal to assist the regular officers in keeping order. The business portion of the town is in the valley. The post is up on the hill, which is a beautiful location. There are 96 negro troops of the Tenth Cavalry stationed here,

commanded by Capt. Lee, said to be a relative of the
late General Robert E. Lee. Captain Lee is genial,
pleasant and sociable gentlemen. There are in the place
three dry goods stores, one confectionary [sic], one drug
and hardware house, one hotel, restaurant, one wagon
and blacksmith shop, ten saloons and one music hall.
This is headquarters for the buffalo hunters. There have
been 75,000 hides shipped from this place, and there
about 30,000 yet to be shipped.[25]

Honest mistakes do sometimes happen when journalists write their
copy, and even when oldtimers are asked to recount the past. In that
same vein, not everything mentioned by the oldtimer was meant to be
taken literally. Time and again it is an aspect overlooked. Sometimes the
oldtimer's remarks were spoken just to convey an overall feeling or
impression, an idea of how things really were—at least how they saw
them. Metaphoric verbiage was a technique habitually employed. It is a
communication device common today.

When our neighbor says it rained "cats and dogs" we know the
implication of his message. Participating in a game of "chicken" does
not necessitate a trip to the barnyard, nor does obtaining vital data
"straight from the horse's mouth" mandate an appearance at the livery
stable. Specifically speaking of busy Fort Griffin two of very many
sterling examples come to mind. Emmett Roberts said:

Fort Griffin was the rendezvous for all this country. It
was a veritable robber's hole. They would throw a
blanket over your head and take your money in a flash.[26]

Emmett Roberts' inference was not that the badmen were literally
circulating throughout The Flat with a revolver at the end of one arm
and a woolen blanket tucked under the other. Rather that human
vultures were there to take unfair advantage of a person not on guard. A
fellow visiting The Flat could be robbed at the point of a pistol. An
insensible inebriate laying on the boardwalk in a drunken stupor might
have been the tempting target of a pickpocket. However the
representative scenario would be that an unsuspecting lad come to town
was more likely to loose his money due to the underhanded antics of
gamblers and girls, not necessarily quilt carrying armed robbers. The
same evaluation may be said of R. A. Slack's comment:

A killing was one of the ordinary expected events of the
night, on which [once] the comments were over, and the

incident closed by the time the blood had been mopped up from the floor.[27]

Mr. Slack's remarks taken in the literal sense would leave an impression that in addition to a barkeep, every Fort Griffin saloon owner employed a fellow equipped with a mop and bucket just to sponge up blood. That was not the case. Simply he meant—much as it is today—once an initial curiosity was satisfied everyone then went their own way. There is a certain comfort level associated with provocatively challenging an oldtimers' remembrances from afar, not in the flesh—and to judgmentally criticize how he put those words down on paper. The distinguished Texas historian and educator Rex W. Strickland remembered and reminded:

> After all, thousands of persons who can write a grammatically correct sentence have never killed a buffalo much less skinned one.[28]

Mr. Strickland's remarks are meaningful. They are applicable to much broader issues than an oldtimer's grammar. Armchair critics may find it quite painless *now* to call a grizzled peace keeper or ne'er-do-well a liar. Would they have been so aggressively inclined *then*? For Lottie Deno's biographical sketch there are several fellows—and a few ladies—that actually knew her. We are fortunate heirs to their preserved experiences and observations.

Henry Herron, a Shackelford County deputy sheriff sometimes posted at The Flat, said he knew Lottie Deno from the time she arrived on the Jacksboro stage, until the day she left town. Herron, *perhaps* not yet privy to, nor too much enamored with a profusion of latter day folklore, offhandedly characterized Lottie Deno in a simple but plain spoken manner: "She had her shanty in the vicinity of other women residing along the river. Lottie was good looking, but I would hardly call her pretty. She went about neatly dressed and conducted herself like a lady on the streets."[29] Edgar Rye's *The Quirt and the Spur: Vanishing Shadows Of The Texas Frontier* is with good reason categorized as a "fractured fairy tale," nevertheless there's little doubt the author actually knew Lottie Deno.[30] Rye's characterization of Lottie Deno as a "female monstrosity" is something that would have best been explained by him; others saw her differently.[31] More charitably Rye does say that Lottie was "an attractive, medium-sized woman, with an abundance of dark, red hair and black, sparkling eyes."[32] Another who knew Lottie, a well known buffalo hunter, had no dreamscape agenda when he spoke of Deno's physical appearance: "She was not overly prepossessing, she was a sort of hawk nosed little red headed sort of woman, round faced."[33]

Adding to this chatter a lady, Sallie Reynolds Matthews, fell short of prettifying Miss Deno, saying she "was a fairly good looking woman."[34] Regarding Lottie's public image—physically—another oldtimer simply said: "I knew Lottie well, and I do not hesitate to say right here that she was a wonderful woman. She was on the portly side, a fine looker, and in manners a typical Southern lady, but didn't always live up to her appearances."[35] Suggesting that Lottie "didn't always live up to her appearances," was but the oldtimer's hint for the reader to look between the lines. The same historical informant, himself a Shackelford County lawman, went on to say that Lottie Deno kept him appraised about the "doings and whereabouts of outlaws who frequented the Flat."[36] Significance of that statement is twofold and evident; Lottie was looking out for her own interest and she was a member in good standing with The Flat's underworld clique, not the Sunday school and quilting circles. Lottie "was shunned by the better class."[37] Miss Deno was a well known fixture in The Flat, a place buffalo hunter Frank Lloyd called "a pretty rollicky town, yes."[38]

For 20th-Century writings about Lottie Deno it is put forward that she delicately preserved an unapproachable "aloofness," having very little interaction with the male gender outside of a card game. An implied suggestion that Lottie was leading a life of celibacy is just that, an obliquely weak attempt to obfuscate reality. It is pure fabrication that makes for a saintly story, but one lacking substantive truth or common sense. There is not any evidence to support the hypothesis that Lottie Deno was a common whore, taking on all comers willy-nilly. "Lottie was strictly a high-class tart who didn't compete with the other girls for the cheap trade."[39] Nor is there believable reason to think that Lottie lived an abnormal life of sexual self-denial, religiously practicing total abstinence. True, several of the oldtimers yet living in Shackelford County when interviewed implied that Lottie had but limited dealings with Fort Griffin's menfolk, apart from gambling. Could there really be a practical motive for concocting such an improbable fairy tale? One historian thinks so! A lifelong Shackelford County resident researcher and author suggests a possibility. When some of the old men—those with wives and having grand children and great grand children—were interviewed regarding days spent at The Flat, at their height of hormonal exuberance, those guys might have had to admit knowing Lottie Deno. However, those same fellows well knew the advisability of saying the old girl did not "entertain" men.[40] An oldtimer, one far removed in both distance and time, had not the slightest hesitancy with revealing his take—characterizing Lottie's behavior and naming names.

Tennessee born buffalo hunter Sam Baldwin, in his early thirties at the time he knew Lottie at Fort Griffin, submitted to a request for an interview when he was an old man. At his home near Lordsburg, New

Mexico, Mr. Baldwin talked with traveling grassroots historians Earl
Vandale and Hervey Chesley. Since that most enlightening discussion,
well over half a century ago, with time to historically check his stories, a
well-respected 21ˢᵗ-Century scholar and writer grades Mr. Sam Baldwin's
remembrances of the Fort Griffin days as "generally reliable."[41]

Sam Baldwin made a sweeping comment, followed by one with
specificity which doesn't demand clarification: "You know, it was the
idea of every whore or prostitute to get a man of some reputation. So
Lottie acquired Jim."[42] The "Jim" was a "blond-headed thin-faced, tall
slim fellow," sometimes gambler and bartender who would go down in
the history books as James "Limpy Jim" Smith. Mr. Sam Baldwin asserts
that on one occasion he was present when Mr. Tom Sherman, a
notorious sporting man who had brought a bevy of working-girls to The
Flat, began teasing Limpy Jim about Lottie's fidelity—or the lack
thereof:

> Well, as to whether Lottie dated the men or just ran a
> dance hall—there was an old ex-dance hall proprietor
> named Tom Sherman. He had [had] a dance hall in
> Fort Dodge. Old Tom and I were in there one day—he
> run a saloon—he went into this dance hall, Lottie's
> saloon [at The Flat], and Smith was behind the counter,
> and Tom began by saying, "Another mule was in the
> stall last night, wasn't there?" Jim didn't know what to
> say. He had to give it up that she had dated another
> fellow. The men that had the money, she took them on.
> That was her style. She had a dance hall and saloon, and
> she had a room back of the dance hall.[43]

Sam Baldwin wasn't the least bit reticent: "Jim Smith was nothing that I
knew of, just a gambler. That was Limpy Smith. He was the one that
was with Lottie Deeno [*sic*]. He wasn't her husband, just staying with
her."[44] Chronologically lining up Lottie Deno's string of romantic
relationships in the proper order is a troubling task but not pertinent for
straightening out the mythology. Lottie Deno was no man hater.

Lottie's personal involvement with Limpy Jim Smith was an off and
on again affair; one of convenience—if not of the heart. Though there is
little hard proof to confirm the story, it is generally accepted tradition
that Lottie was also the mistress of a Shackelford County saloon man,
John Hugo "Shaney" Shanssey. Pat Casey, another bar owner in The
Flat has also been named as one of Lottie's paramours.[45] Creditability
for romantically linking Lottie and Shaney is enhanced after noting that
before his appearance at The Flat, just like Lottie, John had been a
sporting element resident at Jacksboro. While there were they friends or

lovers—or both? After selling his Jacksboro saloon to W. A. Beason during January 1876, Shaney moved his liquor selling and gambling undertakings to The Flat. There he invested in the town's most disreputable dive, the Bee Hive.[46] The former pugilist and future mayor of Yuma, Arizona, also had a joint financial interest with Charley Myers in another Fort Griffin whiskey emporium, the Cattle Exchange Saloon.[47] Shackelford County deputy sheriff Henry Herron, although to some extent cryptic, more or less adds conformation: "However, I do know that she [Lottie Deno] had the name in the underworld of being a kept woman, and that her keeper was a prominent saloon keeper, a married man."[48]

No mention of The Flat would be complete without citing a sign hanging outside the legendary Bee Hive. Depending on the particular version chosen for citation—and there are several—it reads something like:

> Within this Hive, we are alive.
> Good whiskey makes us funny.
> Get your horse tied, come inside.
> And taste the flavor of our honey.

Inside, the Bee Hive was a buzz of activity—not all wholesome. The Flat was known far and wide as the "Babylon of the Border."[49] Rollie Burns visited Fort Griffin during 1877, while Lottie Deno was there. He declared that among the freighters, buffalo hunters and cowboys another group could be found there, the unsavory adventurers and desperadoes: "Robbery was frequently perpetrated in broad daylight, and at night the 'Flats' was a din of ribaldry, lewd women, designing gamblers, and drunken thieves."[50] There was no dearth of girls and gamblers and gun carrying hotheads. There is no historical doubt that barkeep and gambler Mike Fogarty, at Mr. Shanssey's behest, oversaw the day to day business of operating the saloon and its gaming tables.[51] There is, however, every reason to question a fanciful claim that Mike Forgarty and the previously mentioned Frank Thurmond from San Antonio, were one and the same person. Several writers have professed such and, not unexpectedly, the assertion is absent any citation to source material.[52] If it were true, it would serve as the needed touch of romanticism, one necessary to convert an overdue and detached look at Lottie Deno's sordid-sided life at The Flat into an unsullied love story. There is not unreasonableness associated with marketing a firm suggestion that the burden of proof rest with the person making the allegation. If gambler Frank Thurmond was using an alias of Mike Fogarty, there should be a basis for saying so. At least one nonpartisan researcher and writer, a person that should know, forthrightly commented that there is not any trustworthy evidence at all to indicate that Frank Thurmond ever placed a foot in Fort Griffin: "None whatsoever!"[53]

Frank Thurmond will down the road play a leading role in Lottie Deno's story, however it did not take place at Fort Griffin. Even a mild suggestion that Frank Thurmond would shame the family name by hiding from it belies a misinterpretation of his persona. There is a factual basis for declaring that Frank Thurmond had not assumed any undercover identity. Later he would join the Cattle Raisers Association under his rightful name.[54]

Acknowledging that Lottie Deno played poker and faro at The Flat, in the Bee Hive and other gambling halls is not troubling. Her contemporaries, among the several other things, confirm her card playing. Two women tender their corroboration. Elizabeth Smith, wife of the incredibly adventurous Henry Clay "Hank" Smith and affectionately known throughout West Texas and at Fort Griffin as "Aunt Hank," remarked that Lottie was mysterious, but she gambled with the men.[55] Sallie Reynolds Matthews penned that Lottie "at the game of cards was more than a match for the best of them."[56] Lottie was something else, too! Lottie was smart.

She may have always aspired to bigger and better things, but her well documented tenure at Fort Griffin is where that part of Lottie's attitude becomes measurable. Unlike many of her working-girl associates, those who would find themselves desperately trapped in a life of immorality and indulgence, Lottie must have realized the good sense in a change of course. Lottie's resetting the compass was not birthed in an overnight shift of morality, but one directed with an eye to the future. She began buying real estate and investing. In one instance she sold property—Lot 5, Block 3 Veals' Addition—to James Murphy, apparently holding on to two other town lots.[57] Lottie Deno also acquired partial interest in a Fort Griffin dance hall/saloon—*boarding house*—The Gus.[58] One can only wonder if Lottie's dance hall, The Gus, was the hot spot mentioned by oldtimer J. W. Woody:

> Old Fort Griffin was a tough place. I've seen men and women dancing there in the dance halls without a bit of clothing on.[59]

Hardly a real estate mogul and definitely not abandoning the card rooms and back rooms, Lottie Deno was stepping ahead of The Flat's other girls-of-the-night. An overwhelming majority of those fair damsels were unwisely giving in to their heartbreaking weakness for alcohol and/or drugs. Their keenness to own pretty items, colorful clothes and dazzling gold trinkets was monetarily debilitating.[60] Many of the girls were hopelessly mired in the quicksand of poverty, unwilling or unable to extricate themselves. Lottie Deno had re-calibrated her sights a great deal higher, aiming for much more than twilight years spent in squalor and shamelessness. Lottie's time at The Flat was the beginning of a transitional period in her remarkable life's story, but not one free of problems; legal, financial or emotional. Destiny had dealt her hand. She would play it well, not necessarily honestly—but beneficially. Improbable as whimsical stories of her background might be, a salient truth remains: For a girl trying to attain monetary self-sufficiency and social respectability Lottie Deno was stubbornly intent on success. For that she deserves credit.

Lottie Deno merits recognition too as being an unflustered girl; one nonchalantly squaring off and facing the prospects of danger everyday. Certainly for the 21st-Century reader Edgar Rye's propensity to exploit melodramatic dialogue is distracting. However, to altogether disregard or devalue the general meaning of his story because of writing style in vogue for the times is unfair. The plausibility of one of Mr. Rye's tales about Lottie Deno rests not in the excessively dramatized details, but its overall message. How much literary license Rye incorporated into the following affair may be debatable. The fact Lottie at times kept hard company is not arguable.

Purportedly Monta [Monte] Bill and Smoky Joe were the last players standing pat in a high-stakes poker game at Lottie's table, upstairs in the Wilson & Matthews Saloon:

> All interest centered around the game where "Monta Bill" and "Smoky Joe" were pitted against each other. Five hundred dollars was in the pot and the other players dropped out. "Monta" challenged "Smoky" to raise the limit. "Smoky" agreed and bet his last dollar on the results. "Monta" called his hand and laid down three aces and a pair of queens. "Smoky" dropped his hand to the handle of his six-shooter and yelled, "Bunkoed by a sneaking coyote from the 'Bad Lands,' who rings in a 'cold deck' and marked cards when he plays with a gentleman! Take that pot, John" he yelled to the negro porter. "No, you can't play that game of 'bluff' on me," shouted "Monta" in defiance, as he jerked his gun from its scabbard. Both guns flashed at the same time, and the crowd rushed for the stairway. Lottie pushed back from the table and ran to the corner of the room out of range of the bullets, where she remained until the shooting was over, and was the first to greet the sheriff when he entered, and found both men stretched upon the floor in pools of blood. "Why

didn't you 'vamoose' when they pulled their 'barkers,' Lottie?" "Oh, it was too late, sheriff; and I was safe out of range in the corner." "Well, you have your nerve on, all right, old girl. I don't believe I would have carted to take my chances in that scrimmage." "Perhaps not, sheriff, but you are not a desperate woman."[61]

Before this episode is dismissed as factually deficient several relevant particulars are worthy of note, as well as its generalized quintessence. There was at The Flat a real person known locally as Smoky Joe, an indisputable fact supported by Shackelford County courthouse records.[62] Too, John C. Jacobs, a former Shackelford County deputy sheriff, personally knew Smoky Joe and reported what must have been the same incident, but failed to name names other than Lottie Deno's and the then current sheriff, W. R. "Bill" Cruger's.

> One night there was a double killing in the gambling hall where she dealt faro. When the smoke of guns had cleared, Sheriff Bill Cruger arrived and found Lottie seated at her place at the table, with two mortally wounded men lying on the floor and the hall otherwise deserted. Lottie was not the least excited or perturbed, and told the sheriff the full details of the affair. The stack of silver in the jackpot had vanished, too.[63]

The whereabouts of the mislaid money should not come as any surprise, Lottie Deno was a "desperate woman."[64] There was no toll on the road to Heaven or Hell. Dead men didn't need *deniro*.[65] With two oldtimers declaring Lottie was present and conformation that Smoky Joe was a bona fide Fort Griffin troublemaker, removing the narrative from a too farfetched category is not impractical. With both Monte Bill and Smoky Joe dead, who would serve as a *complainant*? A pair of unlucky dead men, each responsible for the other's demise, equates to no criminal charges—no courthouse records. A technically pure revisionist with an agenda would discount the episode, absent any eyewitnesses' *depositions* and/or docket books' entries.[66] But, for capturing the real essence of Lottie Deno's saga such an approach misses one of the main themes of her story. The so-called Gambling Queen of Hearts was intermingling with a host of colorful characters and not all of them were nice people. If Edgar Rye and John Jacobs were correct and Lottie had witnessed Monte Bill and Smoky Joe die on the dingy barroom floor, such is life. On the other hand, if they were downright lying or mistaken or consciously exaggerating, it still is not unreasonable to suppose that Lottie, some night, somewhere, was present when hot words or hurt feeling resulted in fisticuffs, a stabbing, a shooting, or a fingernail scratching and hair-pulling cat fight. She may have on occasion even been a profanity screaming participant in such badness. Lottie Deno was no angel! That is the broader point! As is the fact she was making an effort in her small way to get out—to climb out of those brutal and boorish surroundings, ascending to a livelihood that would leave wagering and whoring behind. A life that someday would rate as respectable.

Henry C. Jacobs and family. Mr. Jacobs was Shackelford County's first sheriff. *Courtesy Ginger McCullar.*

Charles Rath atop buffalo hides at Kansas railhead. The demand was near insatiable. *Courtesy Nita Stewart Haley Memorial Library.*

John W. Poe was one of the notable Old West fellows hunting buffalo in West Texas and was a frequent visitor at The Flat. He characterized the town for his wife, Sophie, who later wrote: "From end to end, on both sides, the street was walled with saloons, gambling dens, dance halls and supply stores....all jammed together like *sampans* on the banks of a Chinese river." *Courtesy Nita Stewart Haley Memorial Library.*

Frank Conrad. Fort Griffin
merchant and hide buyer.
*Courtesy Sharon
Cunningham and Dixie
Gun Works.*

Advertisement for the
Conrad and Rath store
at Fort Griffin. *Courtesy
Sharon Cunningham and
Dixie Gun Works.*

Sharps Buffalo Rifle. This one, serial number 160120, was shipped to Frank Conrad at Fort Griffin on September 5, 1877. *Courtesy Sharon Cunningham and Dixie Gun Works.*

Latter day photograph of what was left of the Conrad and Rath store at Fort Griffin. *Courtesy Sharon Cunningham and Dixie Gun Works.*

J. Wright Mooar, renowned buffalo hunter and a man that aggressively defended hide-hunting as a profession and but pure business, not wanton sport. Mr. Mooar personally knew Lottie Deno. *Courtesy Nita Stewart Haley Memorial Library.*

Buffalo Hunter's camp southwest of Fort Griffin. Obviously it was a stinky business. Nevertheless it was a business, not a sporting lark. *Courtesy Robert E. Nail, Jr. Collection—Archives of the Old Jail Art Center.*

In from the frontier an ox-train of buffalo hides is brokered at Weatherford, Texas. *Courtesy Nita Stewart Haley Memorial Library.*

L. to R. Charles Baldwin, Moorman Baldwin, and their father, Sam Baldwin, and Earl Vandale. As a buffalo hunter working out of Fort Griffin the elder Mr. Baldwin knew Miss Lottie Deno and some of her "personal" friends. Here he is winding up an interview at Lordsburg, New Mexico, about the old days with interviewer Vandale and Hervey E. Chesley [not pictured, probably snapping the shutter]. *Courtesy Nita Stewart Haley Memorial Library.*

One of the numerous nefarious characters frequenting Fort Griffin, John Selman, the rascally associate of a Texas sheriff gone bad. Mr. Selman was ultimately the killer of Mr. John Wesley Hardin at El Paso, Texas. *Courtesy Jim Earle.*

Believed to be the only known photograph of Fort Griffin "working girls." Taken from the personal scrapbook of El Paso madam Alice Abbott and captioned "Beauties of Griffin." *Courtesy Robert G. McCubbin.*

Endnotes Chapter 6

[1] Rainman, "The Legend Of Lottie Deno." *The West.* December 1965. 18.

[2] Henry Herron to J. R. Webb. "I [Henry Herron] was deputy sheriff when she [Lottie Deno] arrived on the Jacksboro stage and when she left there [The Flat]. She had her shanty in the vicinity of other women residing along the river." J. R. Webb Papers, Rupert Richardson Research Center, Hardin-Simmons University, Abilene, Texas. 50; Lester W. Galbreath, *Fort Griffin And The Clear Fork Country: 100 Years of History, 1850-1950, On 25 Miles Of The Clear Fork Of The Brazos River.* 15. During a face to face interview with this author, Mr. Lester W. Galbreath, Fort Griffin State Park, Superintendent [Retired], confirmed that Lottie Deno, while at The Flat, resided along the Clear Fork of the Brazos with other working-girls in a row of prostitutes' cribs.

[3] Charles Robinson, III, *The Frontier World of Fort Griffin: The Life and Death of a Western Town.* 86; Roberts, *Doc Holliday: The Life And Legend.* "She [Lottie] was a mysterious, well-mannered, and attractive woman who was both a whore and immune to the rough and rowdy climate of the saloons and gambling halls." 82; Barton, *Pistol Packin' Preachers.* "Some lawmen liked her [Lottie Deno], but others thought she dipped into the brothel business as well as gambling." 140; Sara R. Massey, *Texas Women On The Cattle Trails.* "The nearest town, called 'the Flats,' was visited by everyone from Pat Garrett, then a buffalo skinner, to the famous woman poker player, Lottie Deno." 44.

[4] Gourney, *Texas Boundaries: Evolution of the State's Counties.* 81.

[5] Thomas T. Smith, *The U. S. Army & the Texas Frontier Economy, 1845-1900.* 81.

[6] Gourney, *Texas Boundaries: Evolution of the State's Counties.* 81.

[7] Uglow, *Standing In The Gap: Army Outposts, Picket Stations, And The Pacification Of The Texas Frontier, 1866-1886.* 106; Frazer, *Forts Of The West: Military Forts and Presidios and Posts Commonly Called Forts West of the Mississippi River to 1898.* Frazer says Fort Griffin was named after Colonel Griffin rather than General Griffin. 151; Smith, *The Old Army In Texas: A Research Guide to the U. S. Army in Nineteenth-Century Texas* concurs with Frazer: "...the name of the post was changed on February 6, 1868, to honor the Fifth Military District Commander, Col. Charles Griffin, Thirty-fifth Infantry, who died September 15, 1867." 66.

[8] Kraisinger, *The Western: The Greatest Texas Cattle Trail, 1874-1886.* 7. And various other maps throughout this comprehensive and well-researched volume; J. Marvin Hunter, *The Trail Drivers of Texas.* "All of the old trail drivers will remember Fort Griffin in Shackelford County, which was the last organized county on the [Western] trail, and all herds had to be inspected at the crossing of the Clear Fork of the Brazos, near the mouth of Tecumpsee. The writer at one time had the honor of being inspector there, and the memory of many pleasant events come back over the fleeting years as I [John C. Jacobs] sit here and write." 665; Diedra Newcomb, "Life In Old Fort Griffin." *Old Timer.* May 1981. "The opening of the Western Cattle Trail which started in the neighborhood of San Antonio and continued northward presented the people of Fort Griffin with glittering opportunities and a dangerous problem of law and order." 27.

[9] Gourney, *Texas Boundaries: Evolution of the State's Counties.* Throckmorton County would be organized on March 18, 1879; Baylor County on April 12, 1879; and Wilbarger County on October 10, 1881. 75, 82.

[10] William Curry Holden, *Alkali Trails*. "Doan's Store on Red River was the only supply station between Fort Griffin and Kansas, but drovers used it only in emergencies, having stocked their chuck wagons at Fort Griffin." 188, n. 4.

[11] Shirley Caldwell, Bob Green and Reilly Nail, *For 500 Years: The Shackelford County Courthouse*. "Starting in 1874 hundred of thousands of longhorn cattle and horses from South Texas were driven to Kansas and Nebraska over the Western Cattle Trail, sometimes called the Dodge City Trail. Trail drivers and cowboys stopped to quench their thirst at the 'Flat.' Griffin became a main supply point on the trail. Drovers and drifters could enjoy the company of some of the local ladies....at one of the town's saloons. Some of the west's most notorious names were drawn into the swirl at Griffin...." 16.

[12] Frances Mayhugh Holden, *Lambshead Before Interwoven: A Texas Range Chronicle, 1848-1878*. "Both sides of the street were lined with saloons, hotels, gambling halls, dance halls, small businesses, and lawyers' and doctors' offices. Scattered about behind these establishments was the 'red light' district, the palaces of sin where the madams and their girls displayed and dispensed their charms. Some were only one room, where an independent operator plied her trade, but most were larger establishments supervised by a madam. The Flat clearly offered antidotes to the monotony of the trail." 102.

[13] Don H. Biggers, [Joan Farmer, ed.] *Shackelford County Sketches*. 29

[14] DeArment, *Bravo of the Brazos: John Larn of Fort Griffin, Texas*. 89-93; Newton J. Jones to J. R. Webb, and Phin W. Reynolds to J. R. Webb, Henry Herron to J. R. Webb. Webb Papers; Several of the so-called old-timer's remembrances can be found in *Tracks Along the Clear Fork: Stories From Shackelford and Throckmorton Counties*, edited by Lawrence Clayton & Joan Halford Farmer; Joan Halford Farmer, *Fort Griffin: Wildest Town On The Prairie*. 15.

[15] J. Wright Moor's 1928 address to the West Texas Historical Association's annual meeting at Abilene, Texas. The entire text of the speech is repeated as "Frontier Experiences of J. Wright Moor," in the June 1928 edition of the *West Texas Historical Association Year Book*. 89-92; J. D. Rittenhouse, *Maverick Tales: True Storeis of Early Texas*. "J. Wright Mooar, who preferred to be called Wright, turned out to be a natural buffalo hunter. He not only knew how to hunt, but—more important—he could organize and run a businesslike outfit." 158.

[16] John Chadbourne Irwin to J. R. Webb. 1934. Webb Papers. "You ask what was Ft. Griffin's most prosperous time. I think it was 1876-1877." 41.

[17] Ibid. Holden, *Alkali Trails*. "The destruction of the [buffalo] herds went on at an increasing rate throughout 1876 and 1877...The *Frontier Echo* estimated there were 1500 outfits on the range west of Fort Griffin in February, 1877. The greatest slaughter came in the winter of 1877-1878. More than 100,000 hides were taken in the months of December and January on the Texas range." 13.

[18] Joe S. McCombs [Contributors Ben O. Grant & J. R. Webb], "On The Cattle Trail And Buffalo Range, Joe S. McCombs. *West Texas Historical Association Yearbook*. Volume XI. [November 1935]. 100.

[19] W. L. Evans, "A Journey to Fort Griffin in 1876." *Frontier Times*. May 1926. 32.

[20] Ben O. Grant, *A Early History of Shackelford County*. Master of Arts Thesis. 1936. Hardin-Simmons University. Abilene, Texas. Quoting *The Frontier Echo*, November 16, 1877. 70.

[21] Ibid. 71.

[22] Doug Perkins and Nancy Ward, *Brave Men & Cold Steel: A History of Range Detectives and Their Peacemakers*. 12; Bob Alexander, *Fearless Dave Allison: Border Lawman*. "There [Graham, Texas] at the county courthouse, or by other accounts under a noble Oak tree, cattlemen, distraught over an unprecedented and seemingly

infectious rash of cattle thievery, met to discuss issues regarding mutual protection." 20; Mary Whatley Clarke, *The Palo Pinto Story*. 88.

[23] Carrie J. Crouch, *A History of Young County, Texas*. "The principal plan that developed from the first meeting was that Northwest Texas be divided into six districts with men selected for each district to look after the stray cattle and hold them for the owners." 139.

[24] *By-Laws, Rules, Regulations and Names of Members of the Cattle Raisers Association of Texas*. 17. For additional information on Stribling, see, Eula Haskew, "Stribling And Kirkland Of Fort Griffin." *West Texas Historical Association Yearbook*. Volume XXXII. [October 1956] 55-69.

[25] *Weekly Colorado Citizen*, May 10, 1877. Courtesy, Chuck Parsons.

[26] Emmett Roberts, "Frontier Experiences Of Emmett Roberts Of Nugent, Texas." *West Texas Historical Association Yearbook*. June 1927. 52.

[27] Ty Cashion, "(Gun)Smoke Gets in your Eyes: A Revisionist Look at 'Violent' Fort Griffin." *Southwestern Historical Quarterly*. Volume XCIX. No. I. [July 1995]. Quoting the *Dallas Morning News* of June 1, 1930. 89.

[28] Rex W. Strickland [Ed.], "The Recollections Of W. S. Glenn, Buffalo Hunter." *Panhandle-Plains Historical Review*. Volume XXII. 1949.16.

[29] J. R. Webb, "Henry Herron, Pioneer And Peace Officer During Fort Griffin Days." *West Texas Historical Association Yearbook*. Volume XX. [October 1944]. 30.

[30] Rye, *The Quirt and the Spur: Vanishing Shadows Of The Texas Frontier*. "In 1909, thirty-three years after his own wide-eyed arrival on the northwester Texas frontier, former judge and editor Rye introduced the *Quirt and the Spur* to a public eager to rediscover the 1870s landscape around Fort Griffin, a time and place fast fading from memory. What Rye delivered was a fractured fairy tale, but one that appealed strongly to the popular appetites of the day." Back cover. Shrewdly the book is classified Texana/Fiction.

[31] Ibid. "Prominent among the wild, dare-devil, reckless characters who frequented the resorts in the Flat, was a female monstrosity known by the name of Lottie Deno." 70.

[32] Ibid. 71.

[33] Sam Baldwin to Earl Vandale and Hervey Chesley, July 11, 1941. 36. Courtesy, Nita Stewart Memorial Library, Midland, Texas. Part, but not all of Baldwin's remarks about Lottie Deno, may be found in Hervey E. Chesley's *Trails Traveled—Tales Told: Adventuring With the Old-Timers*. 91-99. Several of the less than complementary things Baldwin had to say about Lottie Deno apparently were edited from the transcript and not included in the book—either for spatial reasons or a polite deference to prudence.

[34] Sallie Reynolds Matthews, *Interwoven: A Pioneer Chronicle*. 109.

[35] Hunter, *The Story of Lottie Deno: Her Life and Times*. 37.

[36] Ibid.

[37] Matthews, *Interwoven: A Pioneer Chronicle*. 110.

[38] Frank Lloyd, Tularosa, New Mexico, to J. Evetts Haley and Hervey Chesley, June 12, 1939. 17. Courtesy Nita Stewart Haley Memorial Library.

[39] Rainman, "The Legend Of Lottie Deno." 58.

[40] Interview with Joan Farmer, Albany, Texas.

[41] Roberts, *Doc Holliday: The Life And Legend*. 86. For a thumbnail sketch of the most interesting life of Sam Baldwin see Gilbert, Remiger & Cunningham, *Encyclopedia of Buffalo Hunters and Skinners*. Volume I. 13-14.

[42] Sam Baldwin to Earl Vandale and Hervey Chesley.

[43] Ibid. 36; Tanner, *Doc Holliday: A Family Portrait*. "The following year she left Wichita and was working in Tom Sherman's Dance Hall in Dodge City under her new name, Kate Elder." 111; Roberts, *Doc Holliday: The Life And Legend*. "She was one

of the girls in Tom Sherman's dance hall, having moved from Dodge along the wagon road when the Sweetwater camp was established." 77; John R. Cook, *The Border and the Buffalo* adds that Limpy Jim Smith was an "ex-road-agent from Montana," which either means he had been employed by a stagecoach company or had given up the life of a stagecoach robber. 200. Though as of yet not provable there is certainly the chance that Lottie—the woman with a purposefully mysterious past—was connected in some way with Tom Sherman in Kansas. Such an affiliation would not be surprising. Additional data on Tom Sherman may be found in Roger Myers' "Between Wichita and Dodge: The Travels and Friends of Kate Elder." NOLA *Quarterly* [April-June 2007] 22-27.

44 Ibid. 9.

45 Robert K. DeArment, "John Shanssey: From Prize Ring To Politics. *Old West.* March 1999. Quoting a date not cited edition of the *Fort Griffin Echo:* "The round face and rotund body of John Shanssey made its appearance on our streets yesterday. Shaney and family are now residents of the thriving village of Colorado [Colorado City, Texas] where he will open a first class hotel…" 25-29. Rainman, "The Legend of Lottie Deno." "Pat Casey took a shine to Lottie." 19.

46 Ibid. 27.

47 Ibid. Mark Dworkin, "Wyatt Earp's 1897 Yuma and Cibola Sojourns." *Western Outlaw-Lawman History Association Journal.* Volume XIV. Number I. [Spring 2005]. "It is possible that Shanssey was involved in two saloons in Fort Griffin." 63, n. 14; *Arizona Sentinel,* January 6, 1899. "Elected mayor: John Shanssey, no opposition." Also subsequent editions of the *Arizona Sentinel* reflect Shanssey's reelection to the mayoral position at Yuma, Arizona Territory; January 5, 1900; January 11, 1901; July 5, 1905; November 7, 1906; *Yuma County Arizona Magazine,* 1905. Photograph captioned: "J. H. Shanssey, Mayor of Yuma." 4.

48 Henry Herron to J. R. Webb. 44. A later rendition of the same story adds, "….a married man whose name I will not mention." 75.

49 C. L. Sonnichsen, "Justice After Dark." *True West.* January-February 1966. "This story begins about the time the first pangs of civilization began to be felt in the neighborhood of Old Fort Griffin, a hundred and some odd miles west of Fort Worth, Texas, and known far and wide as the Babylon of the Border." 18; Leon Claire Metz, *John Selman: Texas Gunfighter* characterized The Flat as the "Sodom of the Plains." 48.

50 W. C. Holden, *Rollie Burns or An Account Of The Ranching Industry On The South Plains.* 54-55.

51 DeArment, "John Shannesy: From Prize Ring To Politics. "At Griffin he [Shanssey] purchased a two room adobe building on the main street, opened a combination saloon and gambling house called the Bee Hive, and employed gambling man Mike Fogarty to manage it." 27.

52 Rose, *Lottie Deno: Gambling Queen of Hearts.* "Mike Fogarty was in fact Frank Thurmond." 40; Roberts, *Doc Holliday: The Life and Legend.* "Lottie may have followed a former Georgian named Frank Thurmond, who was also a San Antonio gambler on the run, to Griffin. Using the alias Mike Fogarty, he was employed periodically as a bartender at the Bee Hive…" 83; Roberts who does provide his readers with citation to source material, for this instance endnotes to Rose's *Lottie Deno: Gambling Queen of Hearts.* 435, n. 101; Chris Enss, *The Lady Was a Gambler: True Stories of Notorious Women of the Old West,* picks up on the unsupported theme that Frank Thurmond and Mike Fogarty were one in the same person: "Lottie hosted a regular game at the Bee Hive Saloon in Fort Griffith [*sic:* Griffin] and was treated like royalty by the men who frequented the business. Bartender Mike Fogarty treated her especially well—Mike Fogarty was, in fact, Frank Thurmond. Still fearful

of being found out by the law, who knew the pair had been romantically involved in the past, Thurmond and Lottie would steal away to a nearby town for secret rendezvous." 56. An assertion that Frank Thurmond, wanted for murder, would openly tend bar at The Flat with its highly mobile and transit crowd, and then move to a nearby town [which there wasn't] for a secret tryst with Lottie Deno is, indeed, a stretch of credulity.

[53] Interview with Lester W. Galbreath, Superintendent [Retired], Fort Griffin State Park. Mr. Galbreath who has researched and written extensively on Fort Griffin the fort, Fort Griffin the town, as well as the Clear Fork country of Shackelford County and surrounding counties, is emphatic that he has seen no creditable evidence even mildly suggesting Frank Thurmond's presence at Fort Griffin, or that Thurmond used the name Forgarty. Mr. Galbreath stated that on at least one occasion in consultation with an inquiring author he shared that information, only to have it completely and, outrageously, disregarded because the fiction was more appealing than the fact. Like any competent historian Mr. Galbreath stands ready to readjust his thinking should new information be developed that would fundamentally support a different conclusion. Likewise, should new evidence surface, this writer would gladly change her opinion and incorporate the fresh material into future journalistic projects.

[54] *By-Laws, Rules, Regulations and Names of Members of the Cattle Raisers Association of Texas.* 29 & 121. Thurmond was an Association member after he had left Texas and taken up residence in New Mexico Territory. Certainly it cannot categorically be said that Frank had never used an alias, but there is not evidence to support such an assertion, and reasonableness suggests its improbability.

[55] John R. Hutto, "Mrs. Elizabeth (Aunt Hank) Smith." *West Texas Historical Association Yearbook.* Volume XV. [October 1939] 42; The reference to Lottie Deno may also be found in the book-length work of W. Hubert Curry, *Sun Rising on the West: The Saga of Henry Clay and Elizabeth Smith.* 132.

[56] Matthews, *Interwoven: A Pioneer Chronicle.* 109.

[57] Shackelford County Deed Book A. Page 206. Charlotte J. Tompkins to James Murphy. June 1877. Courtesy, Julia Putnam; Cahsion, *A Texas Frontier: The Clear Fork Country and Fort Griffin, 1849-1887.* "She had purchased three other lots in 1877." 330, n. 18.

[58] Cashion, *A Texas Frontier: The Clear Fork Country and Fort Griffin, 1849-1887.* "In this pitiable environment Charlotte Tompkins briefly enjoyed part control of a boarding house, the Gus, as well as a saloon." 196.

[59] J. W. Woody to J. Evetts Haley, Snyder, Texas, October 19, 1926. 4. Courtesy Nita Stewart Haley Memorial Library.

[60] Cashion, *A Texas Frontier: The Clear Fork Country and Fort Griffin, 1849-1887.* 195; Butler, *Daughters of Joy, Sisters of Misery: Prostitutes in the American West, 1865-90.* "Alcoholism and drug addiction went hand in hand in prostitutes' lives." 67.

[61] Rye, *The Quirt and the Spur: Vanishing Shadows Of The Texas Frontier.* 72.

[62] Shackelford County Court of Law. *The State of Texas vs. George Smith & Smokey Joe.* Cause Number 17. Minutes of County Court Number 1, Page 12.

[63] Hunter, *The Story of Lottie Deno: Her Life and Times.* 45. Also, "John Jacobs informed the author that he knew many of the colorful characters in and around old Fort Griffin, among them Smokey Joe,...." 35.

[64] Frank Collinson, *Life In The Saddle.* "As she [Lottie] left the gambling hall she carried hidden in her clothes not only her own winnings of the evening but the pot of more than one thousand dollars that had caused the shooting between Monte Bill and Smoky Joe." 90.

[65] Rose, *Lottie Deno: Gambling Queen of Hearts.* "In several versions of the story, the money that was on the table that night disappeared. Lottie was the only one left in the

room, and most think she quietly slipped in into her purse, then left for the evening."
43.
[66] Ty Cashion, "Rewriting the Wild West for a New History." *Journal of the West*.
October. 1995. The author's take on this affair is quite simple. Mr. Cashion believes it
is pure fabrication. One point of his argument is: "The letters from John C. Jacobs, on
which Hunter relied heavily for intimate details of Deno's life at Fort Griffin, suggest
that he really did not know her very well at all. For instance, Jacobs asserted that Deno
told him her real name and then swore him to secrecy. Actually her name—posted all
over the District Court dockets—was no secret to anyone aware of her legal troubles."
57; How well John C. Jacobs knew Lottie Deno is not the issue in this particular case.
Identifying her as being present when violence took place speaks not at all to the depth
of their friendship—or any other relationship whatever it might have been. Mr.
Cashion placing stock in Jacobs' not actually using Lottie's real name is reasonable, but
imperfect. Jacobs was from Gallatin County, Kentucky, the same county listed as
Lottie's birthplace on her *Certificate of Death*. Would not the possibility of Jacobs
doing the "gentlemanly thing," and withholding disparaging information be worth
considering? More especially if he knew any of Lottie's family members in their home
county? Since Lottie's reputation was somewhat sullied, Mr. Jacobs *might not* have
wanted to be credited as the person responsible for negatively outting Lottie to
posterity. That prospect gains credence when it is remembered that it was Jacobs who
said that Lottie had the manners of a typical Southern lady, but "didn't always live up
to appearances." Mr. Cashion says Jacobs "...really did not know her [Lottie] very
well at all." Jacobs says, "I knew Lottie well..." Additionally it's key to note that John
C. Jacobs and J. Marvin Hunter began having their discussions about Lottie Deno in
1927, 32 years before Hunter's *The Story of Lottie Deno: Her Life and Times* was
posthumously published by Hunter's children—well before Lottie Deno was made
into the popularized Wild West personality of today. There had been, of course,
mentions of her in Rye's *Quirt and the Spur* and she had been blended into a
fictionalized character, Faro Nell, in Lewis' *Wolfville* series. Assuredly Jacobs was not
overly imbued with a desire to connect himself to the publicity about Lottie, a
phenomenon that was yet over a quarter century into the future. Mr. Cashion, in this
same vein, remarks, "Although court and county records are silent about Lottie Deno,
they speak at length about Charlotte Tompkins." 59. The author is half right, they do
speak to *The State of Texas vs. Charlotte J. Tompkins*, but also see, *The State of
Texas vs. Lotta Deno*, Cause Number 26, November 5, 1877, Shackelford County,
"Keeping a Disorderly House." In speaking to Edgar Rye's knowledge about Lottie,
Mr. Cashion, says: "He [Rye] lived in nearby Albany, where he was justice of the peace
and editor of the *Tomahawk*. Although he frequently visited Fort Griffin, his character
sketch of Deno was hardly based on familiarity with her." 59, n. I. This writer cannot
speak to the "familiarity" between Rye and Deno, absent a sound basis. However, it
does not seem unreasonable to believe that the two knew each other. Rye, among other
things, was a Shackelford County criminal justice official, "frequently" visiting Fort
Griffin, and Lottie Deno was, during that same time-frame a flamboyant resident of
Fort Griffin, and under one name or another was a frequent skirmisher with the
county's legal system. Moreover, Mr. Cashion asserts: "Even though a man known only
as 'Smokey Joe' did exist, court records show that he fled town following a charge of
aggravated assault before Lottie ever arrived at Fort Griffin." 57. If Mr. Cashion is
referencing *The State of Texas vs. George Smith & Smokey Joe*, Cause Number 17,
Aggravated Assault, Shackelford County, the court record does not seem to suggest
where Smokey Joe went. On Tuesday, December 5th, 1876, Cause Number 17,
Aggravated Assault, in the case styled *The State of Texas vs. George Smith & Smokey
Joe* a judicial decision was rendered; it was officially "Dismissed."

Chapter 7

"A Reckless and Dissipated Son"

Pruning the extent of Miss Deno's involvement in the next Fort Griffin escapade is maddening, but achievable. Exploring the legend and the facts are crucial for understanding what is a fascinating tale. Evenhanded study will shatter a myth that has swirled around Miss Lottie Deno for years. The scrutiny will also generate questions that are unanswerable. However there are a number of indisputable truths.

One of those is that John A. "Johnny" Golden, Alabama born and East Texas raised, made his appearance at Fort Griffin during 1877.[1] Edgar Rye self-assuredly wrote in the *Quirt and the Spur* that Johnny Golden was "...the scion of a rich Boston family, and a dissolute castaway."[2] Johnny Golden was from Boston, but most likely Boston, Texas, in the central section of Bowie County between the towns of Old Boston and New Boston. Why he made a trip to The Flat may be the crux of an important matter. There is an enormous exchange of conjecture and few known facts about the Fort Griffin life of Johnny Golden. Earlier Mr. Golden had made the professional acquaintance of Major John B. Jones, Commander of the well-known Frontier Battalion [Texas Rangers]. J. E. Hines, 1st Sergeant, Company B, from his post in Throckmorton County confirms:[3]

John Golden who you had under arrest at one time at Griffin...[4]

Major Jones had arrested John Golden on criminal charges stemming from an indictment for Assault to Kill during February of 1876, in Travis County [Austin], Texas.[5] At the time of Golden's arrest, May 25, 1877, Jones had been assisted by Company A Sergeant George Washington "Cap" Arrington.[6] Like so many of the gals and guys populating the western frontiers, even Sergeant Arrington had assumed an alias. He had left his birth name and an unsavory incident in Alabama behind.[7] Unable to secure a witness who could make a positive identification of Mr. Golden, the Texas Rangers released him from custody.[8] If Johnny Golden had been clairvoyant he would have gladly jumped right back into the handcuffs and leg-irons. Had the lawmen connected this John Golden to the John Golden wanted for theft, also in Travis County, Shackelford County's early history would have been written with an altogether different spin.[9] At any rate, regardless pending legal difficulties elsewhere, Johnny Golden was at Fort Griffin, foot loose and fancy free, apparently having already left one female companion behind at Pittsburg, Texas.[10]

Johnny Golden was a "nice looking boy, had a little money to spend, and spent if freely."[11] Johnny was so very nice looking and so very well fixed he was an irresistible catch, at least so thought Miss Deno: "Lottie fell for him and the talk was that she would have nothing to do with the saloon keeper."[12] Saloon man John Shanssey suffered miserably from being smitten. Lottie's misplaced affections touched a raw nerve. The stinging insult and injured pride were compounded in Shanssey's mind; he had provided the furnishings and furniture for her little shanty overlooking the Clear Fork.[13] Shanssey smoldered, so says some of the gossip.

Shackelford County's ex-lawman, John Jacobs, tells a diametrically dissimilar story. According to Mr. Jacobs, Johnny Golden was but a sleazy creature roaming throughout Shackelford County, serving as a "go-between for outlaws and crooks." Johnny Golden, the "young Jew....was not in Lottie Deno's class, but that Lottie had known him elsewhere, and that he held some kind of club over her was quite apparent to me [Jacobs]."[14] Lottie had sought John Jacobs' shoulder to cry on, sobbing that somewhere on the outlaw trail she had an estranged husband dodging the law, probably in Mexico. Fluttering eyelashes and coquettish glances accented her helplessness. Lottie coyly confided to Mr. Jacobs that she had just received a letter from her husband—who miraculously knew just where to send the missive. Desperately he wanted to reunite, go west, and make "a new start." Johnny Golden was the fly in the ointment. Golden knew of her husband's troubles and she was having to "keep him pacified," lest he meanly spill the beans and ruin all: Blackmail![15] That is the story she told an all ears and compassionate John Jacobs. It was a tale of despair. Even one of Miss Deno's most benevolent biographers is compelled to concede that Lottie enlightened Jacobs with "this bizarre combination of lies and half-truths..."[16] Occasionally it is written that Golden was Lottie Deno's estranged husband—or at least an ex-lover—who had finally tracked her down: A nightmare returned. Lacking any validation and generously giving Lottie Deno a husband is a gift best forsaken until there is legitimized proof of matrimony, an inconvenience that has thus far failed to materialize.[17] There will be a point when she marries, but there is no creditable evidence to stand up an inference that she was a widow, divorcee—or a bigamist—when the ceremony took place.

Since Lottie Deno's life at The Flat revolves around poker tables, faro layouts and roulette wheels, it is fitting to toss in the wild card: Big Bill Gilson. After turning over Jacksboro's Town Marshal's position to Dick Harley, Gilson meandered into Shackelford County, finagling himself appointment as a County Constable. His policing beat was The Flat. Raw and wild as the town was, Big Bill Gilson seemed to be an ideal choice, though his methods could be weighed as heavy handed. At Jacksboro, Big Bill had shown he was not a man to trifle with:

> Some of the haughty Negro soldiers often came over to town in bunches, and neither the white nor the colored people had protection from them, but after Marshal Gilson put a few bullets into them, they were less active.[18]

Besides his hulking physical frame, his hardnosed way of thinking and little "Betsy" his sawed-off shotgun with a pistol grip, Big Bill Gilson brought with him an affinity for working-girls.[19] Congenial linkage between prostitutes and policemen was not any anomaly. It was real; a trait not uncommon to many peace keepers of the day. Even some of the best, well, best known, frontier lawmen promenaded through towns' red-light districts pimping profit from prostitutes' antics.[20] Big Bill Gilson fit the profile perfectly. It is not illogical to wonder if Lottie Deno had also spoken with Big Bill concerning her growing apprehension about blackmailer Golden? He was, as she was whining, the barb in her bustle.

At The Flat on the night of July 20th or during wee morning hours of the 21st, 1877, Big Bill Gilson, accompanied by Shackelford County deputy sheriff Jim Draper, arrested Johnny Golden.[21] Though there was a crude but secure jailhouse nearby on Griffin Avenue, the two officers for some reason never explained had decided to march Golden uphill to the military post and lock him in the guardhouse. That was Gilson's and Draper's story! Johnny Golden made it not too far past Hank Smith's Wagon Yard, behind the Occidental Hotel.[22] In the darkness gunfire ended Golden's life. The lawmen's prisoner had foolishly tried to escape. That was Gilson's and Draper's story! "The two officers were exonerated in the hearing before the justice of the peace the next day."[23] Although Mr. Gilson and Mr. Draper were cleared legally not too many folks believed their version as to what had happened.[24] What was believable is that Johnny Golden was dead. Telegraph wires hummed a somber message throughout Texas:

> John Golden, son of Judge James Golden, of Pittsburg [Texas], was killed last night in attempting to escape from the town marshal and deputy sheriff while they were taking him to the guard house. *Galveston Daily News*, July 24, 1877.

> John Golden was killed at Fort Griffin on the 21st inst. in attempting to escape from the town marshal and a

deputy sheriff while being conveyed to the guard house.
Schulenberg Argus, July 27, 1877.

Graham, Texas, July 21—Last night, at Griffin, John
Golden, was being conveyed to the guard house by
Marshal Gibson [*sic*] and a Deputy Sheriff, when he
attempted to escape and was killed. He claimed to be a
son of a prominent Pittsburg [not Pittsburgh] Judge.
Daily Fort Worth Democrat, July 22, 1877.

John Jacobs said when Lottie Deno was made aware of Golden's death
she became "greatly distressed."[25] Whether it was because of her
unselfish altruism, sheer grief, or a guilty conscience is unknowable, but
Lottie extended a helping hand. Mr. Jacobs asserted the distraught
Lottie Deno gave him $65 to pay for Golden's funeral expenses and buy
the dead boy a suit of clothes.[26] Almost before Johnny Golden was
planted in the local cemetery the rumors and gossip cropped up.

The most prevalent theory is that John Shanssey was the brains
behind the scene: "The underworld rumor was that Lottie's former lover
had paid a specific sum to have Johnnie [*sic*] put away."[27] Local chitchat
put the price for killing Golden at $250.[28] The allegation accusing Mr.
Shanssey *may* be true, but it rests on an insecure foundation of hearsay
and innuendo, not facts: "No evidence was obtained and nothing was
ever done about it."[29]

John Jacobs further remarked that Lottie "seemed in a way to blame
herself with his death, and was inconsolable."[30] Lottie Deno might very
well have suffered pangs of guilt. If indeed John H. Shanssey, green-eyed
with jealousy, had played a key role in Johnny Golden's mysterious
death, surely Lottie could fathom the cause and effect; her act of
bedroom betrayal, her ex-lover's work of blind revenge. On the other
hand, blurting out her contrived story to John Jacobs with crocodile
tears, telling of Golden's threat of blackmail unless she kept him
"pacified" smacks of an unflattering picture. Did she moan about
Johnny Golden to Big Bill Gilson, too? Did Lottie complain, hopeful
that someone would simply run Golden out of The Flat and out of her
life? She was circulating with hardened frontier lawmen and sporting
folks. Did she get more than she bargained for? Or, even more sinister, if
Lottie Deno was really the gloomy and vulnerable victim of a
blackmailer who really had the motive for an execution? Did those
fluttering eyelashes and that seductive coyness entice others to act in her
behalf?

A fact anecdotally alleged, but somewhat supported by primary
source review is herewith repeated. Johnny Golden's father, upon
learning of his son's death, initiated a trip to investigate, but only made

it as far as Fort Worth. There Mr. Golden was "advised not to go to Fort Griffin, for he might meet the same fate as his son."[31] Whether or not the senior Mr. Golden even hinted at really making a trip to The Flat is unknowable. He did, however, pen a letter of inquiry. Shackelford County Sheriff Bill Cruger received and shared the heartrending epistle:

> —A letter was received by the Sheriff from the father of John Golden, making enquiry [sic] respecting the fate of his son, who was killed in Griffin some time past while trying to lead the officer who had him in charge, into ambush. The letter was read in the hearing of your correspondent, and never has it been my lot to listen to a more pathetic appeal to learn the truth of a sad affair, the sad condition of the mother now lying at the point of death from the effect produced on hearing the news, make up a mournful story of disappointment, and shows how often a reckless and dissipated son blasts the hopes of fond parents.[32]

Another of the legendary portions of Lottie Deno's story peels away with the gunning down of Johnny Golden. Allegedly, Lottie was so distraught over Johnny's death that she went into a piteous state of mourning, almost becoming reclusive as she pined away in her little shanty overlooking the Clear Fork. If John Jacobs' testimony is to be believed Lottie Deno was so distressed that she could not bring herself to attend Johnny's graveside service.[33] Perhaps her nonattendance at Johnny Golden's burial was that turning point for local fellows to drape Lottie with another nickname, "The Frozen Heart of Fort Griffin," a disdainful moniker at least one essayist alleges she carried.[34] Another writer eloquently but erroneously panders to the mystique of Miss Deno: "She was a strange one. Cold as ice, warm as silk, silent as a passing ship…."[35] Despite contrived myths, Johnny Golden was dead. Now Lottie would be totally free! With John Golden no longer a threat she could simply run away from The Flat, reunite with that husband she had mentioned to John Jacobs and make her "new start." Curiously, she didn't! Folklore colliding with factuality is often a bothersome detail. Most troubling in Lottie's story is a commonly repeated tall tale: Not too soon after Johnny Golden was killed, Lottie Deno vanished from The Flat.[36] Such an assertion has a warm and comforting glow of idyllic romanticism. Sorry to say it flies squarely in the face of contrary evidence. Conscientious attention to chronology in this particular case is uncomplicated. Well onto a year after Mr. John Golden was eradicated, lawmen and lawyers could still find Lottie Deno at The Flat, not moping about, but playing cards—and whatever!

Since there is substantiation that Limpy Jim Smith would continue to play a key role in Lottie Deno's conflicted life a concise update is necessary. Recognizing the financial potential associated with being as close as possible to buffalo hunters' booming Sharps rifles, Charley Rath had opened a trading post and hide buying station about fifty miles west of Fort Griffin. A few others followed suit. Where there were men there was money. In but a short time the collection of austere buildings was known as Rath City, or less frequently as Reynolds City.[37] It was not a pretty place, not according to buffalo hunter Frank Lloyd:

> There wasn't no town at Reynolds City except a bunch
> of houses and a saloon and a barber shop. The whole
> thing was built out of summer hides. They wasn't no
> good. The hides got dry and didn't smell.[38]

Charley Rath had brought fifty wagons to the site, loaded with "gunpowder, lead, food, whiskey, and lumber for a store, saloon, and [not surprisingly] brothel."[39] Although George Aiken and a fellow named Henry Fleming operated saloons, the particular proprietor of the lewd dance hall and whorehouse is misplaced. Outwardly Rath City was even more crude and more rude than The Flat, but it was busy. While Lottie was raking in cash at Fort Griffin, and whilst someone raked dirt over John Golden's coffin that year of 1877, at Rath City hunters trafficked over a million dollars in buffalo robes and tanned skins.[40] Something else contributing to the West Texas frontier economy was being brought to Rath City.

Girls! There was a brisk traffic between Fort Griffin and Rath City, not only in stinking brown hides but perfumed fair ones as well. In an effort to keep the buffalo hunters happily spending, a "new set of girls" was brought to Rath City weekly. They came and went with ease on freight wagons or coaches specifically dedicated to their travel.[41] Cadmus Brown remembered with barely repressible glee:

> Why, the men went calico minded as soon as they got a
> whiff of that Hoyt's cologne, and they swung those gals
> so fast that they got dust in their pockets.[42]

While there is no hard evidence to prove Lottie Deno was promenading or prostituting or poker playing at Rath City, it does not seem too fanciful to think she might have made the trip from time to time. She was a gambler and dance hall owner; the sweet taste of that easy money at Rath City would have been enticing. The hide town's allure was strong enough to draw Lottie's sometimes boyfriend Limpy Jim Smith. That arrival would mark Rath City's first killing.

Following the death of buffalo hunter Marshall Sewell during a Comanche raid, his infuriated contemporaries launched an 1877 campaign of retaliation. It is an adventure and misadventure that has been more than adequately covered in countless scholarly and popular publications.[43] One of those contemporaries, Tom Lumpkin, however, decided he did not want to play that game. Somewhat stupidly for a fellow in a camp comprised of hardened hunters and harlots, Tom became mouthy, saying:

Well, I have not lost any Indians and I don't propose to hunt any.[44]

Knowing whether or not Lottie Deno was in or nearby Henry Fleming's saloon in Rath City on April 27th after the hunters returned from their embittered campaign is not relevant, Limpy Jim Smith was. Drinking heavily, Tom Lumpkin continued making derogatory comments about the buffalo hunters' Indian chasing maneuvers. Charlie Hart, who was getting an amateur haircut in a corner chair, took exception. Tom Lumpkin pulled a revolver from his belt and shot Hart, breaking his arm. Limpy Jim Smith jumped in, and pushed novice barber Willis Crawford out of the way. Then Limpy Jim began shooting at Lumpkin, who continued to fire as he backed out the doorway and onto the street. Mr. Smith followed. Outside, Limpy Jim emptied his pistol, some of his bullets actually scoring hits. Because of bad whiskey and blustering remarks Tom Lumpkin forfeited his life that day. Subsequent to the burial Limpy Jim Smith, accompanied by witnesses he knew would see things his way, traveled to Fort Griffin [or Albany] and turned himself over to Shackelford County's legal authorities. Lumpkin's killing was ruled a "justifiable homicide."[45]

If Limpy Jim Smith was a scrapper, so, too, was Lottie Deno. Working girls' spats, the spitting and scratching, were not aberrations. Prostitutes in this regard were no different from the men, frequently racking up places on the court's docket for being drunk and disorderly, abusive language and, more gravely, assault or murder charges.[46] A quick glance at just one session of the Justice of the Peace minutes at Fort Griffin is enlightening, almost funny if it were not so emblematically sad:

Jennie Knowles, fighting in a public place, plead guilty, fine and costs $12.95.

Annie Timmons, using profane and indecent language in a public place. Jury trial, fine and costs $28.50.

Jennie Knowles, using profane and indecent language in a public place. Jury trial, fine and cots $24.45.

Ellen Anderson, fighting, plead guilty, fine and costs $9.65.

Ellen Anderson, using vulgar and profane language in a public place, plead guilty, fine and costs $11.75.[47]

With tongue in cheek a noted historian quite cleverly analyzed the court's proceedings: "From this docket we might infer that Jennie and Ellen were doing the fighting, and Annie was doing the talking."[48] Lottie Deno had an ongoing feud with another of Fort Griffin's dominate females of the sporting sorority; Madge Morgan.[49] Whether Lottie and Madge ever resorted to biting, scratching or hair-pulling is indeterminate. If not with Madge, then with another gal from the Lost Sisterhood—absent proper groundwork—it is bizarrely alleged that Lottie came up short during one squabble. Purportedly she was hit hard in the face with a brass cuspidor, permanently loosing the use of one eye. The paucity of evidence is as loud as the clanking noise made by the nauseating spittoon bouncing and rolling across the barroom's floor.[50] In this instance, mythology, along with the nasty tobacco spit, is all that is swirling around inside the receptacle.

Also rolling back into to The Flat was Doc Holliday. The gambling dentist made his quiet reentry into The Flat during September 1877.[51] While there Doc checked into Hank and Elizabeth Smith's Occidental Hotel. Keeping with a partial aspect of the traditional image given Mr. Holliday may be found in the hotel owner's ledger book; Doc's bar tab exceeded his room rent by a $100.[52] The minor criminal charges that prompted his earlier flight from town had been dismissed the preceding November.[53] At the time Doc Holliday reemerged Mr. John Golden had been dead more than a month. Lottie Deno was gaily back on the love market.

Somewhere along the gambling circuit Doc Holliday had become entangled with a first-rate whore, Big Nose Kate Fisher [Elder]. Kate was idling time at The Flat, while idle gossip was hinting of a sexual—if not romantic—linkage between Miss Lottie Deno and Mr. John Henry Holliday. The ex-deputy of Shackelford County, John C. Jacobs, who claims with authority to be in on the know, toning down his language for the intended puritanical audience, spotlighted a hot-tempered squabble between Big Nose Kate and the Frozen Heart of Fort Griffin. It was the culmination of smoldering jealously ignited. Kate, "a notoriously lewd character," accosted Lottie and lit the fuse for a bombastic tirade; reproaching her for a dalliance with the dentist. Paraphrasing Jacobs, sweet little Miss Deno responded in kind: "Why, you low-down stinking bitch! If I stepped in soft cow shit, I would not even clean my foot on that bastard! I'll show you a thing or two." One of those things or two was a revolver cleverly hidden somewhere in the billowy folds of Lottie's ornately embroidered Parisian gown. Not to be outdone or overawed Big Nose Kate likewise produced a handgun. Acting with undaunted courage or unthinking imprudence Doc Holliday jumped squarely between the posturing hellcats and "prevented a tragedy."[54]

Out of hand dismissing the veracity of such an altercation might be tempting. Several unassailable truths justify evenhanded scrutiny. A respected scholar particularly focused on the business of prostitution in the Old West says: "Elder and Holliday were both in Fort Griffin in 1877."[55] Lottie Deno was there, too! Other factors seem relevant to the topic. First and foremost is the fact that John Jacobs and Lottie Deno were contemporaries. Jacobs unambiguously said: "I recall one instance when Lottie Deno lost her usual serene temper and went for her gun..." One of the baseline studies of Big Nose Kate Elder is the often cited journal article "The O. K. Corral Fight At Tombstone: A Footnote By Kate Elder," which appeared in a 1970s edition of *Arizona and the West*. A letter allegedly written by Big Nose Kate to Mrs. W. J. Martin is quoted in the commentary. Big Nose Kate said: "I went in to see once where he [Holliday] was with another woman. I had a big knife with me and said I'd rip her open...Doc came away from her."[56] Could this have been the wrangle alluded to by John Jacobs? Interesting! From a woman's perspective it seems that Lottie's sarcastic remarks were not designed as an outright denial of any affair with Doc, but a graceless and catty effort meant to belittle Big Nose Kate. By the time Big Nose Kate and Holliday became an "item," there already had been a Lottie and Doc history at Jacksboro—just what it was is the mystery?

Another installment putting Lottie Deno and Doc Holliday together is also dependent on John Jacobs' memory. In a 1928 letter to J. Marvin Hunter, Mr. Jacobs distinctly recalled:

> In your recent letter you asked if faro was a popular game at old Fort Griffin. It certainly was popular; every gambling house there had a faro bank. I remember well one instance where a lot of money changed hands, and Lottie Deno coming out about three thousand dollars ahead, winning it all from Doc Holliday at the Bee Hive. It seems that Holliday had won over three thousand dollars and the layout from Mike Fogarty, who operated the gambling resort when Lottie Deno,

who was lookout for Fogarty, proposed to Holliday that she be given a chance to recoup Fogarty's losses. Holliday agreed to this, and the game was resumed, with a fifty dollar limit. The game did not last very long, for Lottie Deno copped every bet, and left Doc Holliday completely strapped, for the time being at least, for he was not one who let poor luck get him down and keep him there. He got into a poker game the next night and won $500 and a diamond ring from an army officer stationed at the fort. This fellow Holliday was a consumptive and a hard drinker, but neither liquor nor the bugs seemed to faze him. He could at times be the most genteel, affable chap you ever saw, and at other times he was sour and surly, and would just as soon cut your throat with a villainous looking knife he always carried, or shoot you with a .41-caliber double-barreled derringer he always kept in his vest pocket....[57]

Many thematic writers—those focusing on the Old West—seem not to have any problem accepting Mr. Jacobs' characterization of Doc Holliday as being a "hard drinker," sometimes "sour and surly," and a dangerous fellow who would "cut you" or "shoot you." It fits well within the accepted framework of what a real gunfighting gambler is supposed to be. On the other hand, an iconic gunmen loosing $3000 to a mere woman is most perplexing to he-men ingrained with perceptions as to how the legendary Wild West really was! The account of Mr. Holliday being outfoxed at the card table by a little lady is usually personified as being but an "apocryphal" story; one that is mythical or made up. A reality check is not inappropriate.

While Lottie Deno and Doc Holliday may have been many other things, it is indisputable that they really were frontier era gamblers and barroom habitués. Despite legend building inflation, searching for primary source conformation that either of them attained laudable status as gambling superstars is more than just a little noticeable—by its absence. Renditions of their gaming careers are not overrun with specifics. That they were gamblers, Yes. That they were luminaries, No. Verifiable instances of either one of them ever winning an oversized pile of greenbacks are meager. The game pitting Lottie Deno and Doc Holliday against each other is one of the few—very few—occasions where names are named and the winnings and losses are tabulated. Reading from Jacobs' letter to Mr. Hunter it seems the former was answering a question proposed by the latter regarding faro, and was not being quizzed about Lottie Deno's craft. Mr. Jacobs' remarks appear matter-of-fact. Accepting observer John Jacobs' claim that during one juncture Miss Deno and Mr. Holliday vied for each other's money over a game of chance is not troubling. It is even probable, considering both were gambling at The Flat during the same time and dimensionally the town was tiny. Except for the passing fling of a trail driving cowboy there were not many strangers staying at The Flat. The cardsharps, saloon owners, bartenders and whores were on a first name basis. That assortment was Lottie's and Doc's crowd. Is it so incredible to think that just once Lottie outwitted Doc? The turn of a card could have gone either way! Or, could Lottie have bequeathed Lady Luck a helping hand—from under the table? Later events will more than support the hypothesis that Lottie bested Doc, and that Doc bore her no enmity for doing so.

Those same later events tend to somewhat support Wyatt Earp's claim that he first met Doc Holliday at Fort Griffin.[58] As Lottie Deno's story unfurls the likelihood that she, too, first met the controversial Wyatt Earp at The Flat is not farfetched. Mr. Earp said that his first meeting with Doc Holliday was at the Cattle Exchange Saloon; the introduction courtesy of Mr. John H. Shanssey.[59] Not long thereafter, Wyatt Earp, as did Doc Holliday and Big Nose Kate, bid folks at The Flat goodbye. Miss Lottie Deno stayed behind doing what she did best; coyly using her feminine guile to subsist in a guy's world. Mr. Holliday and Mr. Earp and she would come together again.

Another of the unsavory characters Lottie Deno no doubt met while plying her trades at The Flat was not at all controversial. There was nothing iffy about Jessie Tye, aka Hurricane Minnie. Everyone knew she was a first-rate whore. Minnie was also the lawfully wedded wife of William A. "Hurricane Bill" Martin, the most notorious horse thief ranging throughout northwest Texas and Indian Territory.[60] Hurricane Bill was cunning:

> Bill had never stolen any horses near Griffin; like a wise
> old wolf he hunted a long way from his den. He would
> be gone for weeks and suddenly turn up with two or
> three good horses.[61]

Hurricane Bill may not have routinely ridden into The Flat leading a string of locally stolen horses, but when in town he was not a nice person. Once while drunk he and another fellow, Mike O'Brien, traded long-range rifle shots with each other. During the gunplay Mike, who "had lots of gall," was sitting in the middle of the street taking pot-shots at Hurricane Bill. Composedly he called for spectator Bill Campbell to bring him a shot of whiskey, which the frightened onlooker did. The fiery taste of liquor may have settled his nerves, but it did not improve

Mr. Mike's marksmanship. The preposterous bombardment ended minus any injuries to anyone but the gunbattle is forever scarred into The Flat's history—or folklore.[62] During another disturbance Hurricane Bill ran afoul of Big Bill Gilson. Guns were discharged. Martin ended up in the jail. After making bail Hurricane Bill ran away, but later turned informer on fellow comrades, threatening to furnish a membership list of Shackelford County's much written about brigade of vigilantes.[63] Hurricane Minnie, never faithful, not secretly transferred her pliant charms to area badman John Selman.[64] The sudden switch of her pliable affections was not under wraps:

> Wherever a whore by the name of Hurricane Minnie is
> around, there will John Selman be.[65]

Hurricane Minnie, after John Selman struck out for points further west, returned to her former profession, the world's oldest.[66] Lottie Deno did not take a cue from those sporting ne'er-do-wells who had made The Flat but a stopover. They, one and all, would wind up skirmishing with the criminal justice system elsewhere. Miss Lottie Deno would fight her legal battles—in the near term—on familiar home turf in Shackelford County. Lottie's pensive standing before the judiciary's bench would not be a singular incident, but a reoccurring string of appearances.

Major John B. Jones, Commander Frontier Battalion [Texas Rangers]. He arrested Mr. Johnny Golden at Fort Griffin. *Courtesy Chuck Parsons.*

Much like Lottie Deno and Frank Canton, Texas Ranger George Washington "Cap" Arrington [pictured above] had somewhere along the way left his birth name behind after an unsavory incident, successfully reincarnating himself for a Lone Star law enforcing career. He, along with Major Jones, arrested Mr. Golden. *Courtesy Chuck Parsons.*

John C. Jacobs, early buffalo hunter and Shackelford County resident. Mr. Jacobs personally knew Lottie Deno; in fact it was to him she complained about Johnny Golden with an implausible story. Mr. Jacobs also detailed a poker game between Miss Lottie and Mr. John Henry "Doc" Holliday. *Courtesy Nita Stewart Haley Memorial Library.*

Mr. Henry Clay "Hank" Smith, early day Southwest pioneer. Mr. Golden was killed behind Smith's Occidental Hotel and wagon yard at The Flat. It was here, too, that the contentious Mr. John Henry "Doc" Holliday stayed, registering quite a sizable bill for liquor. *Courtesy Nita Stewart Haley Memorial Library.*

Old jail at Fort Griffin with restored iron door. *Author's photo.*

Mr. John Shanssey, Fort Griffin saloon operator and one of Lottie Deno's purported lovers. *Courtesy Arizona Historical Society, Rio Colorado Division.*

Innocence lost: An early photograph of Mary Katharine Harony Cummings [seated], aka "Big Nose Kate," aka Kate Elder, aka Kate Fisher, Doc Holliday's sometime paramour and, perhaps, a near combatant with Lottie Deno at Fort Griffin. Kate's sister Wilhelmina is also pictured. *Courtesy Sharlot Hall Museum Archives.*

The quite spacious ranch house of Shackelford County Sheriff John Larn, a lawman turned outlaw. *Courtesy Julia Putnam.*

Mr. John Larn, the sheriff turned bad. He was murdered by vigilantes in his jail cell at Albany, Texas. *Courtesy Julia Putnam.*

The author at the Throckmorton County grave site of Shackelford County's ex-sheriff, John Larn. *Courtesy Bob Alexander.*

Endnotes Chapter 7

[1] United States Census 1870, Upsur County, Texas. Precinct Number 3. Pittsburg Post Office.

[2] Rye, *The Quirt and the Spur.* 73; United States Census 1860, Bowie County, Texas.

[3] J. E. Hines, Sergeant, Company B, Frontier Battalion, Throckmortion County, Texas, to Major John B. Jones, Commander, Frontier Battalion. July 31, 1877. Courtesy Texas State Library and Archives Commission, Austin, Texas.

[4] Ibid. The letter is appraising Jones of Golden's death, an event subsequently covered in this text.

[5] James B. Gillett, *Fugitives From Justice: The Notebook of Texas Ranger Sergeant James B. Gillett.* "Golden, John. Assault to kill; committed October, '75; indicted February, '76." 171; Rose, *Lottie Deno: Gambling Queen of Hearts* had a different version though she does not cite a source. "In October 1876, Johnny Golden killed a man. His name appears in 'A List of Fugitives from Justice,' issued by the governor in 1876. Johnny had fled the scene but was captured and arraigned for the murder in February 1877. He was able to escape, however, and in April Johnny headed toward Fort Griffin...." 55.

[6] Monthly Return for May 1877, submitted by Captain Neal Coldwell, Company A, Frontier Battalion. Texas State Library & Archives. Austin, Texas.

[7] Allen G. Hatley, "Cap Arrington: Adventurer, Ranger and Sheriff." *Wild West.* June 2001. "But there was still more to George Washington Arrington than met the eye, for he had been born John C. Orrick, Jr., on December 23, 1844. He had changed his name to Arrignton while on the run for killing a black man named Alex Webb back in Alabama in 1867." 50

[8] Monthly Return, May 1877, Company A, Frontier Battalion. "May 25, 1877, John Golden, Asslt to Kill, Travis County, Sergt Arrington, Failure to identify and was released."

[9] Gillett, *Fugitives From Justice: The Notebook of Texas Ranger James B. Gillett.* "Golden, John...Theft." 172.

[10] United States Census, 1870, Upsur County, Texas. Precinct Number 3. Pittsburg Post Office. Clearly this census report is not an absolute assurance that this was the John Golden of Fort Griffin infamy, but as of yet it seems to be the closest match.

[11] Henry Herron to J. R. Webb. Webb Papers. 51.

[12] Ibid.

[13] DeArment, "John Shanssey: From Prize Ring to Politics." 27.

[14] Hunter, *The Story of Lottie Deno: Her Life And Times.* 39.

[15] Ibid.

[16] Rose, *Lottie Deno: Gambling Queen of Hearts.* 57.

[17] Ibid. "There is no evidence that Lottie ever married Johnny Golden...."; DeArment, "John Shanssey: From Prize Ring to Politics." "To a few of her closest admirers, including Shanssey and John Jacobs, she confided that Golden, an itinerant gambler, was her lawful husband." 27.

[18] Huckabay, *Ninety-Four Years In Jack County, 1854-1948.* 149.

[19] *The Frontier Echo*, September 1, 1876. "Adams found Gilson asleep at Rosa Lee's [a known prostitute with an arrest record] and called him up but Gilson said if he had anything to say to him, to come in."; Robert K. DeArment, *Bravo of the Brazos: John Larn of Fort Griffin, Texas.* "...and 'Old Besty,' the marshal's [Gilson's] gun, tore a hole in the ceiling of the saloon," and "...of how Gilson, a hard drinker,..." 102 & 139.

[20] Roger Jay, "The Peoria Bummer, Wyatt Earp's Lost Year." *Wild West.* August. 2003.

[21] J. E. Hines, 1st Sergeant, Company B, Frontier Battalion, Throckmorton County, Texas, to Major John B. Jones, Commander, Frontier Battalion, July 31, 1877. "....[John Golden] was shot and killed the night of July 20th...."; Several newspaper editions give the date of Golden's death as July 21st rather than the 20th.

[22] Curry, *Sun Rising on the West: The Saga of Henry Clay and Elizabeth Smith.* 132.

[23] Hunter, *The Story of Lottie Deno: Her Life and Times.* 39.

[24] Newton Josephus Jones to J. R. Webb, March 15, 1947. Webb Papers. "Yes, I was in camp near Ft. Griffin when Johnnie [*sic*] was killed and remember about the killing. William Gilson and Jim Draper were supposed to have killed him. However, as I remember it, Gilson said that Golden broke to run after they had arrested him and were taking him up [to] the guard house. But no one believed but that he was shot down in cold blood." 9. For an implausible scenario explaining John Golden's death see the 4th of August 1877 edition of the *Dallas Weekly Herald.* The newspaper correspondent, James W. Grahame, writing under the pseudonym "Comanche Jim" spins a fanciful conspiracy theory; unfortunately insurmountable contradictions are also contained in the text. For an excellently researched biographical sketch of James Grahame, the colorful "Comanche Jim," see, Chuck Parsons "James W. Grahame— From Birmingham, England To Fort Griffin: An Englishman Finds Adventure in Texas." *English Westerners' Society Special Publication No. 11A.* [2005]

[25] Hunter, *The Story of Lottie Deno: Her Life and Times.* 39.

[26] Ibid.

[27] Henry Herron to J. R. Webb. Webb Papers. 51.

[28] DeArment, "John Shanssey: From Prize Ring To Politics." "According to Henry Herron, later sheriff at Griffin, John Shanssey ordered the execution of Golden and paid the officers $250." 27.

[29] Henry Herron to J. R. Webb. Webb Papers. 51.

[30] Hunter, *The Story of Lottie Deno: Her Life and Times.* 39. Rose, *Lottie Deno: Gambling Queen of Hearts.* "Talk was that she blamed herself for the killing." 59.

[31] Henry Herron to J. R. Webb. Webb Papers. 51.

[32] *Weatherford Exponent,* October 6, 1877. Though W. R. "Bill" Cruger was not specifically mentioned in the news item, the reference was under the heading, "Echoes from Albany," and the letter "was received by the Sheriff." Bill Cruger was the Shackelford County Sheriff at the time the story appeared in the newspaper and Albany was the county seat. See, Tise, *Texas County Sheriffs.* 462.

[33] Hunter, *The Story of Lottie Deno: Her Life and Times.* "Lottie remained in her room as the hack carrying the remains was driven out to the cemetery, where simple burial services were held." 40.

[34] Louise Cheney, "The Frozen Heart Of Fort Griffin." *Real West.* September 1973. "Soon males in the Flat pinned a sobriquet, The Frozen Heart of Fort Griffin, upon her [Lottie], a name she carried as so long as she remained in the Flat." 42. Correspondingly another nickname was doled out to Lottie in Valerie Owen's "The Frozen Face Of Fort Griffin," *Texas Co-op Power.* February 1969. The prose is strikingly similar: "Soon the males of the Flat pinned on her [Lottie] the sobriquet, The Frozen Face of Fort Griffin, a name she wore during her stay in the Flat." 4.

[35] F. Stanley [Stanley Crocchiola], *The Deming Story.* 15.

[36] Preston Lewis, "Lottie Deno, Gambler." *True West.* September 1987. 20; Rose, *Lottie Deno: Gambling Queen of Hearts.* Curiously the author has Lottie Deno leaving Fort Griffin for good on May 25, 1877, two months before Johnny Golden was killed; perhaps, a typographical error?

[37] Naomi H. Kincade, "Rath City." *West Texas Historical Association Yearbook.* Volume XXIV [October 1948] "Although Rath City, or Reynolds City as it was also called, was short-lived, it did a thriving business in the heyday of the great buffalo kill in the central West Texas region." 40; Frederick W. Rathjen, *The Texas Panhandle Frontier.* "About eighty hunters followed Rath south, and although Rath City did not replace Fort Griffin, it did get a terrific share of the hide business—perhaps in excess of one million dollars' worth in 1877." 171.

[38] Frank Lloyd, Tularosa, New Mexico, to J. Evetts Haley, June 13, 1935. 8. Courtesy Nita Stewart Memorial Library.

[39] Jerry Eckhart, "Rath City: Texas Hide Town." *True West.* September 1992. 42.

[40] Kincade, "Rath City." 40; Frederick Nolan, *Tascosa: Its Life and Gaudy Times.* "Rath City consisted of six sod buildings huddled together beside the trail to Fort Griffin. On the west side of the road were George Aiken's saloon and [Henry] Fleming's saloon and dance hall." 33.

[41] Gary Ford, "Rath City: A Brief But Important Time In History." *Back To Rath's Trail.* June. 2000. 2-3; Eckhart, "Rath City: Texas Hide Town." "Painted women came from Fort Griffin for dances and parties, while many Griffinites traveled to Rath Ctiy just to see the excitement." 44-45.

[42] Kincade, "Rath City." 46; Nolan, *Tascosa: Its Life and Gaudy Times.* "And very soon after that the saloon operators, the dance hall outfits with about forty women, and ne'er do wells also came.'" 33.

[43] Perhaps the best article length account may be found in Sharon Cunningham's excellently researched and written piece "Yellow House Canyon Fight: Buffalo Hunters vs. Plains Indians," which appeared in the June 2003 edition of *Wild West;* Author Preston Lewis also did a most commendable job in his two part article: "Bluster's Last Stand: The Battle of Yellow house Canyon," *True West,* April & May 1992.

[44] John R. Cook, *The Border and the Buffalo.* 201.

[45] Sharon Cunningham, Union City, Tennessee, to author, April 29, 2004; In most instances Tom Lumpkin is cited as "Lumpkins." This tidbit of incorrectness was amiably straightened out by Cheryl Lewis, an area researcher and expert on Rath City. Cheryl Lewis, Hamlin, Texas, to author, May 21, 2004; Eckhart, "Rath City: Texas Hide Town." 43-44; Ida Ellen Rath, *The Rath Trail,* 148; Cook, *Border and the Buffalo.* 234; Ed Bartholomew, *Western Hard-Cases: Or, Gunfighters Named Smith.* 73; Galbreath, *Campfire Tales: True Stories From The Western Frontier.* 75-76; Author Galbreath gives the name of the man wounded by Lumpkin as Oleson.

[46] Butler, *Daughters of Joy, Sisters of Misery: Prostitutes in the American West, 1865-90.* 67; Karen Holliday Tanner & John D. Tanner, Jr., "The Case of Ada Hulmes: Murder and Scandal in New Mexico." *Wild West.* December 2003. 55.

[47] W. C. Holden, "Law And Lawlessness On The Texas Frontier, 1875-1890." *Southwestern Historical Quarterly.* October 1940. Quoting the *Albany Echo.* 200.

[48] Ibid.

[49] Rainman, "The Legend of Lottie Deno." "Lottie's most bitter enemy was Old Madge Morgan, who operated a brothel and looked with envy on the beautiful redhead and the money she made." 58.

[50] To this author's knowledge the assertion that Lottie Deno had an eye knocked out by a flying cuspidor first appeared in Frank X. Tolbert's column in the *Dallas Morning News,* June 10, 1956; followed by Charles Robinson's 1992 *The Frontier World of Fort Griffin* [88]; and then, without citation to source, repeated in C. F. Eckhardt's 1999 *Tales of Badmen, Bad Women and Bad Places: Four Centuries of Texas Outlawry.* 64.

[51] Roberts, *Doc Holliday: The Life An Legend.* "Doc's recovery was marked by another arrest for gambling in Dallas in September, and this time he decided to move on. His destination was Fort Griffin." 81-83.

[52] Curry, *Sun Rising on the West, The Saga of Henry Clay and Elizabeth Smith.* 133. And, on page 211:
"Interesting Sidelight. The 1877 ledger for the hotel, café, bar, livery stable, has the following account page:"

Doc Holiday
First entry was September 14, 1877 for drinks, 50 cents.
Entries continued until September 21, 1877, all for drinks, $22.00

[53] Roberts, *Doc Holliday: The Life And Legend.* 81.
[54] Hunter, *The Story of Lottie Deno: Her Life and Times.* The actual quotation reads: "Why, you low-down slinking slut!' screamed Lottie, 'if I should step in soft cow manure, I would not even clean by foot on that bastard! I'll show you a thing or two!" 41; Patrick A. Bowmaster, "A Fresh Look at 'Big Nose Kate'", National Association For Outlaw And Lawman History, Inc. [NOLA], *Quarterly.* July-September. 1998.
[55] Jay Moynahan, *Just Call Me Kate: The Stories of Four Kates of Negotiable Virtue.* 28.
[56] A. W. Bork & Glen Boyer [Editors], "The O. K. Corral Fight At Tombstone: A Footnote By Kate Elder." *Arizona and the West.* [Spring 1977]. 76, n. 9.
[57] John C. Jacobs, San Antonio, Texas, to J. Marvin Hunter, Bandera, Texas, July 17,1928. Entire letter quoted in Hunters' *The Story of Lottie Deno: Her Life and Times.* 58.
[58] Roberts, *Doc Holliday: The Life And Legend.* 86.
[59] Casey Tefertiller, *Wyatt Earp: The Life Behind The Legend.* 17-18; Tanner, *Doc Holliday: A Family Portrait.* 113.
[60] Robert K. DeArment, "'Hurricane Bill' Martin: Horse Thief." *True West.* June 1991. 38-45.
[61] Ibid. Quoting Frank Collinson: In Collinson's *Life In The Saddle,* Frank repeats: "Hurricane Bill was a wise old wolf and hunted a long way from the home range." 95.
[62] Galbreath, *Campfire Tales: True Stories From The Western Frontier.* 15.
[63] DeArment, "'Hurricane Bill' Martin: Horse Thief." 44.
[64] Metz, *John Selman: Texas Gunfighter.* 55; Clifton Caldwell, *Fort Davis: A Family Fort.* "By 1876, Selman had taken up with a Fort Griffin prostitute known as Hurricane Minnie." 15.
[65] Ibid. Citing a wanted notice for John Selman; John Meadows, Alamogordo, New Mexico to J. Evetts Haley, June 13, 1935: "A whore named Hurricane Minnie, she jumped on a bareback horse and give the thing away to Selman by daylight...This whore give him warning, and he took advantage of it too." 5-6. Courtesy Nita Stewart Haley Memorial Library.
[66] DeArment, "'Hurricane Bill' Martin: Horse Thief." 44.

Chapter 8

"Go Hence Without Delay"

On November 5, 1877, someone acting as bailiff for the Shackelford County court, likely Sheriff Bill Cruger, called the next case on the docket: Cause Number 26, *The State of Texas vs. Lotta Deno*, Keeping a Disorderly House.[1] Referring to a 19th-Century edition of *The Penal Code of the State of Texas* and reviewing Article 339 is appropriate for knowing what law Lottie Deno was alleged to have violated:

> Art. 339: A disorderly house is one kept for the purpose of public prostitution, or as a common resort for prostitutes and vagabonds.
> Art. 340: Any room or part of a building, or other place appropriated or used for either of the purposes above enumerated, is a disorderly house within the meaning of this chapter.
> Art. 341: Any person who shall keep, or be in any way concerned in keeping a disorderly house, as defined above, shall be punished by fine not less than one hundred nor more than five hundred dollars.[2]

The statute was not vague. It was not a violation of gambling laws, as some authors of folklore sometime write when their favorite hero or heroine is so charged. For whatever reason Lottie Deno had decided this heretofore routine criminal action was not going to be a pushover for the prosecutor. She did not propose to spend any money paying a fine or to spend any time in jail in lieu of that fine. Whatever may be said of Lottie—good or bad—she was her own girl. Lottie was headstrong! Her attorney filing an exception to the criminal indictment [information] was over-ruled, and the court's hearing of supplemental motions was scheduled for the next day.[3]

Whether or not it was pure bluff, which Lottie Deno was accustomed to doing, is but vague. However it worked! The prosecutor dismissed the case. The judge ruled:

> *This day came the parties by their Attorneys and the Plaintiff says that for the following reasons—To Wit—"That after a thorough examination I find that a case cannot be sustained against her," it is therefore considered by the Court that the Plaintiff take nothing*

144

by the Suit, and that the defendant go hence without delay.—Discharged.[4]

It would be but speculative to analyze Lottie's thoughts about "going hence without delay." The victory would be hollow. Lottie's courtroom clashes were far from finished. Despite conventional myth, courthouse records reflect Lottie Deno would be dancing across the Fort Griffin stage long after Johnny Golden had been gunned down and laid to rest. Grief had not prompted her departure. Greed compelled her stay.

Several of Lottie's like-minded sisters were also dancing into and out of the Shackelford County courtroom. Prostitutes such as Sway-backed Mag, Nancy Sharpe, Lizzie Harvey, Ellen Gentry, Maggie Marshal, Molly McCabe, who like Lottie had moved in from Jacksboro, Nannie Rivers, Annie Holden, the Dickerson gals, Sarah and Annie [mother and daughter], Lou Baker, Ann Timmons, Mollie Grace, Indian Kate Gamel and, not at all unexpectedly, Hurricane Minnie Martin—just to identify a few.[5] There was also an upright element living in and around Fort Griffin. A few were inclined to espouse their righteous cause of temperance and condemn the town's wickedness, but their voices were weak in a town wholly dependent on gratifying decadent demands. Of Fort Griffin depravity it has been written: "Only the economic force behind the vices of prostitution, gambling, and unbroken revelry kept the local dives in business."[6] Such an assertion is unarguable, but its application to The Flat is but generic. Then or now traditional vice is always fueled by pecuniary energy.

Perhaps Lottie's next move was intended as an act of deliberate defiance; an in your face affront to the snobbish and moralistic denizens crusading against the evils of drink, the gullibility of gambling with professionals, and the impiety of paying for play. Miss Lottie Deno sponsored a "masque ball" on the very same night another dance for the more respectable people was taking place at a Fort Griffin hotel.[7] Which event drew the biggest crowd is unanswerable? Although not befitting the manufactured image of a Southern Belle decked out in the latest cut from Paris' fashion houses it does appear that Lottie Deno was "shunned by the better class."[8] During the time she was ginning cash at The Flat it seems that Lottie did not even "try to mix with them," the decent and upstanding folks.[9]

Lottie did, however, develop a female friendship outside the *demimonde*. John C. Jacobs wrote:

> ....her only intimate woman friend being the wife of an army sergeant, a refined, matronly woman, who sometimes came down from the fort in a carriage and they would spend most of the afternoon driving about

the countryside or over to Albany, but always returned before sunset.[10]

Because an army wife would not stoop so low as to socialize with the likes of Lottie Deno, the assertion of such a friendship has been ridiculed as being unfeasible and impossible.[11] Spreading a categorical blanket wears thin. Taking a meaningless buggy ride to Albany with a "matronly woman" to see the sights or go shopping does not invoke images of sensationalism. It does not add any wildness to the story about Miss Lottie or The Flat. If it were not true—at least in part— why would Mr. Jacobs have mentioned it? What is to be gained by such trivia? Traveling between the two towns was not hazardous. The threat of Indian raids in the region was a thing of the past. Outlaws? It does not seem too likely they would molest Lottie Deno. On balance she knew quite a lot about their "doings and whereabouts." And, it does not seem any badmen would have bothered another of The Flat's notorious madams, Indian Kate Gamel, had she too decided to make such an afternoon excursion. What girl doesn't like to shop? Even the badly behaved girls liked to splurge sometimes. Shackelford County deputy sheriff Henry Herron had Indian Kate's number:

> I was to learn that she stood in with some of the officers of the law for protection. Also I was to learn that her house was a rendezvous for cutthroats and murders and all other lawless characters. She would double-cross the officers as well as the criminals when it suited her purposes, but quite naturally she would favor the criminals.[12]

Indian Kate, naughty as she might have been, was not the only double-crosser to be found in the Clear Fork country. Shackelford County's second sheriff, John M. Larn, having tendered his resignation March 20th [1877] was drawing no little attention to himself.[13] He had landed a military contract to supply beef for Fort Griffin. Operating a cattle ranch in nearby Throckmorton County ex-sheriff Larn with punctuality furnished livestock to the fort's commissary officer. The headcount for his herd remained static. Such was not the case for neighboring stockmen. Their day by day computation was steadily registering in the red.[14] Though the Clear Fork's climate was most often invigorating and healthful it was not a wholesome environment for the horse or cow thief. Shackelford County may or may not have won first prize for the most extralegal executions in Texas, but it came close. The northwest section of Texas was a fermenting hotbed of vigilante justice. Acting as the region's surrogate conscience, editor Robson of *The Frontier Echo* reflected public opinion about how to deal with livestock thieves:

> ....Hang 'em first; then if they persist in their innocent amusement, cremate them. If that does not put the kibosh on 'em, we don't know what will.[15]

John Larn began looking over his shoulder. Area vigilantes, The Tin-Hat Mob, were casting the evil-eye in his direction. Lottie may have had good reason to think also.

Although it had happened before Lottie's arrival at The Flat, working under a theory that "bad meat draws flies," some local affiliates had posted an explicit warning sign: "We've given notice that no prostitutes will be suffered to come among us. Several have come in the last few days. We know the parties who persuaded them to come. When we strike, look out. We wait a little."[16] Whether or not the forewarning to working-girls was just an appeasement to the concerns of Shackelford County's wives and mothers is enigmatic. Such protests of indignation for public consumption were but common, more often than not followed by a sly wink. On the other hand, the Tin-Hat Mob's callous threat to cow and horse thieves was real. Little could Lottie Deno worry about those fellows' legal problems, she had more than her fair share.

A civil—not criminal—lawsuit naming Miss Lottie Deno as the defendant was called for trial in Shackelford County on January 23rd, 1878. Cause No. 22, was styled *Geo. O. Matthews vs. Charlotte Tompkins*. Pinpointing with absolute accuracy why Matthews was suing Lottie is pesky, determining a request for damages is not: $290.[17]

The following month, on February 18th 1878, another Shackelford County legal action was called for disposition. This time it was not a civil case. County authorities had filed the familiar criminal accusation: *The State of Texas vs. Charlotte Tompkins*, Cause No. 29, Keeping a Disorderly House. Through her lawyers Lottie alleged that she was temporarily incapacitated due to illness and unable to attend court. The pale assertion was bolstered, in a written format, by Lottie Deno's physician.[18] The court noted:

> *This day came the parties by their Attorneys, and then came on to be heard the motion for a continuance now here made by the said defendant and the affidavit in support thereof being read, it is ordered by the Court that this cause be continued until the next term of this Court...*[19]

On the 18th day of March, her criminal case was once again scheduled for adjudication. For this docket call Lottie Deno was present and standing before the judge as evidenced by the following excerpt from Shackelford County's record book: *"And now comes the State by her Attorneys and the defendant in person and by Attorneys and announces themselves ready for trial...."*[20] As a sidebar it must be mentioned that her in person presence at court once again refutes romantically glorified myth; the allegation that Lottie Deno fled The Flat in a state of despair shortly after Johnny Golden's death the preceding year. The judge impaneled a jury of "good and lawful men, citizens of Shackelford County" to hear Lottie's case. Laboriously Judge W. H. Ledbetter began listening to a litany of hopeful defense motions designed to have the charges dismissed. All of the defense motions filed in Lottie's behalf were over-ruled. The trial commenced after the court accepted and recorded Miss Lottie's plea of *not guilty*. The prosecution and defense teams presented and argued their cases. Then both sides closed. The trial judge issued his written instructions to the six man jury. The jurymen retired to deliberate. It may have been a deliberative process, but it was not long and drawn out. It was, from start to finish, a one day affair. Foreman of the jury, S. S. McCatherine, signed the verdict form:

> *We, the Jury, find the Defendant "Guilty" and [affix?] her punishment by fine at $100.*[21]

Lottie Deno was committed to the custody of Sheriff Bill Cruger, to be held until the *"said fine and costs be paid."*[22] Court adjourned! Exactly just how long Lottie was detained in an arrest status is indefinite. Probability would suggest she never saw the inside of a cell. Most likely her attorneys posted a bond in lieu of Lottie's fine. With certainty, the day after her conviction for Keeping a Disorderly House, Lottie's legal counsel filed paperwork with the court seeking a new trial. Once again arguments were made before the court, and once again the judge over-ruled the motion. Lottie's lawyer then filed notice for a remedy by the Court of Criminal Appeals for the State of Texas.[23]

Filing notice of appeal put Lottie's criminal case on hold. However, the civil action *Geo. O. Matthews vs. Charlotte Tompkins* was yet unresolved. It was to be heard during the March session of Shackelford County's District Court. On March 20th the case was placed before the judge for disposition. Matthews asked that the matter be heard by a jury. His request that was granted:

> *The Jury having been duly impaneled and sworn according to law with and truly to try the issue joined between the parties, having heard evidence, arguments*

of Counsel, and by consent of parties a written charge
of the Court having been waived, retired to consider of
and returned in open Court the following verdict:

We the Jury render verdict in favor of Plaintiff for $100.[24]

For whatever reason the jury had reduced the settlement damages by $190. Furthermore the court ordered that the $100 due Matthews from the jury's award accrue interest at the rate of 8% per annum until paid by the defendant.[25] Mythically it was written in the 20th-Century that Lottie Deno had been the unconditional darling of Fort Griffin; gaily gambling her way through life as a faultless frontier princess, revered and respected by everyone. Her brushes with the Texas legal system in both civil and criminal actions reveal the truth. She was not perched atop any pedestal. Lottie Deno was not loved by everybody, especially by those she owed money. Fighting the criminal case for Keeping A Disorderly House was not helpful either. Miss Deno was supposed to "go along to get along," not legally spar with the system—that is what society at The Flat expected. Perhaps reassessing some of those Shackelford County realities prompted Lottie to began thinking of once again changing her address.

Economically, circumstances at The Flat were shifting. There were believable rumors circulating that Fort Griffin was to be permanently closed; Indian raids were no longer much of a threat in northwest Texas.[26] Drovers were noticeably being replaced by another breed of cowboy, those employed year around by Shackelford County's ranchers.[27] Buffalo hunting on the Southern Plains, heretofore a big industry, was beginning to play out. The wholesale extermination was near finished. With such shrinkage the bone business had supplanted the hide-hunting business. Throughout West Texas enterprising freighters were filling their wagon-beds high with bleached buffalo bones, free for the taking. Eastern markets were insatiably consuming ton after ton of the skeletal remains "at fertilizer plants to grind into bone meal, for fresh Texas bones at refineries for calcium phosphate to neutralize cane juice acid and to decolor sugar, for choice Texas bones at bone china furnaces for calcium phosphate ash, and for firm Texas bones at button factories."[28] The Flat was undergoing a transition, a financial turn down. With the promise of a railroad Albany was on the economic upswing. Even the ever pugnacious John Shanssey, "a gentleman and a good man" was contemplating a move down the road to Palo Pinto County where he intended on opening a "first class saloon."[29]

The ex-sheriff of Shackelford County, John Larn, wasn't allowed the dignity or the opportunity of making a move to Palo Pinto County—or anywhere else. Like a mischievous child caught with a hand in the cookie jar, John Larn had been apprehended—allegedly—with seriously incriminating evidence; cow hides wearing the wrong brands. Placed in the Shackelford County jail at Albany on June 23, 1878, Mr. John Larn knew his fate was sealed tight. Doomed! He had been up to just too much meanness, knew just too much about too many people and their taking part in too many things—namely nighttime lynching. The Texas Rangers were not even going to take a hand in saving his hide; they had been instructed by Adjutant General William W. Steel, then through their boss Major John B. Jones, to do nothing; "let the county officials and local citizenry work out this problem." The local folks worked through the problem. Before he could implicate anyone John Larn was mortally gunned down in his jail cell. The killers were vigilantes, some of Shackelford County's most upright and no doubt uptight citizens.[30] After that rejoinder some of The Flat's badmen and bad girls could see the worthwhile wisdom in disbursing—before something bad happened to them. Lottie Deno and some of her crowd were listening to an echo reverberating from South Texas. The emanating sound was sweet; money was changing hands.

Kinney County, Texas, lay southwest of Fort Griffin. It was border country, a winding sliver of the Rio Grande River made up part of Kinney County's southern edge. Named for Henry Lawrence Kinney the founder of Corpus Christi, Kinney County was created before the Civil War [1850] but not organized until February 7, 1874.[31] Within Kinney County's boundaries were settings that seductively beckoned an enterprising girl like Lottie Deno. A military garrison, Fort Clark, was there. Nearby was Los Moras Creek and just across that the customary civilian settlement, Brackettville [formerly just Bracket]. Maintaining the image of its promiscuous sisters, San Angela, Jacksboro and The Flat, the little town was tough and tempestuous. Even as small as it was Brackettville had fifteen saloons and could usually count her rambling throng of professional gamblers at about fifty—at any given time.[32] The number of whores?. Anybody's guess! Brackettville was artfully characterized: "The town was soiled but lively. It had few morals but plenty of money. Some damned it, and some worshiped it."[33] Written with a spicy pinch of literary license, a contemporary account for the *Galveston Daily News* painted an 1878 word portrait:

> ...They want a newspaper at Brackt [*sic*], Kinney county. Mr. W. W. Arnett writes to the San Antonio *Express*: Brackett is a fast place. There are seven dry goods stores, twelve or more retail whiskey shops, 80 regular thoroughbred monte dealers. The justice of the peace for this precinct has had up before him for misdemeanors 393 cases since 1876; has assessed fines

to the amount of $2000 or more that has been collected. The county judge has been doing a good county business in the way of fining monte dealers. Why, sir, it is nothing strange to hear from fifty to one hundred shots fired here any night and to hear next morning of two or three men and as many women being shot, or robbed, or thrown into Los Moras spring to feed the fish and flavor the water. Six men broke jail last night and seven are still there. All this is nothing to what a reporter could see and learn if he was here. Then why not come to Brackett and have a paper that would be spicy? Why, if that fellow Sweet, who tells about the recorder's court in San Antonio, were here in our justice's court one week he would never go back again.[34]

The newspaperman's piece carried a ring of truth. A reality brought home after noting that the Kinney County Sheriff, John P. Fries, while in Brackettville had been fatally gunned down by unknown assassins.[35] Some folks knew and labeled unpolished Brackettville "in the glory days, as a 'metropolis' of the border."[36] It was the right spot for an enterprising gal like Lottie Deno. Brackettville was such a fast village that the Army "placed metal cages around town and in back alleys to hold its unruly troops—keeping them off the streets and out of further trouble—until they could be hauled with aching heads back to their duty posts again."[37] One solider, enlisted man Jasper Ewing Brady, recalled:

> Saloons were on every corner and plenty in between. Dance halls, brothels—let your imagination run riot and you may approximate what this town was in those hectic days. Two dance halls stood out—the Blue Goose and the Gray Mule. There were several kinds of dances indulged in that are not seen on stage or ballroom floor. There was cheap liquor, cards, all kinds of gambling, women and no legal restraint...The morning after pay day there were 110 men confined in the guardhouse, or under arrest charged with every crime in the calendar, from drunkenness and A.W. O. L. up to and including attempted murder.[38]

Brackettville was nothing more than a "collection of adobe houses, shacks, huts, jacales, picket stores, whiskey shops, and gambling saloons," inhabited by a "mixture of half-bloods, blacks, whites, Mexicans, and discharged soldiers..."[39] Despite fanciful myth about

Lottie Deno's life of splendor and elegance, Brackettville was representative of the type places she liked to set up housekeeping. She had a fondness in her heart for isolated posts; those where soldiers' money was funneled into the parasitically prone sin-towns.

At least one of the many violent episodes taking place at Brackettville bears repeating. In an interesting fashion it is historically significant. There is a possibility that Lottie Deno was acquainted, at least minimally, with one of the story's star players.

Claron Augustus Windus, a Wisconsin born boy with a musical aptitude, had lied about his birthday and entered the U. S. Army at the tender age of fifteen, after already having served as a civilian drummer boy during the Civil War. Claron became a troop bugler, Company L, 6th U.S. Cavalry. His first duty station was Fort Richardson, within walking distance of Jacksboro. Several years later, while so stationed and on a "scout," Windus was part of a command that was chasing the band of Indians who had earlier attacked a stagecoach just west of the fort. During the pursuit Windus and his comrades were ambushed by hostile Indians on the Little Wichita River; the odds were four to one in favor of the colorfully painted warriors. Displaying coolness under fire, Claron Windus first assisted the Medical Officer, George W. Hatch, with caring for the wounded. Then, acting as an orderly, under a barrage of bullets he dashed back and forth relaying verbal messages for and from various platoon commanders. Furthermore he took a leading role in clearing Indian sharpshooters from a hilltop. If that were not enough, he volunteered to ride to Fort Richardson carrying the alarm so reinforcements could be dispatched. For his heroic actions [along with others] Claron A. Windus was awarded the Congressional Medal of Honor.[40]

After leaving the army Windus freighted for awhile at Jacksboro, San Angela and Dallas, before settling at Brackettville. Kinney County Sheriff L. C. Crowell offered Windus a job as deputy sheriff and Claron accepted. Familiarly known throughout the border country as "Deputy Gus," Windus made an enviable name for himself as a no nonsense lawman, even on one occasion arresting the commander of Fort Clark himself, Colonel Edward Hatch. Another arrest, however, would be one for the record book.[41]

Adam Payne [Paine], a private in the legendary Seminole-Negro Indian Scouts, had discharged from military service at Fort Clark. Adam then moved to Brownsville, Cameron County, Texas, near the state's southernmost tip on the Gulf Coast. Like Claron Windus, Adam Payne was, too, an admired recipient of the Congressional Medal of Honor. His bravery on the battlefield had been tested on several occasions, but during an affray near Quitaque Peak in West Texas is where he earned the medal: Payne stubbornly fought off a superior force of Indians enabling four of his fellow scouts to escape total annihilation. At Brownsville the "cool and daring" Payne hauled supplies to the U. S. Army's Fort Brown while working as a civilian subcontractor. There were also unverified rumors that Payne had degenerated into the role of a livestock thief, "stealing horses and cattle and running them into Mexico."[42] In addition to his highly prized Medal of Honor, Payne carried an oversized and razor-sharp knife. During a quarrel with an 8th Cavalry private on Christmas Eve, 1875, Adam Payne fatally stabbed the soldier and fled across the Rio Grande. A murder warrant for Payne's arrest was quickly issued in Cameron County. Mexican authorities arrested him, but during a tropical storm the momentary prisoner escaped and fled back to more familiar ground, the Seminole-Negro village on the outskirts of Brackettville's saloon strip. Several fugitives were laying low in the close-knit community, an indisputable fact already well-known by Sheriff Crowell. Receiving specific information from an informant that Adam Payne and other wanted men would be at a New Year's Eve celebration to drunkenly greet 1877, the sheriff acted. Accompanied by Gus Windus and a civilian volunteer posseman, teamster James Thomas, Sheriff Crowell maneuvered into an unseen position within the Seminole-Negro encampment. When Adam Payne and another fugitive, Frank Enoch, plus several others unnamed, walked into a clearing the lawmen made their presence known. During the process of manacling prisoners a scuffle broke out, one initiated by Mr. Payne and Mr. Enoch. Rather than have his shotgun forcefully taken and turned against him, deputy Windus intentionally pulled the twin triggers. The weapon's discharge liberally peppered both Adam and Frank with buckshot.[43] The range was so short that Mr. Payne's clothing was set afire, smoldering as he fell to the ground.[44] Both prisoners died, Payne instantly, Enoch a short time later. The sad historic irony should not be overlooked. This was and is the only known example of a Congressional Medal of Honor recipient killing another Congressional Medal of Honor recipient.[45]

Yet owing money to George Matthews and her criminal case still awaiting a final disposition by the Texas Court of Criminal Appeals, Lottie Deno once more packed those fine Parisian fashions in her trunk and deserted The Flat. Miss Deno was heading toward Brackettville— but not alone! Limpy Jim Smith was back in the picture, at least according to Sam Baldwin:

> Lottie came over there, she and Jim Smith, when that boom come at Fort Clark. She went down there...There was lots of others that went with them. This partner of mine [Robert "Happy Bob" Fambro], that was killed up here [Shakespear, New Mexico], he

went at the same time. He didn't go with her, but a whole lot would go together. Quite a long ways down there. What caused the boom down there, the government was about to have a war with Mexico—the government was going to put in a thirty or forty company post there, mostly cavalry, and some buildings were going to be put up. That was in '78.[46]

Sam Baldwin's timeline dovetails perfectly with Lottie's taking leave of The Flat and her arrival at Brackettville. Edgar Rye wrote in *The Quirt and the Spur* that Lottie Deno had mysteriously forsaken Fort Griffin. Adding that for quite awhile "no one felt at liberty to open the shanty and investigate" her disappearance.[47] Although it was unintended, Rye's implication is clear; no one was concerned about Lottie Deno dropping out of The Flat's limelight. Only later did Shackelford County Sheriff Bill Cruger, accompanied by George Matthews [who she owed money to], open Lottie's quarters and discover that the nest had been abandoned. It has been alleged that Sheriff Cruger found a note pinned to the folded and tucked bedding signed by the ever charitable Miss Lottie Deno, saying: "Sell this outfit and give the money to some one in need of assistance."[48] Rye's charming touch fits well with Lottie Deno mythology, but not too well with what other contemporaries had to say; or what simple logic would suggest. Mr. Henry Herron's remarks, while not absolute, are insightful: "When she left, it was afterwards reported that she left her furniture to the poor, but I knew nothing of this."[49] That oldtimer characterized as being "generally reliable," buffalo hunter Sam Baldwin, was even more direct: "I don't know whether she left all her stuff in her room or not. You say you have heard she left a note asking them to sell the place and give the money to the poor. I never heard that. She did not know what became of it."[50] Sam Baldwin's last sentence seems to imply that he had even discussed the matter of Lottie's material possessions with her. John Jacobs asserts that he knew of Lottie's plan to leave The Flat behind in her memories. He even gave her a larger leather-covered trunk to pack some of her things in for the long trip. Mr. Jacobs does not mention Lottie's alleged philanthropic note.[51] Common sense would tend to hint that Miss Lottie Deno, who always journeyed from one sin town to the next by stagecoach, "traveled light" and really didn't own any property to give to the poor. Such a premise takes on more credibility if a preeminent Old West historian's findings are accepted at face value: "It was Shanssey who provided the house in which she set up her game, and it was Shanssey who found her a cabin on the edge of town in which to live, and provided the furniture to furnish it."[52] Whether there was or was not a note, from The Flat dear Miss Lottie Deno had departed.

Despite folklore her whereabouts were not secret. Sam Baldwin knew she was at Brackettville. So too did others—and there was/is a paper trail. It has been written that Lottie Deno left The Flat because she owed money. A much more reasonable statement would be that she left town owing money. Her real reasons may have been many and varied. On the 2ⁿᵈ day of October 1878, attorneys acting in behalf of George Matthews, who understandably was desirous that Lottie Deno comply with the judgment and hand over money due him, composed a letter of inquiry. C. K. Stribling and George A. Kirkland, as a partnership were Stribling & Kirkland, Fort Griffin's leading law firm. They were representing plaintiff Matthews. The overland distance to Brackettville from Fort Griffin was considerable. The attorneys wanted to avoid making a time consuming trip. They wrote to Mr. William E. Friedlander, Post Trader, at Fort Clark. George Matthews' lawyers asked:

> We have a judgment against Charlotte J. Tompkins ("Lottie Deno") now of Brackettsville [*sic*] and formerly from here for near $200—Can the money be made if we should forward judgment—If not in your line will you do us the favor to hand this to some reliable attorney.[53]

The statement "now of Brackettville" is not inexact. Sam Baldwin had been right. Miss Deno had moved to Brackettville. The relocation should come as no great surprise, Lottie was a connoisseur and the Kinney County seat offered a smorgasbord of paying prospects—for a poker player or a prostitute. Finding Lottie was not the problem. Inducing her to surrender the money, that may have been an altogether different bottle of perfume. Mr. Friedlander referred Matthews' lawyers to Laurence Hagarty, the Kinney County Attorney. On November 4, 1878, Stribling & Kirkland wrote Mr. Hagarty: "We have a judgment for near $200—against Charlotte Tompkins alias 'Lottie Deno'. Can you make same out of her? If so we will send it to you."[54] Mr. Hagarty did little or nothing to collect money from Lottie. Establishing Lottie's continued presence at Brackettville is not even somewhat iffy, a local attorney, W. L. Clamp, wrote George A. Kirkland on April 2, 1879: "I think that something can be made out of Lottie D- Please send me another [updated] execution & I will try, & see what can be collected."[55] Attorney Clamp also expressed practical interest in trying to work out an *Offer In Compromise* with Lottie; would she be willing to pay a lesser amount?[56] The question, would he take less, was referred to George Matthews.[57] Unfortunately we have no answer whether Mr.

Matthews would or would not, nor if he did or did not, finally settle his civil lawsuit with Lottie.

There was, however, a definitive resolution regarding Miss Deno's appellate case. The Texas Court of Criminal Appeals ruled:

Charlotte Tompkins v. The State

> The charge as set forth in the information is in these words, viz.: "Did then and there commit the offense of willfully, knowingly, unlawfully, and fraudulently keeping a disorderly house for the purpose of public prostitution, or as a common resort for prostitutes and vagabonds, " etc.

> The information is fatally defective in two respects: First, "it does not charge that the accused *did keep* a disorderly house, etc., but that she was *guilty of the offense of keeping*, etc.—a statement of a conclusion drawn from facts, rather than as statement of the facts from which the law draws the conclusion." Second, the offense attempted to be stated is charged disjunctively. "If a statute makes it a crime to do this or that, mentioning several things disjunctively, the indictment may, indeed, as a general rule, embrace the whole in a single count; but in doing so it must use the conjunction 'and' where 'or' occurs in the statute, else it will be defective as being uncertain.

> For these reasons the judgment of the lower court is not only reversed, but the case is also dismissed.[58]

Legal technicality—in this case—had saved Lottie Deno from suffering any punishment for Keeping A Disorderly House. Complying with Texas state law regarding gambling and prostitution violations was not what Miss Lottie Deno cared to do. She was out to make money, and there were free-spending soldiers at Brackettville. Thus far overlooked by Lottie's well-meaning chroniclers, other courtroom skirmishes pitting Miss Deno against the state of Texas, this time in Kinney County, are extant.

At Brackettville on January 29, 1879, another case of Keeping A Disorderly House was filed against Lottie. Kinney County Cause Number 216 was legally styled, *The State of Texas vs. Lottie Tompkins, alias Lottie Deno*. A Capias Warrant was issued. The sheriff of Kinney County, Frank S. "F. S." Fritter, had no trouble locating

Lottie. Sheriff Fritter certified the warrant had been executed by "arresting the within named defendant who gave bond."[59] After Lottie's sureties had posted the necessary collateral guaranteeing her court appearance, Miss Lottie was released from custody, but remained at Brackettville.[60] So there is not any undue or unintended confusion, specifics from the *complaint* read:

> ....*and for the county of Kinney and state of Texas and presents to inform and gives the court to understand that the said Lottie Thompkins alias Lottie Deno late of the County aforesaid and in said County of Kinney and state of Texas on the twenty first day of the month of January in the year of our Lord one thousand eight hundred and seventy nine did then and there unlawfully Keep a disorderly house, said house being then and there kept for the purpose of public prostitution and as a common resort for prostitutes contrary to the statute in such case made and provided and against the peace and dignity of the state.*[61]

Phraseology "late of the County aforesaid" does not mean she had departed Brackettville. It is but legalese clarifying the fact that Lottie Deno was there when the crime had been committed. A subsequent criminal filing for an altogether different type violation—six months later—pinpoints Lottie's whereabouts; still at Brackettville. Emboldened by the successful role of an appellant in the Shackelford County case, Lottie asked for and was granted a jury trial regarding the prostitution charges lodged against her in Kinney County. On March 3rd, 1879, the jury heard the case and their verdict was read in open court: "Find the defendant guilty and assess the fine at the lowest penalty of the law [$100]."[62] Apparently she paid the imposed fine, but Lottie's legal nightmares in Kinney County were not over.

All of Lottie Deno's known brushes with the law, thus far, have revolved around allegations that she Kept A Disorderly House—the legal terminology indicating she was at worst a common prostitute, at best an enterprising madam. Legal language defining that violation of the Texas State Penal Code is not vague. Certainly it may now—after the myth—seem unbecoming to link Miss Deno to the flesh trade, nevertheless primary source documents leave little doubt, nor leeway to believe otherwise. Lottie's next skirmish with the criminal justice system is more in line with what has been previously written about her. Miss Lottie Deno has been portrayed as a frontier gambler par excellent in annals of the Old West, though this is the first and only time that she was ever charged with an infraction of any state or territorial gaming laws. Under oath Kinney County Sheriff Fritter alleged in a sworn *complaint* that Lottie was yet engaged in illegal activities at Brackettville. On the 1ˢᵗ day of July 1879 at Brackettville, Cause Number 228 was filed: *The State of Texas vs. Lottie Deno*, Exhibiting a Faro Bank. An arrest warrant for Lottie Deno was issued and on the 3ʳᵈ of July she was once more arrested by Sheriff Fritter. Again Lottie posted the requisite bond which triggered her release from custody.[63] Since Lottie Deno has been bequeathed a descriptive name, The Gambling Queen of Hearts, examining one part of Sheriff Fritter's *complaint* is appropriate:

> *...in and for the County of Kinney state of Texas at this term and presents to inform and gives the court to understand that one Lottie Deno late of said County in said County of Kinney in the state of Texas on the twenty fifth day of the month of June in the year of our Lord one thousand eight hundred and seventy nine did then and there unlawfully keep and exhibit a gaming bank, to wit; a Faro Bank, said Faro Bank being then and there kept and exhibited for the unlawful purpose then and there of gaming contrary to the form of the statute in such cases made and provided and against the peace and dignity of the state.[64]*

Quite interestingly, and even lending more validity to Mr. Sam Baldwin's remembrances about Lottie Deno is the fact that one of the witnesses subpoenaed in the Kinney County gambling case was a "James Smith."[65] Tying this Mr. Smith and Lottie's sometimes paramour Limpy Jim Smith together conclusively is an unachievable task; but it seems more than a just a little coincidental. Unfortunately the Kinney County case file regarding Exhibiting A Faro Bank is not near as complete as the Keeping A Disorderly House folder. At this point, whether or not Lottie Deno was convicted, found not guilty, or simply forfeited her bond and ran away is but guesswork.

Consistent with those anecdotal "front porch stories," at least according to the Vivian clan, another gaming ne'er-do-well also made his appearance at Brackettville—for awhile. Purportedly Doc Holliday whiled away a few days gambling at a watering hole known locally as Old Blue's Saloon at Eagle Pass, the border town just to the south of Brackettville. The sporting enterprise had been founded by Blue Vivian and later sold to the infamous King Fisher, a Vivian relative by marriage. After a few crafty card games at Old Blue's Saloon, Mr. Holliday wisely decided to move up the road to Brackettville. There the pickings were fresh and ripe, the tenderfoot plums not near so suspicious of his dexterity. According to the Vivian family oral history, Doc Holliday beat a bevy of Fort Clark's buffalo soldiers out of their payday earnings and saw the wisdom in not daring to tarry too long at Brackettville. He hopped aboard the stagecoach and bid Brackettville adieu—before the black solders sobered up and wised up.[66] Though it is but a sketchy story, uncorroborated by evidence, nevertheless it is fascinating. It is particularly interesting because of Lottie Deno's confirmed appearance at Brackettville. This was not the first occasion that Doc and Lottie would be frequenting the same town at the same time, nor would it be the last!

Miss Lottie Deno's life in Texas had been tumultuous. Overlooking her collisions with the civil and criminal judiciary in Texas may be fitting for a folklorist, but her legal wrecks had fostered authentic nightmares for the Gambling Queen of Hearts. Once again Lottie began wadding those fine Parisian gowns into her new leather-covered trunk. This time, just for good measure, she packed away the name Lottie Deno, too! Carlotta Thompkins turned her dark eyes away from turbulent Texas and looked west—toward New Mexico Territory. She was going "hence without delay!"

Depletion of the buffalo herds opened the doorway to permanent cattle ranches and, correspondingly, a more settled workforce of cowboys. Here L. to R. Berry Campbell, Lee Tuton, and "Tull" Newcomb pose for a delightful photograph. *Courtesy Robert E. Nail, Jr. Collection—Archives of the Old Jail Art Center.*

Another "one of the boys" that managed an entire career horseback in Shackelford and Throckmorton Counties was George W. Newcomb, a genuine old-time cowboy. *Courtesy Martha Fanning.*

As Fort Griffin declined its sister town of Albany captured cherished county seat honors. A spur railroad connection to Albany would sound the final death knell for Fort Griffin. Though technology was advancing throughout the Southwest, it was yet horse and buggy or stagecoach transportation between most towns in West Texas. *Courtesy Robert E. Nail, Jr. Collection—Archives of the Old Jail Art Center.*

On horseback at rear of packed stagecoach is Claron Augustus Windus, a Medal of Honor recipient, Kinney County Deputy Sheriff, and the killer of another Medal of Honor recipient, a former Seminole-Negro Indian Scout, Adam Payne. *Courtesy Diane Dooley.*

Kinney County Sheriff Frank S. Fritter. He arrested Lottie Deno on charges of Keeping A Disorderly House and for Exhibiting A Faro Bank. To date, although her arrests for prostitution violations are plural, this is the only known case where Miss Deno was actually charged with an infraction of gambling laws. *Courtesy Jewel F. Robinson.*

Endnotes Chapter 8

[1] *The State of Texas vs. Lotta Deno,* Cause Number 26, Shackelford County. November 5, 1877. "Lotta Deno" instead of "Lottie Deno" is the way the criminal case is styled.

[2] *Texas Penal Code,* Articles 339, 340 & 341. [Galveston: A. H. Belo & Co., 1879].

[3] *The State of Texas vs. Lotta Deno,* Cause Number 26.

[4] Ibid. November 6, 1877.

[5] *The State of Texas vs. Nancy Sharpe & Sway-backed Mag.* Cause Number 19, Shackelford County Criminal Court, November 11, 1876; *The Fort Griffin Echo,* September 20, 1879, November 29, 1879, and June 19, 1880.

[6] Cashion, "Rewriting the Wild West for a New History." 58.

[7] Matthews, *Interwoven: A Pioneer Chronicle.* 109-110.

[8] Ibid.

[9] Ibid.

[10] Hunter, *The Story of Lottie Deno: Her Life and Times.* 40; Frank X. Tolbert, "The Lieutenant's Letter," *Argosy Magazine* [September 1956] adds another to a circle of Lottie's female friends, a Tonkawas Indian named "Woman." The story is absent source citation and charitably quotes Lottie's dialogue.

[11] Rose, *Lottie Deno Gambling Queen of Hearts.* 63. The author transposes Jacobs' mention of "wife of an army sergeant," with her interpretation, "the wife of an officer." While seemingly but a minor distinction, in truth for the 19th-Century U. S. Army the hierarchical social status afforded spouses of commissioned officers was poles apart from that awarded to the wives of noncoms and enlisted soldiers.

[12] Henry Herron to J. R. Webb. Webb Papers.

[13] Tise, *Texas County Sheriffs.* John Larn was elected Shackelford County Sheriff on February 15, 1876 and served until March 20, 1877, at which time he resigned, being replaced by W. R. "Bill" Cruger. 462.

[14] Certainly exhaustive research by Robert K. DeArment has produced the most complete biography of the sheriff turned outlaw: *Bravo of the Brazos: John Larn of Fort Griffin, Texas.*

[15] Robinson, *The Frontier World of Fort Griffin: The Life and Death of a Western Town.* 109.

[16] Ibid.

[17] Shackelford County Court, *Geo. O. Matthews vs. Charlotte Tompkins,* Cause Number 22.

[18] Interview with Joan Farmer, Albany, Texas; *Albany News,* October 22, 1998. "She [Lottie] did not appear in court as Dr. Culver signed a statement saying 'she was ill and could not attend any business out side her room.'"

[19] *State of Texas vs. Charlotte Tompkins,* Cause No. 29, Shackelford County.

[20] Ibid.

[21] Ibid. The other five jurymen, in addition to foreman S. S. McCatherine, were R. R. Reed, John Sheldon, Henry Palmer, John Johnson, and L. D. McNutt.

[22] Ibid.

[23] Ibid. "And now comes the defendant by her Attorneys and move for a new trial in this cause [No. 29], and the reasons therefor have been read and the arguments of Counsel having been heard the motion was over-ruled by the Court to which defendant excepts and gives notice of appeal."

[24] *Geo. O. Matthews vs. Charlotte J. Tompkins,* Cause Number 22, Shackelford County Court. March 20, 1878.

[25] Ibid. "It is therefore considered by the Court that the said Plaintiff, Geo. O. Mat[t]hews, do have and recover of the said defendant Charlotte Tompkins the sum of one hundred dollars, and that Judgment bear interest at eight per cent per annum from this date, together with his costs in this behalf expended, and that he have his execution."

[26] *The Frontier Echo*, March 1, 1878. "....We understand also that Fort Griffin is to [be] abandoned..."

[27] Ethel Matthews Casey, *Reminiscences*. "All ranch operations were on the open range until the late '70s and early '80s when titles to the land were acquired." 2.

[28] Ralph A. Smith, "The West Texas Bone Business." *West Texas Historical Association Yearbook*. Volume LV. [1979]. 111; Vernon Schmid, "Hides and Bones." *Roundup*. December 2006. 11-12, 18.

[29] *The Fort Griffin Echo*, January 4, 1879.

[30] DeArment, *Bravo of the Brazos: John Larn of Fort Griffin, Texas*. 127-135; Joseph Edwin Blatnon, *John Larn*. 17-20.

[31] Else Sauer, [Editor]., *Kinney County 1852-1977*. 7; Gournay, *Texas Boundaries: Evolution of the State's Counties*. 61. Tise, *Texas County Sheriffs*, provides alternate dates for Kinney County' creation and organization: "Kinney County as created January 28, 1850 from Bexar County....The county was re-created February 2, 1856, then organized December 3, 1869 with Brackettville as the county seat." 312.

[32] Smith, *The U. S. Army & the Texas Frontier Economy, 1845-1900*. 127.

[33] Caleb Pirtle III & Michael F. Cusack, *The Lonely Sentinel: Fort Clark On Texas's Western Frontier*. 43.

[34] *Galveston Daily News*, April 3, 1878. Courtesy, Rick Miller; Roberts, *Doc Holliday: The Life And Legend* quotes part of the same newspaper account describing Brackettville. 87.

[35] Sauer, *Kinney County 1852-1977*. 11; Tise, *Texas County Sheriffs*; "A note in the State Election Register shows Sheriff Fries was murdered October 25, 1870." 312; A *Reward Poster* for the arrest and conviction of the unknown murderers sets the date of the killing as October 25, 1873.

[36] J. Marvin Hunter [Editor], "Brackettville and Old Fort Clark." *Frontier Times*. May 1935. 349.

[37] Pritle & Cusack, *The Lonely Sentinel: Fort Clark On Texas's Western Frontier*. 43.

[38] Sauer, *Kinney County 1852-1977*. 11-12.

[39] Wooster, *Soldiers, Sutlers, and Settlers: Garrison Life On The Texas Frontier*. 79; The more or less classic description of early Brackettville may be found on page 420 in Robert G. Carter's *On the Border with Mackenzie or Winning West Texas from the Comanches*.

Le Boulevard de Brackettville

Opposite the Post, beyond the creek, on a low, flat piece of land, almost in the mesquite chaparral, is a small town named Brackettville, the county seat of Kinney County, the exact counterpart of Jacksboro, near Fort Richardson, the ulcer of every garrison, an inevitable fungus growth, sometimes improved, but scarcely ever eradicated without much care and trouble. Its composition varied somewhat, but there were the inevitable adobe houses, Mexican ranches or "shacks," huts, "jacals" and picket stores, profusely plastered with mud, used for whisky shops, gambling saloons, etc., Mexican "greasers," half-breeds of every hue and complexion, full-blooded descendants of the African persuasion, low down whites and discharged soldiers, with no visible occupation, composed the population, and at night a fusillade of shots warned us that it was unsafe venturing ovedr after dark on the one, crooked, unlighted and wretched street—Le Boulevard de Brackettville.

[40] Charles M. Neal, Jr., *Valor Across The Lone Star: The Congressional Medal of Honor in Frontier Texas*. 334-335; Bill O'Neal, *Fighting Men of the Indian Wars: A Biographical Encyclopedia of the Mountain Men, Soldiers, Cowboys, and Pioneers Who Took Up Arms During America's Westward Expansion*. 27. Author O'Neal places Windus in Company A rather than Company L. For a treatment examining the role of Indians as quasi-soldiers, see, Thomas W. Dunlay, *Wolves for the Blue Soldiers: Indian Scouts and Auxiliaries with the Untied States Army, 1860-90*.

[41] Ibid. "On the third attempt on January 13, 1876, Windus, the former Civil War drummer boy, heavily armed and purportedly wearing his Medal of Honor, elicited from the Civil War general a meek agreement to accompany him to the courthouse to respond to the warrant and post the required bond." 336. Later Claron Windus served as a U. S. Customs Mounted Inspector stationed at Lajitas and Presidio, Texas, in the Big Bend Country; see, Sauer, *Kinney County 1852-1977*. 52.

[42] Kevin Mulroy, *Freedom on the Border: The Seminole Maroons in Florida, the Indian Territory, Coahuila, and Texas*. 152.

[43] Neal, *Valor Across The Lone Star: The Congressional Medal of Honor in Frontier Texas*. 336.

[44] Mulroy, *Freedom on the Border: The Seminole Maroons in Florida, the Indian Territory, Coahuila, and Texas*. 152.

[45] Neal, *Valor Across The Lone Star: The Congressional Medal of Honor in Frontier Texas*. 306 & 336.

[46] Sam Baldwin to Earl Vandale & Hervey Chesley, July 11, 1941; Gilbert, Remiger & Cunningham, *Encyclopedia Of Buffalo Hunters And Skinners*. Volume I. "Baldwin described many others from the buffalo range and other places about whom interviewer Vandale inquired. It was remarkable that he could remember even their names after all those years, and how well he painted a word picture of each man [or women]. 14; Bill Haenn, Kinney County Tax Appraiser, local historian and published author, confirms Baldwin's statement regarding Fort Clark being a significantly staffed post during 1878. Mr. Haenn reports that during that year Fort Clark was a multi-unit post with companies from both cavalry and infantry divisions; approximately 1000 enlisted men and officers.

[47] Rye, *The Quirt and the Spur*. 73.

[48] Ibid. 74.

[49] Henry Herron to J. R. Webb. Webb Papers.

[50] Sam Baldwin to Earl Vandale & Hervey Chesley.

[51] Hunter, *The Story of Lottie Deno: Her Life and Times*. 46-47; Matthews in *Interwoven: A Pioneer Chronicle* repeats the tale about the note. 110; Rose, *Lottie Deno: Gambling Queen of Hearts* also replicates the supposed note's wording. 62.

[52] DeArment, "John Shanssey: From Prize Ring to Politics." 27.

[53] Stribling & Kirkland to William E. Friedlander, October 2, 1878. Letter Press Of Stribling And Kirkland and Stribling And Spears, 1878-1879. Courtesy, The Center For American History, The University of Texas At Austin.

[54] Striblin & Kirkland to L. Hagarty, County Attorney, Brackettville, Texas, November 4, 1878. Letter Press Of Stribling And Kirkland and Stribling And Spears, 1878-1879.

[55] W. L. Clamp, Brackettville, Texas, to G. A. Kirkland, Buffalo Gap, Texas, April 2, 1879. Letter Press Of Stribling & Spears, April-June 1879. Letters Received.

[56] Ibid. "…and if you are willing to take less than the face of the a/c, by way of compromise say what you are willing to do."

[57] G. A. Kirkland, Buffalo Gap, Texas, to Messrs Stribling & [Samuel] Spears, April 14, 1879. Letter Press Of Stribling & Spears, April-June 1879. Letters Received.

[58] Tompkins v. State, 4 Tex. Ct. App. 161 (1878). Rick Miller to author, March 20, 2007: "Back in those days, prosecutors, in bringing an indictment for a grand jury, had to be very careful and precise in the language used, and courts of appeal were very stringent. For example 'leaden balls' were always alleged in shooting cases. Today, a prosecutor merely has to track the statute. In Lottie's case, the appellate court found the grand jury only alleged that she was guilty of an offense when it should have been alleged that she *did* the offense. Also, an old rule is that one alleges conjunctively, but charges the jury disjunctively. 'And' should be used in an indictment, but the jury would be charged with 'or.' Confused?"

[59] Capias Warrant Number 216. *The State of Texas vs. Lottie Tompkins alias Lottie Deno.* Kinney County, Brackettvile, Texas. Courtesy Dora Elia Sandoval, County/District Clerk, Kinney County. Brackettville, Texas.

[60] Case file *The State of Texas vs. Lottie Thompkins aka Lottie Deno.* Keeping A Disorderly House. County Court at Law, Kinney County, Texas. Cause Number 216. County/District Clerk, Kinney County, Brackettville, Texas.

[61] Ibid. The case file is most complete.

[62] Ibid.

[63] Case file *The State of Texas vs. Lottie Deno.* Exhibiting A Faro Bank. County Court at Law, Kinney County, Texas. Cause Number 228. Courtesy Dora Elia Sandoval, County/District Clerk, Kinney County, Brackettivlle, Texas.

[64] Ibid.

[65] Ibid.

[66] Personal interview with Lawrence Vivian at Rapid City, South Dakota, Thursday, July 26, 2007.

Chapter 9

"Shooting Promiscuously at the Piano"

There is a gap when Miss Carlotta Thompkins' dainty little footprints are lost to scrutiny. Once again she was on the move. Although her destination may be established, every now and then a revisionist will baselessly try to infer otherwise.[1] Sam Baldwin, who had migrated to New Mexico Territory, a gentlemen who was acquainted with Carlotta, knew just where she went:

> I don't know what become of Lottie and [Limpy] Jim [Smith] at Fort Clark. From what I could find out she came over there to Silver City.... [2]

Another oldtimer, the renowned buffalo hunter J. Wright Mooar, also knew where she had set up housekeeping. Carlotta had told him so during a chance encounter at El Paso.[3] The where was Silver City, New Mexico Territory. Just what route she took and who she traveled with in getting there is lacking absolute clarity. A factor that is indisputable, however, is that it was a grueling trip—and dangerous, too! There were not railroad lines across the western portions of Texas or the southern section of New Mexico Territory at that time. From Brackettville there were two pathways to Silver City. The quickest, but the most convoluted trip, would have been to travel east rather than west by stagecoach, catch a northbound train in Central Texas, ride to Topeka, Kansas, then make connection with a southwestern bound Atchison, Topeka & Santa Fe train into New Mexico Territory. Still, at the inching railroad's terminus, wherever it was at that time, the last leg of the trip to La Mesilla would have to be completed by stepping into a stagecoach. From there it was a hazardous 105 mile dash by four or six horse coach to Silver City. The other route from Brackettville was much shorter in actual distance, but much longer in travel time: Straight across West Texas by stagecoach over rudimentary military roadways.[4] No matter the origination point reaching La Mesilla was the true objective. At La Mesilla the traveler could head north to Santa Fe or west toward Tucson and California. The well-worn road to Silver City intersected with the western route near the Mimbres River. At Brackettville the real danger from Comanches or Kiowas yet hostile was minimal to nonexistent. West of Kinney County, however, in fact all across West Texas and completely throughout southern New Mexico Territory, there was still the very real prospect of an attack by Apaches.

After learning that the Grant County Grand Jury at Silver City had indicted him for horse theft and murder, Warm Springs Apache leader Victorio bolted the Mescalero Reservation in the picturesque and pine forested Sacramento Mountains of south central New Mexico Territory.[5] Victorio's raids throughout southwestern New Mexico Territory during the late summer and early fall of 1879 had gripped the whole region in a reign of terror.[6] John Ringo and Joe Olney, aka Joe Hill, veterans of Mason County's bloody Hoo Doo War in Texas, just like Carlotta Thompkins had chosen the fall of 1879 to migrate to New Mexico Territory. There is not any evidence to support a belief that Miss Carlotta was traveling with the same wagon train laboring toward Silver City, one barely escaping destruction at the hands of Victorio's warriors. John Ringo and Joe Olney had ridden with that party as welcomed reinforcements. The added travelers had made an impression on the journeying Texans. Jennie Parks Ringgold who later penned an Old West classic passed along a bit of family lore:

> Father often said that John Ringo, who afterward figured in Tombstone's early history, was a man with many good traits. Ringo possessed one quality which counted for much in those days; his word could be absolutely depended upon. He had good principles and a higher standard of morals than most outlaws. He loomed far above the opposing gang of outlaws—the Earps, Doc Holliday, and the Curly Bill faction in Tombstone's early days. Even in his own gang Ringo was a man apart from the others.[7]

The frightened family made it to Silver City, although utterly destitute—not even having a change, just the clothes on their backs.[8] Apaches had pillaged their abandoned wagons while the travelers had run for cover. At Silver City a relief fund was started for the lucky, but penniless and beleaguered people. Carlotta had by way of quaint La Mesilla, Fort Cummings and Dick Hudson's celebrated Hot Springs managed to make it to busy Silver City.[9] At long last she could once more unpack those garishly elegant but terribly wrinkled Parisian fashions. According to at least one preeminent Old West historian's account, Carlotta Thompkins had rekindled her relationship with San Antonio gambler Frank Thurmond and the agreeable pair had ventured into Silver City arm in arm.[10] Carlotta and Limpy Jim Smith had parted company, for keeps. A separate, but primary source, indicates Frank Thurmond had preceded Carlotta to New Mexico Territory by several years.[11] By the time Carlotta Thompkins appeared in New Mexico Territory—or quite soon thereafter—she and Frank Thurmond were, in fact, an "item." At Silver City they fast set themselves up in the Gem, "a combination saloon, dance hall and theater." Frank dealt faro and Carlotta served as the "lookout, occasionally taking a turn at the box."[12] Lottie and Frank were also regular players at the near legendary Centennial Saloon.[13] Besides the congenial company of Carlotta, Frank Thurmond had another constant companion, a finely-honed and sharp-pointed Bowie knife. It guaranteed that his widely known and earned reputation as man "that would give ground to no one," wasn't foolishly insulted.[14]

Miss Carlotta Thompkins had taken up residence in a town with a promise of respectability. San Angela, Jacksboro, and Brackettville would grow into places of decency and decorum, but such was not the case while Carlotta had been there selling her wares and wagering. Of course San Antonio would eclipse those places, but during the immediate post Civil War period, when Carlotta had been a resident, the city was suffering its growing pains amid the hated Yankee imposed Reconstruction. As for poor Fort Griffin? By the time Carlotta reached New Mexico Territory its heyday was but a memory, Albany was now Shackelford County's flowering municipality.

Much like those other cities making up Carlotta's gambling program, Silver City had an authentic history of being stocked with more than an ample assortment of colorful frontier types. Some were outrageously bad characters. One renowned historian captured the essence: "Silver City was a town with all its hair on, its population a mixture of the most fearless and the most desperate men on the frontier."[15] There were good folks, too, and they were at last beginning to wrest belligerence and lawless transgressions away from that contrasting societal element. When Miss Thompkins stepped off that stagecoach the town of near eighteen hundred people was much different than the hodgepodge of log cabins and adobe houses of just ten years before. It was a place on the move—ideally located in the pulsating heart of New Mexico Territory's southwestern mining and cattle country. At Silver City, much to Carlotta's delight she could count "three churches, three schools, three quartz mills, twelve stores, two hotels, four restaurants, four livery stables and corrals, one planing mill, sixteen saloons, four blacksmiths, one jeweler, two drug stores, one cracker factory, three dance halls, one furniture factory, two foundries, one machine shop, three wheelwrights, two banks, and no vacant houses."[16] Pledging that Silver City would really be a place "built to last," the city council passed an ordinance that all future construction within the incorporated town limits must be of either adobe or brick—no tinderbox wood frame or log buildings allowed.[17] There is little doubt, while Carlotta Thompkins sat in on those card games and obediently served as the lookout for Frank Thurmond's faro games, she was also sizing up the right time to make a break from the sporting life.

And a sporting life Silver City had! Aside from Don Juan Ward's place, with a dance hall on one end and gambling room on the other, separated in the middle by the "wet goods and cashier's department," there were plenty of places to gaily socialize with a straight in one hand and a straight whiskey in the other. There was Old Bill McGeary's Saloon, which during an earlier time had also seen triple duty as a sometimes courtroom, sometimes schoolhouse, and sometimes site to hear a lively Sunday sermon. There, too, was "Richard 'Dick' Howlett's place, along with such spots as the Blue Goose, the Red Onion, Joe Dyer's Orleans Club, James Copely's Bedrock, the Centennial, the Kentuck, Fred Shelton's Sample Room, the Monarch Saloon, the Cottage Saloon, the Keystone, the White House, and Wolcott and Mill's Tap Room—just to name a few."[18] Hard-working saloonkeepers didn't need to keep up with keys; the places were open around the clock—everyday of the week—the doors were never locked.[19]

Though they came and went randomly, Silver City also was home to a bevy of working-girls. In the early days two of the best known madams were Bessie Harper and Kate Stewart. The latter could later claim a loose-knit relationship with Carlotta. Other colleagues making up Silver City's frail sisterhood were Gracie Nash, Claudie Lewis, Antoniette "Nettie" Simon, Ruby Fowler, Edna da Ray, Verdie Bell, Big Jess, Ada Humes [Hulmes], and the strikingly gorgeous Lucy Coronne, that "tall stylish, good looking dame of French extraction."[20]

Silver City lay in Grant County, a geographical subdivision that literally was all of southwestern New Mexico Territory due to its gargantuan size. For law enforcement purposes it was the realm of Sheriff Harvey Howard Whitehill, one of the area's earliest pioneers and politicians.[21] Though he was widely known throughout the Southwest as a participant in many thrilling adventures, Mr. Whitehill is best remembered as the very first lawman to arrest Henry Antrim, aka Billy the Kid. By the time Carlotta had arrived on Silver City's scene, the Kid had long before escaped from the local jail and started down the trail of murder and mythology. For some of the real heavy-duty police work Sheriff Whitehill relied on his Chief Deputy, Dan Tucker. Much like Mr. Whitehill, during the time he lived Mr. Tucker was recognized from Texas to Tombstone as a force to be reckoned with:

> Dan Tucker was appointed Deputy sheriff and at once began to show what kind of stuff he was made of. Hitherto the bad element had "painted the town red," and "shot it up," at their own sweet will, but when Tucker took charge it was not quite such an easy job,

especially after he had given the coroner two or three siftings.[22]

Deputy Dan Tucker really did give the Grant County Coroner more than "two or three siftings."[23] Characterized by one old-timer, it was implicit across all of southwestern New Mexico Territory and points beyond—east and west—that Dan Tucker "never shot a man unless that man had broken a law."[24] And unlike so very many of the now legendary frontier peace officers, lawman Dan Tucker "went single handed into these affairs [gunfights], and it was up to him to use his own judgment; and he did so with an accuracy and precision probably unsurpassed in the West."[25] But the briefest legal inquiries were initiated after these actions and the citizenry "never questioned the manner of his killings."[26] Dan Tucker was known far and wide as "fearless as a man ever gets to be."[27] Anton Mazzanovich said Dan Tucker was "considered a gun fighter as good as anyone I knew of in that section...."[28] An overall assessment of Dan Tucker's law enforcing tact is repeated: "He was the one 'dead game hombre' that was needed at that time, for he was not afraid to kill."[29] Frank Thurmond, too, was not afraid to kill—when necessary—or when provoked.

Eighteen months after her conviction for Keeping A Disorderly House in Kinney County, Texas, Carlotta began keeping an orderly house, one for herself and Frank Thurmond. Standing before Grant County Justice of the Peace for Precinct #3, Isaac Givens, on the 2nd day of December 1880, Carlotta J. Thompkins and Frank Thurmond exchanged wedding vows at Silver City. Witnessing the informal and no frills ceremony were David Ebi and P. N. H. McMillan.[30] From this day forward The Gambling Queen of Hearts would be known by several first names; "Carlotta," "Charlotte," "Lottie," and even "Aunt Lottie," but always as Mrs. Thurmond.

At thirty-five years of age Carlotta had finally managed to begin remaking her life. Disengagement from the past is often difficult. In Carlotta Thurmond's case it would take several more years before the umbilical cord connecting her to the sporting gentry and gals was completely severed. During those intervening years Carlotta lived at the fringe. Her husband was a sporting and saloon man. Carlotta Thurmond had good friends and casual acquaintances yet running in the sporting circles. Several of that stripe would soon run through Silver City for a last goodbye or a grubstake or a scrap of gossip.

Day by day records of Mrs. Lottie Thurmond, as she was often referred to in the local press, embedding herself in Silver City's upper class social strata are sketchy. There is, however, evidence indicating she was mightily trying—and meeting with increasing approval. Lottie Thurmond had foregone the card table for the dinner table. Taking her organizational skills from the back rooms and barrooms to the banquet room, Lottie had made arrangements with the Ancient Order of United Workmen to cater their annual Thanksgiving Ball.[31] She did an outstanding job that holiday season of 1881:

> The supper, prepared by Mrs. Lottie Thurman [sic], was an elegant affair, and gave general satisfaction. In fact, it is well known that she never fails, upon such occasions to secure an abundance of the best the market affords, and to prepare it in the best of style.[32]

By any stretch of imagination Silver City was proving to be that "go ahead town," a safe haven fit for families and futures. Lottie Thurmond was making her place. There were vociferous newspaper editors capable of making the public relations sale. Proudly the townsmen could boast of the Silver City Library Association, as well as the Silver City Dramatic Association and its cast of amateur thespians climbing steps to the Morrill Opera House's stage. Two local photographers, A. S. Addis and H. W. Lucas, were madly marketing "Stereoscopic views of Silver City." The hometown folks and visitors alike were rushing like crazy to Bennett's News Depot to make their purchases of photographic prints before the supply was exhausted.[33] Financial magnates from back "in the states" were pouring money into Silver City's mining economy. Some local fellows were getting well-fixed, becoming tycoons in their own right. Business acumen could pay a handsome dividend at New Mexico Territory's jewel of a township. Outside of the city, besides the dotting mining shafts, the cattle business was taking a foothold. Here, too, good judgment and good luck—plus a little rain—would make a man rich. Silver City was drawing a multitude of wives and husbands to the region; single men—miners and cowboys—by the drove. At the busy gaming tables in wide-awake downtown Frank Thurmond was emptying pockets. Uptown Lottie Thurmond was satisfying hungry tummies, catering first this then that social event. The chances for financial success were panning out so good that Frank wrote home promoting the possibilities to his two brothers, James "Jim" and Harrison.[34]

There was plenty to write home about too! Not only were positive developments at Silver City newsworthy, but fifty miles to the south a nationwide story was seizing headlines. America's second transcontinental railroad had been completed. The Southern Pacific working its way east across Grant County, leaving newly built Lordsburg, New Mexico Territory, behind, had made juncture on March 8th, 1881, with the Atchison, Topeka & Santa Fe line working its way southwest. Where they met a new town was born. The place had been christened Deming, in honor of Mary Ann [Deming] Crocker, the wife of wealthy railroad industrialist Charles Crocker.[35]

Deming was a brand new settlement in the middle of nowhere; thirty miles north of the Mexican border. Expectations for the town were high. Deming was predicted to be one of the greatest cities in the American Southwest due to its round houses and switching yards, a base headquarters for mechanics and tradesmen, and the designated layover spot for numerous passenger and freight trains' attendant employees.[36] Cargo and express traffic thrived. Businessmen and tourists now had a sunny southern route to California. Renowned hotel developer Fred Harvey saw to it that one of his Harvey Houses, staffed by perky and unmarried Harvey girls, was promptly built at Deming. The sprawling Harvey House was the most handsome and commodious depot hotel between Kansas City and San Francisco.[37] The Harvey House complex was

> ...three hundred and fifty feet long, one story high at both ends, the center, two stories high, was two hundred feet long. It had a broad verandah on both sides. It was an architectural gem...The west end of the first story housed the railroad office, telegraph office, waiting rooms. Each end of the platform housed the offices of the Adams Express Company and the Wells Fargo Company. Equidistant from the ends of the depot hotel, just a mile apart, where the round houses, shops, mechanical headquarters of the S. P. and the A. T. & S. F.[38]

Deming was not an atypical frontier village. Before respectability could be permanently seeded the riffraff, rascals and reprobates had to be weeded from town. Flotsam and jetsam making their presence known in new frontier towns was a perennial problem. Deming had its share! One early day newspaperman writing of clear land titles jotted: "Title is a consideration that troubles boom town builders but little, and it did not these. Title was an after-consideration to be tackled by the lawyers and the future. The boomers ran their street lines, set their lot stakes and had Colt and Winchester documents to hold the stakes in place."[39] Another onsite journalist suggested: "Deming morals are not to be discussed in a newspaper—until she has some!"[40] The caveat was ignored. Early on the *Deming Headlight's* editor rebuffed that sage advice and publicly chastised its readers, admonishing them to be distrustful of such human leeches as Big Ed Burns, a killer, con-man and tinhorn gambler.[41] Another character staying at Deming was Anthony "One-Arm" Price whose murder trials were plural not singular; one being for killing a man just to hear the gun go "pop!"[42] Adding to the isolated region's rougher element was a self-styled two-gun man, John Henry Hankins, aka Six-Shooter Smith. Supposedly a sometimes pal of the previously mentioned ne'er-do-well Doc Holliday, Six-Shooter Smith had rightly earned scurrilous status throughout the Southwest.[43] A newspaper editor characterized Six-Shooter Smith as "the big dog with the brass collar."[44] Almost echoing as ludicrous was an ex-railroad man's moniker, Three-Shooter Smith, a protégé of Six-Shooter Smith.[45] An 1881 edition of Las Vegas, New Mexico Territory's *Optic* carried the story, a silhouette of shamelessness:

> We have heard from "Three-Shooter" Smith, the terror of the Membres [*sic*] sink, again. A random correspondent at Deming says: "Three-Shooter" Smith, a pupil and partner of "Six-Shooter," and who has lately been developing into a very bad man, has been captured and conveyed to Silver City. This dandy-"Three Shooter" and some friends made a raid on a rival saloon a few nights ago and made things lively for a while by shooting promiscuously at bottles, pictures, the piano and several other prominent articles about the place.[46]

Also sliding into Deming was another scalawag, John Jefferson "Off-Wheeler" Harlan, sometimes a killer and always a bunco artist.[47] Specifically registering all the acts of badness or naming all the badman hanging out at Deming is not necessary. Soon the upstanding folks at Silver City took note of what was taking place. The Grant County Grand Jury met—and publicly cried: "There seems to be a very bad state of affairs existing in the southern part of this county, near the border of Old Mexico. It almost seems that a law abiding citizen can hardly live there with any safety to himself or property. There seems to be a band of men living in that section of the county, who live by robbing and stealing, and defy the authorities. We ask that our Sheriff and law abiding citizens use every effort possible to suppress this lawlessness...."[48] An editor traveling through Deming may have vaulted his prose with a touch of colorful exaggeration, but the underlying theme of his piece reflected reality:

> But the Indians are not the worst element in Grant County society. The cowboys, or roughs and thieves, are so numerous that no man ventures any distance from the village without his Winchester rifle, ready to repeat 12 or 16 times without reloading. With this

element constantly on the watch for plunder, a man's
life goes for naught.[49]

Sheriff Harvey Whitehill was an astute politician. He surrendered to
political pressure and traveled from Silver City to Deming, taking with
him deputies Dan Tucker and James K. Farrell. After Whitehill's initial
investigation and a few arrests, he and Farrell returned to Silver City.
Dan Tucker remained behind pledging to put a stop to any
disorderliness at Deming. Tucker was the right man for the job.
Although "lawlessness had taken a foothold in Deming," Dan Tucker
patrolling the streets with a double barreled shotgun tucked under one
arm "narrowed the dimensions."[50]

Enumerating all of Dan Tucker's adventurous accomplishments at
Deming would be impossible. Highlighting just a few is representative.
According to one newspaper account, before Dan Tucker killed him,
Charley Hugo had been "deporting himself in a riotous manner and
[had] resisted arrest."[51] Single-handed Dan Tucker confronted five
violently drunken soldiers in from Fort Cummings, the military post
positioned 21 miles northeast of Deming. During the ensuing brawl
Dan Tucker suffered a burned hand from the muzzle blast of a soldier's
pistol. Nevertheless, the news reporter noted that deputy Tucker
"effected the arrests, as he usually does."[52] Later the *New Southwest &
Grant County Herald* would spotlight another incident where Dan
Tucker, acting alone, tackled the problem of dealing with transient
toughs:

> At Deming, on Monday a party of roughs stood a man
> up in broad daylight for his team and entire outfit.
> Deputy Sheriff Tucker hearing of the fact, got down his
> trusty gun and ran the whole gang off.[53]

After two reckless fellows had thoroughly misbehaved at the settlement
of Shakespear, west of Deming, Dan Tucker during separate
confrontations took them both into custody. Deputy Tucker turned
Sandy King and William Rogers "Russian Bill" Tettenborn over to local
citizens. The badmen were lynched in a hotel dinning room.[54] Tucker's
reputation as a hard border lawman soared. Many were Dan's more-or-
less routine arrests, and those prisoners, once tuned loose, chose to leave
Deming; and "few ever returned while Tucker was the law there."[55]
Another desperado that did not depart Deming quickly enough was Jim
Bond, an ex-Texas Ranger but recent badman. Dan Tucker did not
tolerate any misbehavior at Deming, a fact well-known, even in faraway
Kansas. The *Wichita Daily Eagle* updated its readership regarding the
grave matter between Mr. Tucker and Mr. Bond:

A darn fool went and rode through the dining-room in the railroad hotel at Deming flourishing his pistol, and frightened the lady passengers bound west nearly into fits. Dan Tucker found the fellow on the street, covered him with her [shotgun] and called "hands up." The blasted idiot makes a motion for his six-shooter and Dan filled him chuck full of buckshot. He failed to get there, Eli, and now peacefully sleeps beneath the daisies.[56]

Wayne Whitehill, the sheriff's second son, was a person who actually knew Mr. Tucker. As an oldtimer Wayne Whitehill repeated what elders had told him about the Deming depot incident, saying that deputy Dan "had this old shotgun so he just let him have it, shot his [Bond's] head off and the brains went up all over the ceiling."[57] Newspapers from El Paso to Tombstone were carrying reports of Dan Tucker's exploits.[58] By one account in an 1881 El Paso paper it was tabulated that Tucker had arrested thirteen members of the "cowboy gang," during one twenty day period and had issued the errant boys their "walking papers."[59] Displaying a degree of pride, a later edition of that same newspaper observed: "Deputy Sheriff Tucker at Deming, keeps that town free of rough characters."[60] An inflexible message was resonating throughout the Southwest: "The word soon spread all along the border that Dan Tucker had put the clamps on Deming. Lawbreakers and fugitives gave the town a wide berth."[61]

The Thurmonds, too, gave Deming a wide berth—at least for awhile. There was as of yet no railroad connecting Silver City and Deming. At Silver City, where they were residing, there was considerable revenue to be derived from dealing cards and doling out groceries. Frank's gambling was profitable. Lottie had undergone a change of heart—if not conscience—albeit with the helping hands of several persistent Texas prosecutors. Maintaining a respectable catering business and negotiating a rental agreement for the Grand Opening of a restaurant and lodging house was much more reputable than keeping that other kind of house. Lottie's continuous bouts with the legal system had grown tiresome. New Mexico Territory was the foundation provided for Lottie Thurmond's new start; her new lease on life. For now Silver City seemed the perfect place. There would be time to check out Deming—after Dan Tucker had tamed the town!

Another photograph of J. Wright Mooar. He conversed with Lottie Deno about her "new life" in New Mexico Territory. *Courtesy Nita Stewart Haley Memorial Library.*

John Ringo [L.] and Joe Olney, aka Joe Hill [R.], Texas Hill Country veterans of the bloody Mason County War, traveled to Grant County, New Mexico Territory during 1879 as did Miss Lottie Deno. *Courtesy Robert G. McCubbin* [Ringo photo] *and David Johnson* [Olney photo].

Traffic to booming Silver City, New Mexico Territory was brisk. *Courtesy Silver City Museum.*

Frank J. Thurmond. A gambler, saloon man, and mining speculator. He married Carlotta J. Thompkins [Lottie Deno] at Silver City, New Mexico Territory in December 1880. From *Lottie Deno: Her Life and Times* by J. Marvin Hunter. Frank was described as "a man you couldn't cry in front of." *Courtesy the Hunter Family.*

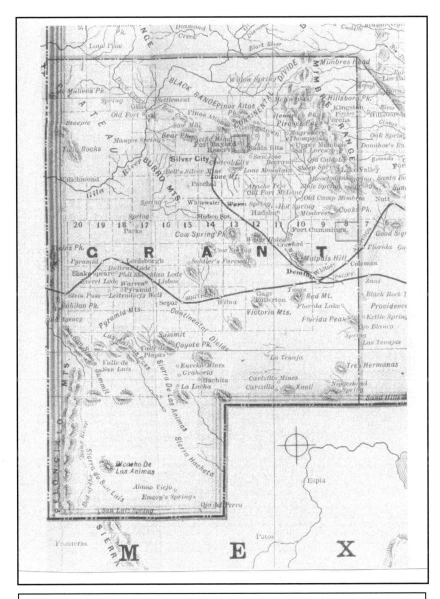

Massive in size, Grant County was all of southwestern New Mexico Territory. Although this is an 1885 Railroad Map, when Lottie Deno arrived in the territory there were no railway lines across southern New Mexico Territory. The connection made at Deming didn't take place until 1881, and it was 1883 before narrow gauge tracks were laid between bustling Silver City and Deming. Note the close proximity of Florida Station, established in 1881 on the Santa Fe line and old Fort Cummings. Walter V. Hayt Railroad and Township Map. *Courtesy, Silver City Museum.*

Silver City during the mid-1880s. *Courtesy Silver City Public Library.*

Silver City's well-known Southern Hotel and the scene of a least one shooting. *Courtesy Nita Stewart Haley Memorial Library.*

Mrs. Frank Thurmond [Lottie Deno] is standing far right in the doorway of the New Cash Store in Silver City, New Mexico Territory. *Courtesy Silver City Museum.*

Because of brick construction and a prohibition against wood frame buildings, Silver City was taking on the overall appearance of an "Eastern" town. *Courtesy Silver City Museum.*

Silver City's citizens were trying mightily to make southwestern New Mexico Territory "civilized." Here amateur thespians take a curtain-call at the Morrill Opera House. *Courtesy Nita Stewart Haley Memorial Library.*

The Centennial Saloon at Silver City. Frank Thurmond was gambling here when three Grant County lawmen fatally gunned down another Grant County deputy. Frank was subpoenaed to testify, and did so. *Courtesy Silver City Museum.*

The Harvey House Hotel at Deming. This is the location that Deputy Dan Tucker shotgunned out of the saddle "a darn fool and blasted idiot." *Courtesy Deming/Luna Mimbres Museum.*

Sheriff Harvey H. Whitehill. He was an early day Grant County pioneer, peace officer and politician. Commonly credited as the first man ever to arrest Billy the Kid is how Mr. Whitehill is often characterized: He was much more. *Courtesy Silver City Museum.*

Endnotes Chapter 9

[1] Cashion, "Rewriting the Wild West for a New History." Mr. Cashion captions a known photograph of Carlotta Thompkins, aka Lottie Deno this way: "Charlotte Tompkins Thurmond, who claimed to be the 'long lost' Lottie Deno." 54. To this author's knowledge Mrs. Thurmond never claimed to be the mysterious Lottie Deno.
[2] Sam Baldwin to Earl Vandale & Hervey Chesley.
[3] Hunter, "The Lottie Deno I Knew." "She told him she had quit gambling, had married a New Mexico ranchman, joined the church, and had settled down to a peaceful life." 34; The fact that Carlotta Thompkins [Mrs. Frank Thurmond] made trips to El Paso, Texas, may be confirmed: *New Southwest & Grant County Herald*, December 9, 1882. "Mrs. Lottie Thurman [*sic*] has gone to El Paso."
[4] Alexander, *Desert Desperadoes: The Banditti Of Southwestern New Mexico*. 91-92.
[5] *Grant County Herald*, July 19, 1879; Grant County Criminal District Court Book. Posting of Indictments, July 17th and 18th, 1879. Courtesy New Mexico State Records Center & Archives. Santa Fe.
[6] Donald Howard Couchman, *Cooke's Peak—Pasaron Por Aqui: A Focus On United States History In Southwestern New Mexico*. "During 1879, continued Indian depredations culminated in the short vicious wars between the Untied States military and the Apaches, serially led by Victorio, Nana, Loco, and others." 199; Daniel D. Aranda, a specialist on Victorio's raids has published two outstanding articles on this outbreak; "An Episode From Victorio's War" [*Real West*, February 1984] and "Apache Depredations in Doña Ana County: An Incident in Victorio's War" [*Southern New Mexico Historical Review*, January 1996]; For participation of Doña County's fighting Lopez family in the Victorio War, see Bob Alexander's *Lawmen, Outlaws & S. O. Bs*. Volume II. Chapter 10.
[7] Jennie Parks Ringgold, *Frontier Days In The Southwest*. 15.
[8] *Grant County Herald*, October 25, 1879.
[9] Prior to any railroad connection at Silver City, which would not occur until 1883, commercial travel to the city was by stagecoach. For an interesting contemporary account of travel along the dangerous roadway originating at La Mesilla and ending in Silver City [with intermediate stops] the reader is referred to *New Mexico in 1876-1877, A Newspaperman's View: The Travels & Reports of William D. Dawson*, compiled and edited by Robert J. Tórrez; Ron Swartley, *Fort Cummings and Massacre Canyon*. "Fort Cummings became nearly overrun with passing travelers, especially after the war. Increasing numbers of emigrants were heading west to California. Tradespeople, miners and businessmen were coming and going." 19; Couchman, *Cooke's Peak—Pasaron Por Aqui: A Focus On United States History In Southwestern New Mexico*. "Meanwhile, several mail and transportation lines and freighting efforts flourished along the old road, and business was good at each water source. In fact, places such as Slocum's, Fort Cummings, and Rio Mimbres added facilities for overnight guests to their inventory of services and supplies." 196.
[10] DeArment, *Knights Of The Green Cloth: The Saga of the Frontier Gamblers*. "The Thurmonds went to Silver City, New Mexico, that year of 1878." 264. Perhaps, as the author suggests Frank Thurmond and Carlotta Thompkins traveled to New Mexico together, but not as husband and wife—their marriage would take place in Silver City.
[11] *Silver City Enterprise*, June 5, 1908. In Frank's obituary it is remarked that: "Mr. Thurmond was 70 years of age and had resided in this section of the country of the last thirty-three years." That tabulation computes as sometime about 1875. Another newspaper account, the *Deming Headlight* of June 11, 1908, somewhat contradicts the

obituary as carried in the *Silver City Enterprise*. "After the war Mr. Thurmond came to Texas, where he lived for several years, then came with his wife overland to New Mexico, arriving in Silver City July 1, 1880." Again, if Frank and Carlotta traveled to Silver City in July of 1880 it was prior to their legally recorded marriage.

[12] DeArment, *Knights Of The Green Cloth: The Saga of the Frontier Gamblers.* 264.

[13] *The New Southwest & Grant County Herald*, September 9, 1882. Frank Thurmond while gambling at the Centennial witnessed a shooting where a man was killed. Pioneer Foundation Interview, Number 504. Wayne Whitehill to Lou Blachly. "She [Lottie] used to deal there in the Centennial Saloon."

[14] Bob Alexander, *Dangerous Dan Tucker: New Mexico's Deadly Lawman.* 49.

[15] Nolan, *The West of Billy the Kid.* 21.

[16] Susan Berry & Sharman Apt Russell, *Built to Last: An Architectural History of Silver City, New Mexico.* "With the dawn of the 1880s, a new self consciousness was apparent in Silver City; the 'real American Town' had begun to attract attention." 20.

[17] Ibid.

[18] Bob Alexander, "Guns, Girls & Gamblers, Silver City's Wilder Side." *Western Outlaw-Lawman History Association Journal.* Volume XIV. Number 4. [Winter 2005] 16.

[19] Ibid.

[20] Ibid. Karen Holliday Tanner & John D. Tanner, Jr., "The Case of Ada Hulmes: Murder and Scandal in New Mexico." *Wild West.* December 2003.

[21] The standard work on Whitehill is Bob Alexander's *Sheriff Harvey Whitehill: Silver City Stalwart.*

[22] *Silver City Enterprise*, October 17, 1902.

[23] For a tabulation of Dan Tucker's verifiable deathly encounters see Alexander's *Dangerous Dan Tucker: New Mexico's Deadly Lawman.* 162-167. Interestingly in the book's Introduction, Leon Metz characterizes Tucker: "Overall, Tucker was a better lawman, and more dangerous, than such redoubtable, high-profile figures as Wyatt Earp and Wild Bill Hickok. Yet he is practically unheard of today largely because he lacked the ability or the need to exploit himself." 5.

[24] *Silver City Independent*, September 22, 1931.

[25] Ibid.

[26] Ibid. Somewhat amusingly Alexander in *Dangerous Dan Tucker: New Mexico's Deadly Lawman* quoted Edgar Beecher Bronson's tongue in cheek remark that certain Old West gunmen were afflicted with *Triggerfingeritis*, "an acute irritation of the sensory nerves of the index finger of habitual gun-packers; usually fatal—to someone." 30.

[27] *Silver City Enterprise*, September 5, 1902.

[28] Anton Mazzanovich on Lake Valley, New Mexico. Mazzanovich Papers. Arizona Historical Society. Tucson Arizona. Courtesy Tom Gaumer, researcher extrodinare.

[29] *Silver City Independent*, June 12, 1917; Also quoted in *The Silver City Book: "Wild and Woolly Days"* by Susan and David Nelson. 19.

[30] Marriage Record Book, Grant County, New Mexico, 1872-1899. Marriages listed alphabetically by husband's last name, in this instance under tab T, for Thurmond. Courtesy Grant County Clerk, Silver City, New Mexico.

[31] *New Southwest & Grant County Herald*, November 12, 1881.

[32] Ibid. November 26, 1881.

[33] Berry & Russell, *Built to Last: An Architectural History of Silver City, New Mexico.* 20; *Grant County Herald*, April 12, 1880. Bob Alexander, *Six-Guns and Single-Jacks: A History of Silver City and Southwestern New Mexico.* 140-141.

[34] The assertion that Frank wrote home to his brothers James and Harrison is an assumption, but based on a comment in the *Southwest Sentinel* of March 25, 1882: "Two brothers of Frank Thurmond arrived from Texas last week."

[35] William S. Greever, "Railway Development in the Southwest." *New Mexico Historical Review.* Volume 32 [1957]; David F. Myrick, *New Mexico's Railroads—A Historical Survey.* 12.

[36] *Newman's Semi-Weekly*, April 6, 1881. "....the railway yard at Deming will be the largest west of Chicago. It is stated by railway men who have traveled about the west pretty thoroughly that the Deming yard can now lay claim to that distinction."

[37] Lesley Poling-Kempes, *The Harvey Girls: Women Who Opened The West.* "These Harvey Houses, in places like Raton, Deming, San Marcial, Belen, Vaughn, and Clovis were constantly busy with railroad crews, and also served as social centers for the small and often isolated young communities they were part of." 119; Stanley, *The Deming Story.* "The railroad depot hotel was considered the finest of its type between Kansas City and San Francisco." 5.

[38] Stanley, *The Deming Story.* 5.

[39] *Deming Sun*, November 21, 1957.

[40] C. M. Chase, *The Editor's Run In New Mexico and Colorado.* 127.

[41] *Deming Headlight*, March 25, 1882; Dan L. Thrapp, *Encyclopedia of Frontier Biography.* Vol. I. 196. Before coming to the Deming, New Mexico Territory, Ed Burns had literally been run out of Leadville, Colorado; *Colorado Miner*, November 22, 1879; *Fairplay Flume*, November 27, 1879. "Of the seven who were warned out of town by the vigilantes but two—Champ and Ed Burns—have obeyed. The rest express a determination to stay at all hazards."

[42] Alexander, *Desert Desperadoes: The Banditti of Southwestern New Mexico.* 169-170; *Las Vegas Optic*, July 29, 1881; C. A. Gustafson, "Dan Tucker, Deming's Lethal Lawman." *Destination Deming: 1999 Luna County Visitors Guide.*

[43] Citations to Six-Shooter Smith are common in both primary and secondary writings. One contemporary account with a person who actually was present when Smith accidentally discharged his revolver while "showing off," may be found in the Pioneer Foundation Interviews, Wayne Whitehill to Lou Blachly. A primary source linking Six-Shooter Smith and Doc Holliday is the *Denver Tribune*, May 16, 1882.

[44] *Las Vegas Optic*, March 22, 1881.

[45] Phillip J. Rasch, "'Six Shooter' and 'Three Shooter' Smith." *National Association For Outlaw and Lawman History* [NOLA] *Quarterly.* Volume IX. Number 4. [Winter 1985].

[46] *Las Vegas Optic*, April 14, 1881; David Johnson, "The Fifth Ace: H. F. Sills and His Testimony," *NOLA Quarterly*, [April-June 2007] postulates an unsupported theory from an unnamed source that it *may* be possible that Three-Shooter Smith was the nickname of H. F. Sills, a witness at the preliminary hearing regarding the killings near Tombstone's O. K. Corral. 36-37. Credibility must be based on evidence.

[47] Thrapp, *Encyclopedia of Frontier Biography.* Volume III. 616; Alexander, *Dangerous Dan Tucker: New Mexico's Deadly Lawman.* 73.

[48] *New Southwest & Grant County Herald*, July 30, 1881.

[49] Chase, *The Editor's Run In New Mexico and Colorado.* 127.

[50] Alexander, *Dangerous Dan Tucker: New Mexico's Deadly Lawman.* 75; Robert K. DeArment, "Deadly Deputy." *True West.* February 1999. 17; Alexander, *Sheriff Harvey Whitehill: Silver City Stalwart.* 124. Stanley, *The Deming Story.* 3.

[51] David Johnson, *John Ringo.* 121.

[52] *The New Southwest & Grant County Herald*, October 15, 1881.

[53] Ibid. May 21, 1882.

[54] El Paso *Lone Star*, November 16, 1881; Sharman Apt Russell, "Russian Bill: the True Story of an Outlaw." *Journal of the West*. April. 1984; Alexander, *Dangerous Dan Tucker: New Mexico's Deadly Lawman*. 83-86; *Santa Fe New Mexican*, November 12, 1881; *The New Southwest & Grant County Herald*, November 12, 1881; F. Stanley, *The Shakespear Story*. 16.

[55] Thrapp, *Encyclopedia of Frontier Biography*. Volume III. 1443.

[56] *Wichita Daily Eagle*, October 11, 1884. This newspaper article was a reflective piece, highlighting previous events, not necessarily those contemporaneous to its publication.

[57] Pioneer Foundation Interview. Wayne Whitehill to Lou Blachly.

[58] Mentions of Dan Tucker in the El Paso *Lone Star* are numerous; The *Tombstone Epitaph* of October 20, 1881 [just days before the O. K. Corral killings] mentions a shoot-out between one George Brown and a deputy Dan Tucker; For coherent analysis, see, Alexander, *Dangerous Dan Tucker, New Mexico Deadly Lawman*. 78-79.

[59] El Paso *Lone Star*, November 11, 1881.

[60] Ibid. December 3, 1881.

[61] DeArment, "Deadly Deputy." 17.

Chapter 10

"Took Breakfast at the Broadway"

Mrs. Lottie Thurmond won the International Order of Odd Fellows' contract to ensure the grand New Year's Eve ball was a gourmet's triumph. In a January 1882 edition of the *New Southwest & Grant County Herald* she received positive remarks for making the event a "perfect success" and for being "a good housekeeper."[1] Perhaps in light of her shady past Lottie could even squeeze a dollop of humor from the article. She much preferred a nice newspaperman lauding her "housekeeping" aptitudes, rather than a persnickety prosecutor speaking with an arrest warrant to her other "keeping house" talents.

She had found her niche. On or about January 14, 1882, in downtown Silver City, Lottie opened a restaurant, the Broadway, a semi-elegant establishment with a second story that was used to accommodate overnight guests.[2]

Not able to shake loose of her former proclivities as a habitué of nighttime spots, Lottie kept the Broadway open around the clock. The Broadway was the solitary Silver City restaurant keeping the same hours as the saloons and gambling halls. Lottie's fare was reasonably priced; $.50 for a meal from the regular menu, slightly higher it is presumed for "Delicacies of the Season," which could include such delicious items as oysters, fish, and wild game of all kinds. Upstairs were the "clean and well ventilated rooms," at a rate of $7.00 per week—naturally, in advance—the very "best attendance" was guaranteed. Lottie Thurmond's recurrently running ad in the local newspaper suggested that folks should just "drop in and make yourself at home."[3] With Frank's and Lottie's long tenure on the Southwest's gaming circuit there can be little doubt word of their Silver City location and new business quickly spread amongst the sporting crowd. To presume otherwise would expose naiveté. Owning and operating a legitimate business was a far cry from Lottie's earlier life in frontier Texas. She had been in a self-employed business before, yes, but in the beer halls, bordellos and back rooms. Ladies could cross the Broadway's threshold.

So very many of Lottie's former female friends and acquaintances would never find their way out of that sordid life; hopelessly they were mired. Unable to jettison their past, some would fall victim to gunshots or stabbing as a result of unrestrained rage. Other working-girls would be killed by a stray bullet while drunken idiots fired their guns at each other—or indiscriminately. Some, never able to rise above poverty, would wither and die on the frontier West's skid rows. Prices for their sexual favors fell drastically as they aged; robbed of calcium and color.

Acute alcoholism and depression would be no stranger to worn-out girls sliding downhill. Scores would deliberately swallow copious quantities of mind and body numbing laudanum—an opium derivative—intentionally committing suicide; while a few others simply and sadly died from unintended overdoses while trying to momentarily escape life's troubles. Those type of catastrophic misfortunes were not Lottie's cards to play.

This point in her chronology is not the place to suggest that Mrs. Lottie Thurmond was recalibrating her righteous moral compass. That would—at least from outward appearances—come later. Meanwhile, at Silver City she and husband Frank were beginning to calculate the wisdom of diversification. Lottie maintained her interest in the Broadway Restaurant and Frank continued to roll dice and turn cards, but they branched out, too. Examination of Grant County deed books reveals that during 1882 the couple began purchasing and sometimes reselling Silver City town lots.[4] The couple also began speculating in the mining business, a venture that Frank and Lottie would invest in for a number of years to come.[5] Prospects for profitability were good at Silver City. Frank's family heeded that message.

Climbing out of a stagecoach and making an appearance at Silver City's during March of 1882, were Frank's brothers Jim and Harrison from Texas, an arrival exacting notice in the *Southwest Sentinel*.[6] Both were high-rolling sporting men and plunging speculators. Jim Thurmond, along with business partner Ed Preston, would eventually become financially affiliated with one of Tombstone's drinking landmarks, the Oriental Saloon.[7] That the Thurmond boys were not strangers in Tombstone may be extracted from the *Silver City Enterprise*.[8] Also there was a dispatch to the *Southwest Sentinel* from the *Tombstone Epitaph*:

> Quite a number of prominent sporting gents came in from Silver City last evening. Their names are [John] P. Thornton, C. [Charles] Ashton, J. C. [Jim] Thurmond and J. Antrim [Billy the Kid's brother?]. The former has been taking in other camps since last here, and announces his intention to locate here permanently,—
> *Tombstone Epitaph*.[9]

News such at that emanating from turbulent Tombstone seems rather mild when set against the backdrop of an earlier communiqué from Arizona Territory. Until now it has been overlooked, but Lottie's bit part in that saga warrants inclusion. Her role may serve as the podium for an expanded explanation or as an appropriate platform for ancillary questions. A fleeting over-the-shoulder look is necessary.

The shootings near Tombstone's O. K. Corral on October 26, 1881, may not have been the most chronicled gunfight of the Old West at that time, but by now such would be the case. Particulars and minutia surrounding the actual killings have been debated—sometimes hotly—for years. More often than not the participants are partisans. Seldom is a consensus reached. For Lottie's and/or Frank Thurmond's cameo part in this theater of melodrama there should be but little to argue.

On that chilly October afternoon, Mr. Virgil Earp, his two brothers Morgan and Wyatt, accompanied by Doc Holliday, squared off with Frank and Tom McLaury and their nineteen year old pal William "Billy" Clanton. When the shooting stopped the McLaurys and Clanton lay dead. Subsequently Virgil was dismissed as the city's police chief. The Earps and Holliday were formally charged with murder, but after a favorable ruling during a preliminary hearing they were set free. Angered by what they saw as a politically manipulated miscarriage of justice, friends of the deceased men ambushed Virgil Earp, savagely wounding the poor man, but not mortally. Their next attempt at assassination was victorious—but cowardly. An unsuspecting Morgan Earp was fatally gunned down while playing a game of pool. Afterwards Wyatt Earp, joined by his baby brother Warren and Doc Holliday, in consort with "Turkey Creek" Jack Johnson and Sherman McMaster turned certifiable criminals and cold-bloodedly killed Frank Stilwell in Tucson's train yard. After rummaging around in the wilds of southeastern Arizona Territory they executed Florentino Cruz and, maybe, as Mr. Wyatt claimed, killed outlaw Curly Bill. Prosecuting their personal vendetta the men had cleaved unto themselves the mantra of murderers.[10]

The good folks at Tucson were not sympathetic to one crowd of disputable feudists using their backyard to settle old scores with another group of disputable feudists. An Arizona newspaper gave them a blistering spanking.[11] Nor, for that matter, were the folks across the line in New Mexico Territory in accord with the illegality resulting from unrestrained madness. The *Deming Headlight* chided that "the Earp party riddled Frank Stilwell with bullets," and then took their editorial shot across Arizona Territory's bow, declaring:

> Murder is the order of the day in Tombstone and Tucson.[12]

At Tucson arrest warrants charging Wyatt and Warren Earp, Doc Holliday, Turkey Creek Jack and Sherman McMaster with murder were placed in the hands of Pima County Sheriff Robert Havlin "Bob" Paul. The wanted men became hunted men. Deputy Dan Tucker was not overawed with the fugitives' reputations as unsavory and treacherous characters. From his posting at Deming deputy Tucker volunteered his services to Sheriff Paul should he arrest the guys, and find that help was needed in transporting and guarding or even protecting the prisoners.[13] The boys on the dodge did not wish to be arrested. Not unwisely calculating their actuarial odds the fugitives very much feared a somewhat different outcome during a second murder hearing—one at Tucson. Their political clout in Cochise County was about evenly divided.[14] Such was not the case in Pima County. They were cognizant of another irrefutable truth. There was no real warranty as to just who would die next. Would it be Wyatt or Warren or Doc? Tit for tat revenge was the trademark of a feud. A decision was made. There would be no contest in a District Court, or a resolution in the desert. They would run away to Colorado.

With a transcontinental railroad running across southern Arizona and New Mexico Territories the fastest and easiest way for the fugitives to leave Cochise County would have been to board an eastbound Southern Pacific train and ride to Deming. At Deming changing railway lines to the Atchison, Topeka & Santa Fe would provide effortless northbound transportation to Albuquerque and points beyond. There would be a drawback with that plan—for fugitives. Dan Tucker was at Deming:

> ….the Earp crowd in their hasty exit from Tombstone toward Colorado, rather than take the train through Deming—Tucker's Territory—went on horseback the long way around. Apparently they were reluctant to test Tucker's ability to make the arrests Arizona officials desired.[15]

There was, however, a way to bypass Deming and still take advantage of making part of the long trip to Colorado by train. There were other good reasons for taking a devious route. A sly trip into Silver City would no doubt throw lawmen off track and off guard. Too, an old friend had taken up residence there! The fugitives chose to secretly ride—via Mule Creek northwest of town—into Silver City; after dark and undercover:

> Last Saturday evening at 10 o'clock, the Earp Boys' party and Doc Holliday were in Silver City. They went at once to the Exchange Hotel to find a stage agent to make arrangements to leave the next morning on the Deming coach. They slept in a private house up town and took breakfast the next morning in the Broadway restaurant, as they had not registered at any hotel, it was not known they were in town until after their departure.

The party came on horseback, and put up at the Elephant Corral. They were all mounted and armed to the teeth. One of the men when asked his name, answered John Smith, and another Bill Snooks. This excited the suspicion of Mr. White, proprietor of the Corral, and the next morning when they offered to sell him their horses, he refused to buy them, fearing to get himself in trouble. They offered six of their horses for $300, but as the horses were worth more than that, this offer was also looked on as unfavorable to them. They finally sold the six horses to Mr. Miller, who is about to start a livery stable here. This done they spoke to Mr. White about hiring a team to take them to Fort Cummings, but he advised them to go by stage, which they decided to do. The saddles and two horses they failed to sell were left here with Charley Bagsby.[16]

Sensible and impartial review of the newspaper item is not difficult. The "Earp Boys' party and Doc Holliday," using artfully assumed names to avoid arrests, slipped into town. Interesting is the statement that they stayed overnight in "a private house" and the next morning "took breakfast" at the Broadway Restaurant, Mrs. Lottie's illustriously well-known and recurrently advertised business.[17] It has been established that Lottie and Doc Holliday knew each other, by certain accounts quite well. They had both traveled that Texas gambling circuit from one army town to the next. By implication, then, she very well may have also previously known Wyatt Earp from her bawdy days at Fort Griffin. A reunion at Silver City between Lottie and the fugitives raises a plethora of intriguing and thought provoking questions. Were the fugitives looking for her? Were any of those fellows acquainted with Lottie's husband, Frank, a popular sporting man? Or, Frank's brothers, Jim and Harrison? Could they have been seeking a financial helping hand for their devious escape from justice? Did Lottie and/or Frank know the actual whereabouts of the dangerous and proven man-killing deputy, Dan Tucker? What was the general talk on the street; were New Mexico Territory's lawmen hard hunting for them, or hardly looking at all? What said the latest rumor, the freshest gossip? Where could they catch a ride on a northbound Santa Fe if they wanted to skip around Deming altogether? Was a romantic or lustful link even the vaguest of possibilities, a last lonely farewell? The probability of a muted huddle at Silver City is great. Identifying the actual motive for the short-lived get-together is and will remain indistinct. Lottie could keep a secret.

Various writers try to identify the "private house" where the Earp party stayed overnight. The guesswork always falls into the realm of "could have" or "might have." One example of such conjecture suggests that Wyatt Earp spent the night at Sheriff Harvey Whitehill's personal residence, while the rest of the crowd slept at the Grant County Jail. This contention is attributed to an "unverified source."[18] Such a scenario is highly unlikely. Whitehill, whatever else he might have been, was a family man. Neither Mr. Whitehill nor his children during 20th-Century interviews made mention of such dubious overnight guests.[19] It would certainly align with the category of being "unverified," but an unsupported assertion that the fugitives stayed at the "private house" of Lottie and Frank Thurmond would really rate as more believable. Or barring that "unverifiable" supposition, hiding out at Jim Thurmond's and Kate Stewart's place—a private house of ill repute—would be more in line for known sporting characters.[20] The Thurmond brothers, the Earps and Holliday, one and all, consorted and cohabited with women of questionable virtue or a spotted past.

In somewhat the same vein [missing any demonstrable provenance] it has been professed that since there was no railway line between the two towns, behind the scene manipulators arranged for a special stagecoach to secretly transport the fugitives from Silver City to Deming.[21] Sophisticated business executives overtly overstepping the legality line and conspiring to commit such criminally indictable crimes as Obstruction of Justice or acting as Accessories does seem more than a bit doubtful. Never mind a deficiency of evidence. Would it be too unladylike to wonder; if the Earp coterie were so intent on getting to Deming, why did they not just take the train from somewhere in Arizona Territory in the first place? That would have been quick and restful! Or, was the fact that telegraph messages between cooperative lawmen travel much more speedily than locomotives a salient reason for deception?[22] Why inflict on themselves a tortuous roundabout trip to Silver City? Was seeing Frank and/or Lottie Thurmond truly that important? Was there not a really good reason to bypass the town of Deming altogether? Ducking past Dan Tucker—if that was their judgment—would have been sensible for fugitives choosing flight instead of a fight.

"Though sometimes disputed, on-the-ground travel logic suggests the wanted men did take the Deming Coach—as it was called—but not to Deming."[23] The cited newspaper article attests that the Earps and Holliday were making inquiries about getting to Fort Cummings—not Deming—and were advised to take the scheduled stagecoach to that very location, "which they decided to do."[24] From Fort Cummings it was but walking distance to Florida Station, a stop on the Santa Fe Railroad's tracks. If one were heading to the state of Colorado from Fort Cummings, according to one of the paramount scholars of 19th-Century travel in southwestern New Mexico Territory, there would be no good reason "whatsoever" for backtracking umpteen miles to Deming: That trip would be "illogical."[25] For this gang of wanted fellows any trip into Deming might have proven unwise, unfortunate— and unhealthy:

> One old-timer wrote, "He [Dan Tucker] was just a nice man, quiet, didn't bother anybody, but don't bother him!" It is generally believed that Wyatt Earp and his cohorts didn't want "to bother him" either. During their flight to avoid murder prosecutions in Arizona, the fugitives chose to bypass Deming and Dan Tucker.[26]

After taking the coach to Fort Cummings, it has been established that the Earp party survived a train trip to Albuquerque without being arrested. Once there, according to an unsigned, unverified, and an admittedly "still controversial" claim, the fugitives were "kept watch over" by Sheriff Perfecto Armijo and Lou Blonger, who was then standing in as a city lawman for his absent brother, Sam Blonger.[27] *If true*, the connotation is not encouraging. There is reason for making mention of this as it is applicable to Frank's and Lottie's story. The fugitives being "watched over" by on the payroll peace officers has a genteel ring, but is deceiving. Good guys protecting other good guys was not taking place. According to the preeminent historian of Arizona's and New Mexico's territorial sheriffs, Larry D. Ball, Sheriff Perfecto Armijo was later removed from office during a heated political dispute regarding $14,000 of public funds withheld from Bernalillo County.[28] More troubling, however, for upholding any naïve notion about the fugitives' image and of interest for Lottie's story is Mr. Louis H. "Lou" Blonger. The heavy-set gangster of French-Canadian ancestry had migrated from his birthplace in Vermont to the United States' frontiers at an early age, taking up transitory residences in the country's western mining camps and cow towns. From an uninspiring startup Mr. Lou Blonger grew from a rather novice saloon proprietor and painted-princess procurer into, perhaps, the Rocky Mountain West's leading organized crime figure.[29] Mr. Louis Blonger, after a well-recognized career as a Denver crime boss, known in the underworld as "The Fixer," was ultimately convicted of felonies and sent to prison at Canyon City, Colorado. Mr. Blonger could not fix his own predicament. He began pleading for a Governor's Pardon. Lou Blonger's bemoaning pitch was not well received. The prosecutor was scathingly unsympathetic:

> You [Blonger] have been a criminal from the time of your youth. You have been the fixer of the town. You

have prostituted justice. You have bribed judges and jurors, State, City and police officials. You have ruined hundreds of men. With that record, tell me why a death sentence is not your due? As to your plea for parole, I say no, emphatically and for all time no. Before the king of the underworld is pardoned, the penitentiary doors should be torn from their hinges and all other occupants be first turned out. They would be less dangerous than you. You have met your day of judgment and the death sentence is your due. I will fight to the last any attempt to give you leniency of any kind or description.[30]

Whether it be Wyatt Earp or Doc Holliday, having an association with Mr. Lou Blonger is not a helpful feature for one's résumé. *If true,* Mr. Blonger's purported involvement with Frank and Lottie Thurmond adds a taint to their names, as well. Before he died in the penitentiary Blonger had filed the paperwork for a military pension. In that application Blonger stated that from 1883 until 1887 he had resided in the households of Frank Thurmond at Silver City, Deming and Kingston, New Mexico Territory.[31] The fact that Lou Blonger was, among other things, a sporting man is watertight. The same could be said of Mr. Frank Thurmond. The particular time-frame mentioned was between U. S. census reports, but there was a comprehensive 1885 New Mexico Territorial population count, by name and place of residence. Census records—notoriously inaccurate—fail to enumerate Mr. Lou Blonger as a resident in the home of Frank and Lottie Thurmond at Deming. Blonger's declaration that he was with them at Silver City, Deming and Kingston is suspiciously precise. They were there too! Likewise an oldtimer who wrote of those days places both Mr. Blonger and Mr. Thurmond in Kingston—at the same time.[32] So far, Lou Blonger and the Thrumonds have not been directly linked. If such were the case it would range from interesting to incriminating. Prying open that doorway, examining any personal or business relationship between the Thuromonds and Lou Blonger would be noteworthy. Should such an investigation be undertaken, however, it must rely on more than unverified and unidentified allegations, accompanied by controversial innuendo.

For Lottie Thurmond's story there is no compelling necessity to rush after Wyatt and Warren Earp, Doc Holliday, or their other companions in crime. They had planned to flee to Colorado and did just that. Old West history has well recorded their remaining allotment of mediocre misadventures and their whirlwind of self-promotion. On the other hand, that same history records that Lottie and Frank Thurmond would forevermore remain proud New Mexicans. They had no reason to hide; no reason to run away; no reason for puffed excuses.

The Broadway Restaurant under Lottie's direction was evidently a money maker, so much so that after a series of false starts she sold the business to a Mr. Andrews, the former proprietor of a hotel in nearby Santa Rita. Wisely the new owner kept Lottie on the payroll as manager, possibly because she had landed the contract to feed prisoners confined in Grant County's jail.[33] Divesting themselves of the Broadway unfastened the latch for exploratory fiscal options elsewhere. But before that, Frank Thurmond had some unfinished courtroom business to conduct in Silver City.

On August 24, 1882, sheriff's deputies Dan Tucker and Billy McCellan, assisted by Silver City's Town Marshal, Glaudius W. Moore, fatally gunned down another Grant County deputy, James Burns, inside the Centennial Saloon. Not just a few Silver City citizens, including a mad prosecuting attorney, screamed murder. Under the microscope, officers maintained it was a clear-cut case of self-defense.[34] The three surviving lawmen were arrested, an anomaly that irked Dan Tucker:

> Dan Tucker informs us that in the course of his duty as deputy sheriff he has been obliged to kill eight men in this county, besides several in Lincoln and Doña Ana counties, and the killing of Burns, in which he was implicated, was the first time he was ever put under bonds to await examination.[35]

Frank Thurmond had been operating his gambling game at the Centennial Saloon when the shooting erupted. He was subpoenaed to testify. Frank Thurmond was by all accounts a "straight-talker," a man whose outlook on life was focused through a narrow prism. Frank said what he believed and others had best believe he meant what he said. Frank's testimony in the murder trial was also plain-spoken: "He too would have killed Jimmy Burns," he matter-of-factly said.[36] After some time the murder case against Deputy Dan Tucker was dismissed and the other two lawmen were acquitted.

Mr. and Mrs. Frank Thurmond had decided on shifting their dwelling and destiny to Deming. The town had quieted down considerably. Late in 1882, Lottie—apparently by herself—traveled to El Paso, Texas.[37] The true objective of Lottie's trip is unknown. Since Christmas was nearing maybe a little holiday shopping was in order, or furniture was required for their house, or fixtures for their new enterprise, the "wet grocery" store. Idle speculation that while staying in El Paso she visited with one of the Wild West's most notorious madams, Alice "Big Alice" Abbott, will not even be broached. It is clearly known, however, that Big Alice was keeping a photographic scrapbook, one with an intriguing 19th-Century photograph captioned "the beauties of Griffin."[38] The length of Lottie's stay is indeterminate, but Frank was busy; busy with a startup:

> Frank Thurmond has purchased a wholesale liquor house in Deming and will dispose of the stock on hand and probably continue the business. Frank is well known in Silver City, and everybody will be glad to hear of his doing well.[39]

Frank either divested himself of the "wholesale liquor house" or converted it into a retail enterprise. For this financial plunge Mr. Thurmond was joined by a business partner, Mr. George Shepherd. Soon the Cabinet Saloon, with its billiard parlors and club rooms, was a fashionable Deming place to enjoy a game or a drink. The atmosphere was elevated after the acquisition of a "grand square piano" and the hiring of a Silver City lady, Mrs. Moehler, to play it.[40] With future prospects bright at Deming, Frank and Lottie disencumbered themselves of the Silver City town lots, selling them to E. G. Shields, pocketing a significant profit.[41] Turning that money around and diving into Deming real estate investments, Frank and Lottie purchased town lots from Edward M. Harner and his wife, Alma.[42] The Thurmonds were living the good life at Deming, yet for Frank it was the sporting life—danger could ignite at anytime! The story's finer points are lost to history, but the *Silver City Enterprise* reported:

> Frank Thurman [*sic*], one of the oldest and most popular sporting men of this section, and who was recently wounded by the accidental discharge of a revolver, will with Martin Sauber take charge of the Timmer House club rooms. Frank will visit Silver City in a few days when arrangements will be made to make these the handsomest club rooms in New Mexico.[43]

Frank Thurmond was dividing his time between Silver City and Deming. Frank's next round of serious business is a little better documented than his somehow being wounded by the no doubt stupid, but accidental discharge of his or someone else's weapon. As August 1884 Deming temperatures rose, so too did tempers. What started the friction is indeterminate; the fact that a "quarrelsome" Dan Baxter threw a billiard ball at Frank Thurmond is not. Previously mentioned was Frank's incapacity for submissively receiving an insult or attack without responding. Mr. Thurmond did not grab the ivory cue ball and hurl it back at Baxter. Frank whipped out a Bowie knife, and with deftness Mr. Baxter was "badly cut in the abdomen."[44] For nearly a week Dan Baxter lingered in excruciating agony; then he died.[45] For killing Mr. Baxter it is evident that Frank Thrumond did not suffer a severe criminal penalty. Grant County's Cost and Bond Book does reveal Frank's arrest for a charge of Assault With Intent To Commit Murder, but he was ultimately "No Billed" by a Grant County Grand Jury.[46] What is somewhat obscure is whether or not this legal action was for the Baxter case. If not, it might indicate Frank Thurmond had another critical altercation with someone else. He did have a lesser and short-lived row with Mr. Fred Baxter, presumably Dan Baxter's brother. Friends "intervened" and prevented a fatality. Frank Thurmond wasn't a man to trifle with.[47] He was, however, a good man to do business with:

> Harry Moore, well and most favorably known here in Silver City, has purchased the Shepherd interest in the "Cabinet" at Deming, and the firm will be hereafter known as Thurmond & Moore. We understand that Mr. Moore secured the interest, which includes very valuable real estate, at a bargain. Harry Moore is a popular man, and the house will lose nothing of prestige through his connection.[48]

By this time [1884] there was a narrow gauge railroad connecting Silver City and Deming. Travel between the two towns became but routine. Frank and Lottie could easily manage the short back and forth jaunts to Silver City, Frank's brother Jim was residing there; sibling Harrison had married and made himself a home in Deming.[49]

Brother Jim was making quite a favorable name for himself throughout the desert Southwest. He was continually buying and selling real estate, investing in various proprieties, usually an up and running saloon business. Jim was also continually setting up a faro bank at one place or another; Silver City's famous White House Saloon being one prime spot.[50] Jim Thurmond was a pure sporting man. As previously mentioned, he had taken up with a sporting gal, Kate W. Stewart, one of Silver City's better known madams. Jim Thurmond, at least on paper, sold Kate a spacious two-story house on Silver City's Texas Street which the local press would come to bitingly identify as the *mansion-de-joie*. Many citizens of Silver City knew her not as Kate Stewart but as Mrs. Kate Thrumond.[51] All knew how Kate filled her pocketbook:

> Miss Kate Stewart returned from Georgia on Monday, where she went to receive the benefits of a famous Golden Radicator [patent medicine] at present being

sold there. She brought two fair but frail New Orleans damsels with her.[52]

While Frank was operating the Cabinet Saloon at Deming, Jim Thurmond with a partner, Harry Newland, "one of the best known saloon men in the West," assumed charge of Silver City's Centennial. The newspaperman predicted that the boys would "run it in good style."[53] Later Mr. Newland sold his interest, and Jim Thurmond became the Centennial's sole proprietor.[54] While those two had been hashing out financial details, Frank and Lottie had made a pleasurable Thanksgiving Holiday train trip to Indian Territory[55] After the vacation Frank and Lottie returned to Deming. As the new year of 1887 dawned over southwestern New Mexico Territory big news was breaking about the Thurmond families. Frank's brother Harrison had purchased the Timmer House's bar at Silver City, and Mrs. Lottie Thurmond was pregnant, a fact that could not be and was not hidden from family and friends.[56]

Inadvertently or intentionally overlooked, secondary written mentions of Lottie Thurmond's pregnancy are—to this writer's knowledge—nonexistent. In the reasonably large body of work published about this darling of the Wild West's gaming circuit, she is never mentioned as being with child. Nauseating instances of morning sickness and insatiable food cravings at midnight are really not beneficial descriptions in trying to craft the mythological image of a gambling queen. Nevertheless it does put a human face on Lottie, one that all mothers can identify with:

A daughter has been born to Mr. and Mrs. Frank Thurmond, of Deming.[57]

For researching biographers or interested readers that is where the story of Lottie's 1887 motherhood starts and stops. Most likely circumstances surrounding the birth of a precious little girl were unfortunate. There are—to date—no other known mentions of there being any children born to Mrs. Lottie Thurmond. Sorrowfully it's but logical to presume that their daughter died, though no newspaper or other citations have been unearthed which provide categorical conformation. However the presumption is somewhat bolstered by factuality and logic. Several heretofore unpublished photographs of Lottie and Frank Thurmond were located in a museum's archival collection. The images were not catalogued under Frank's or Lottie's names, but rather in an extensive photographic compilation of their extremely close personal friends, the Lindauers, also of Deming. One of the photographs is that of a deceased infant; unidentified, devotedly dressed in an exquisite Christening gown and respectfully reposed on a religiously draped table. At the time it was not an uncommon practice to make such a photograph. Today it would be deemed an unacceptable and thoughtless custom. Paying a reverent touch of editorial discretion precludes publication of the photograph in this volume, although it is readily accessible. Mothers will understand.

Whether or not Lottie's pregnancy sparked Frank's interest in children's education is unknowable. The fact that the saloon man was instrumental in raising money to that end is indisputable. The *Deming Headlight* reported:

> In fact, the first school in Deming was of the subscription type. Mr. John Corbett and Mr. Thurmond collected a sum of $1,700 one afternoon in 1887 to pay for a two-room school which housed 60 pupils....[58]

Frank [L.] and Tom [R.] McLaury. These two brothers, along with Billy Clanton, were killed during the so-called O. K. Corral gunfight at Tombstone, Arizona. It was an event that triggered a series of revenge killings and murders, ultimately forcing Wyatt Earp and Doc Holliday, along with others, to flee Arizona Territory and surreptitiously run through Silver City, New Mexico. *Courtesy Robert G. McCubbin.*

Wyatt Earp [L.] and his younger brother Warren [R.]. Accompanied by other fugitives running ahead of Arizona arrest warrants for murder, Wyatt and Warren sneaked into Silver City and "took breakfast at the Broadway," Lottie's well advertised restaurant. *Courtesy Craig Fouts* [Wyatt Earp] *and Jim Earle* [Warren Earp].

Hudson's Hot Springs [Mimbres Hot Springs], a popular vacationing spot and one of the key hubs for getting into or out of Silver City, New Mexico Territory before a railroad came to that city during 1883. *Courtesy Silver City Museum.*

Louis H. Blonger, a Crime-Lord Supreme. *Courtesy Craig and Scott Johnson.*

Interior view of Deming's Cabinet Saloon, once owned by Frank Thurmond. *Courtesy Deming/Luna Mimbres Museum.*

1. John Hyatt 2. Albert Lindauer 7. "Little" Steve Birchfield
3. Jack Wright 4. Kelly Phillips 8. Hanie Barksdale 9. Dan Hathaway
5. Jimmy George 6. Jim Hyatt   Cabinet Bar   about 1907

Exterior view of the busy Cabinet Saloon at Deming. *Courtesy Deming/Luna Mimbres Museum.*

Endnotes Chapter 10

[1] *The New Southwest & Grant County Herald,* January 21, 1882.

[2] Ibid. January 14, 1882. This is the date that Lottie Thurmond's advertisements for the Broadway Restaurant began appearing in the newspaper; Terry Humble, Bayard, New Mexico to author, April 12, 2007.

[3] Ibid.

[4] Deed Book Number 4, Grant County, Silver City, New Mexico. Pages, 482, 483, and 512,: 482, Frank Thurmond, Lots 4, 5, & 6, Block 206; 483, Frank Thurmond lots 7, 8, 9, 10, 11, & 12, Block 207: 512, Frank and Charlotte J. Thurmond, Lots 9 & 11, Block 207. [It appears that lots 9 & 11 were sold to Edmund G. Shields, and then repurchased by Frank and Lottie].

[5] Grant County Deed Book Number 5. Page 367. William Malsted sold Frank Thurman [*sic*] one half interest of the Perservance Mine in the Lone Mountain Mining District for $2000. Grant County Deed Book Number 9. Page 535. Frank Thurmond sold one third interest in the Black Crook Mine, Central City Mining District, to Benjamin F. Glasswell for $500.

[6] *Southwest Sentinel,* March 25, 1882. "Two brothers of Frank Thurmond arrived from Texas last week."

[7] *Silver City Enterprise,* January 11, 1884. "Jim Thurmond and Ed Preston have purchased the Oriental Saloon of Speck & Bagsby at Tombstone."

[8] Ibid. August 27, 1909. This article—a dispatch from the *Douglas Daily International*—specifically details a poker game that had taken place at Tombstone's Crystal Palace during the 1880s. The players were George Bell, Jim Thurmond, "Patsy" Thornton, and Johnny Speck.

[9] *Southwest Sentinel,* November 28, 1883.

[10] Tefertiller, *Wyatt Earp: The Life Behind The Legend.* "With one shotgun blast in a train yard, the once judicious and temperate lawman had turned killer. By Wyatt Earp's own admission, he shot a man begging for his life. The cowtown marshal who took pride in avoiding bloodshed had become what he once despised: a life-taker. He had crossed his own boundaries of decency, and he seemed to do so with a sense of pride." 227; Alexander, *Desert Desperadoes: The Banditti of Southwestern New Mexico.* "There was not then, nor is there now, any attempt at labeling the [Stilwell] killing as anything other than what it actually was: a calculatingly cold-blooded homicide." 187; Tanner, *Doc Holliday: A Family Portrait.* "Though Wyatt, Doc, and the other posse members may have been acting within the law, they did stretch legality to its limit and possibly beyond. Wyatt never denied being on the revenge trail and savoring it." 178; Roberts, *Doc Holliday: The Life And Legend.* "Doc, Warren, Sherman, and Creek caught up to Wyatt about then, and a volley of gunfire followed, riddling the body of the fallen Stilwell…Stilwell's body was proof enough that Wyatt had never intended to arrest him." 246-247.

[11] Wyatt Earp, And Others, [John Richard Stephens, ed.] *Wyatt Earp Speaks.* Quoting an article in a March 1882 edition of the *Arizona Star.* "If one twentieth part of what is said of them [the Earps] is true, they are certainly no desireable [*sic*] acquisition to any community. They are a roving band; their path is strewn with blood. Strange as it may seem, when they halt in a settlement, stage robberies follow and human life ceased to be sacred." 12.

[12] *Deming Headlight,* March 25, 1882. Frank Stilwell was gunned down at Tucson on March 20, 1882.

[13] John Boessenecker, "Lawman Bob Paul's Doc and Wyatt Connection." *Wild West.* August 2003. "Also that Deputy Sheriff Dan Tucker, at Deming, had agreed to meet me in New Mexico with a strong guard to travel as far in my [Paul's] company as I desired, should I think additional guard necessary." 45.

[14] Harry Sinclair Drago, *The Legend Makers: Tales Of The Old-Time Peace officers And Desperadoes Of The Frontier.* "Tombstone stood divided, as it had never been before." 135.

[15] Thrapp, *Encyclopedia of Frontier Biography.* Volume III. 1443.

[16] *The New Southwest & Grant County Herald,* April 22, 1882; Tanner, *Doc Holliday: A Family Portrait.* "....Doc, the Earps, and the rest of their group surreptitiously arrived in Silver City, New Mexico Territory. They found lodging in a private dwelling. Their arrival in New Mexico was not known to the public until well after their departure...." 183.

[17] The arrival of Wyatt Earp and Doc Holliday at Silver City during April 1882, is abundantly bracketed by Lottie Thurmond's newspapers ads for the Broadway Restaurant. She owned the business prior to their arrival and after their departure; Terry Humble, Bayard, New Mexico to author, October 25, 2005.

[18] Roberts, *Doc Holliday: The Life And Legend.* 268.

[19] Interview with Bob Alexander, author of *Sheriff Harvey Whitehill: Silver City Stalwart.* Mr. Alexander who has written the only full-length—birth to death—biography of Sheriff Whitehill advised that during the course of his research he failed to uncover any data whatsoever that would support such an assertion. In fact, according to Mr. Alexander, primary source material in the form of interviews with Sheriff Whitehill's children would seems to refute any favorable relationship between their father and Wyatt Earp. See, Pioneer Foundation Interview, Number 504, Wayne and Mary Whitehill to Lou Blachly. Although an omission is not necessarily conclusive, during the interview the subject of Wyatt Earp claiming to have killed Curly Bill was discussed, because as a boy Wayne Whitehill had personally met the notorious outlaws Curly Bill and Six-Shooter Smith. Wayne, who would have been ten years old at the time, nor his siblings ever mentioned Wyatt Earp and fellow fugitives spending the night at their residence or at the Grant County Jail during their flight from Arizona. The Whitehill children, as adults, were frequently interviewed by those interested in preserving oral histories and/or journalists seeking facts for their writing projects. Interestingly in response to the question about Earp killing Curly Bill, Wayne Whitehill replied to Lou Blachly: "No, I don't think so. I've read all those tales and things but I don't think Earp ever killed him." Interviews with other children of Sheriff Whitehill—to Mr. Alexander's knowledge—fail to make mention of Wyatt Earp ever spending the night at their house, though they were of an age to be living at home when the alleged sleep-over occurred.

[20] Berry & Russell: *Built to Last: An Architectural History of Silver City.* 32; Pioneer Foundation Interview, Number 112, L. Frank Burris to Lou Blachly. Burris confirms that Kate Stewart was operating a "whorehouse."

[21] Roberts, *Doc Holliday: The Life And Legend.* 268.

[22] That the telegraph was employed as a crime fighting tool is well recognized. Specifically for this case, after Earp and Holliday were located in Colorado, Pima County Bob Paul commented: "...that I had reliable men at Willcox, Bowie, and Deming who were to notify me by telegraph of any cowboy demonstration at those places, and posses would be at those points to render assistance in case of an attack." See. Boessenecker, "Lawman Bob Paul's Doc and Wyatt Connection." 45.

[23] Alexander, *Desert Desperadoes: The Banditti of Southwestern New Mexico.* 190.

[24] *The New Southwest & Grant County Herald,* April 22, 1882.

[25] Telephone interview with authority George Hackler, Las Cruces, New Mexico, author of *The Butterfield Trail In New Mexico*, on August 27, 2007; Robert Julyan, *The Place Names Of New Mexico*. "This former trading site and still-active RR loading point originally was called *Porter Station*, for reasons unknown, then *Cummings*, for *Fort Cummings* nearby." 132; T. M. Pearce, *New Mexico Place Names: A Geographical Dictionary*. "Florida....14 miles NE of Deming. Established 1881 when AT&SF RR was built." 57; Author Bob Alexander who has written several books detailing outlaw/lawman history as it relates to southwestern New Mexico Territory has in the past written that the Earp party during their departure from Silver City, first went to Fort Cummings, and then caught a northbound train at Nutt Station. After learning of the detailed and informative data provided by Mr. Hackler, Mr. Alexander acknowledges he was in error, and now concurs that it is most likely that Earp and Holliday boarded the Albuquerque train at Florida Station.

[26] Leon Claire Metz, *The Encyclopedia Of Lawmen, Outlaws, and Gunfighters*. 251.

[27] Chuck Hornung and Gary Roberts, "The Split: Did Doc & Wyatt Split Because Of A Racial Slur?" *True West*. December 2001. 58-61; Roberts, *Doc Holliday: The Life And Legend*. 270; Ed Bartholomew, *Wyatt Earp: The Man & The Myth*. "There [Albuquerque] Sam Blonger ruled as City Marshal of New Town, with his brother Lou helping, and who was later to be the super conman, the Mr. Big of vice in Denver for many years...." 325.

[28] Larry D. Ball, *Desert Lawmen: The High Sheriffs Of New Mexico And Arizona, 1846-1912*. 58.

[29] Philip S. Van Cise, *Fighting the Underworld*. "He [Lou Blonger] first appeared in Denver in 1880 with his brother Sam as a bartender, then became the proprietor of a saloon with all the early-day accessories of a dance-hall and the necessary girl attendants, roulette wheels and all kinds of gambling. As society became more respectable in the West, the girls were first eliminated, then gambling, until only the saloon was left." 3-12; DeArment, *Knights Of The Green Cloth: The Saga of the Frontier Gamblers*."....a leading member of the Lou Blonger bunco gang in Denver." 362. "Thwarted in his bid to move back into Denver by the powerful Blonger forces in 1896, Soapy Smith gathered around him a coterie of loyal followers and left town for the last time." 381-382.

[30] Ibid. 346-347.

[31] Scott Johnson to author, July 29, 2005. Craig Johnson to author, March 7, 2006. The leading authorities on Lou Blonger and his brother Sam are the Johnson brothers. Their valuable research work in the field is extensive and, commendably, their devotion to sharing those findings with fellow writers or other interested parties is outstanding. Intriguingly several of Lou Blonger's obituaries are posted on the Johnson brothers' website, BlongerBros.com. A notice from the *Denver Post*, April 21, 1924, asserts that in his early years Lou Blonger was a peace officer at San Angelo, Texas. The *Denver Times*, April 22, 1924, awards Lou Blonger the distinction of being "sheriff of a Texas county." Certainly, since Lottie Thompkins was at San Angela [San Angelo] gambling, this morsel of news is fascinating. Unfortunately, Scott Johnson advised on May 13, 2007, that they have not been able to confirm that Lou Blonger was a peace officer anywhere in Texas, at anytime. Nor has the author; Tise, *Texas County Sheriffs* has no listing for any person identified as Blonger. Scott Johnson surmises that the confusions arises from Lou Blonger sometimes filling in for his brother Sam as town marshal in New Mexico Territory, a fact adequately confirmed by primary source review.

[32] James A. McKenna, *Black Range Tales*. 132.

[33] *New Southwest & Grant County Herald*, June 10, 1882; July 8, 1882; October 7, 1882.

[34] Alexander, *Dangerous Dan Tucker: New Mexico's Deadly Lawman.* 98-104. *New Southwest & Grant County Herald,* August 26, 1882.

[35] *Silver City Enterprise,* December 14, 1882.

[36] DeArment, "Deadly Deputy." "....Burns entered the Centennial and went in the back gaming room presided over by house gambler Frank Thurmond." 18; Alexander, *Dangerous Dan Tucker: New Mexico's Deadly Lawman.* 102.

[37] *New Southwest & Grant County Herald,* December 9, 1882. "Mrs. Lottie Thurman [*sic*] has gone to El Paso."

[38] Photograph, included in this text, courtesy Robert G. "Bob" McCubbin. Mr. McCubbin, a renowned collector of rare books and documents purchased Alice Abbott's photographic scrapbook. For biographical information about Alice Abbott the reader is referred to Frost's *The Gentlemen's Club: The Story of Prostitution In El Paso;* Bob Boze Bell, "Clash Of The Madams: Alice Abbott Vs. Etta Clark." *True West,* July 2003. 48-51.

[39] *Silver City Enterprise,* January 11, 1883.

[40] *The Deming Tribune & Lake Valley Herald,* March 6, 1884; *Southwest Sentinel,* September 1, 1883.

[41] Grant County Deed Book, Number 4. Page 607.

[42] Abstract of Title, three lots in Deming Townsite. August 16, 1884. Ed. M. Harner and Alma E. Harner, his wife, to Frank Thurmond and Charlotte J. Thurmond, his wife; Newspaper mentions of Frank Thurmond's real estate transactions are also numerous. "Frank Thurmond to Conway & Posey, lots No. 10, 12, 14, and 16 in block No. 15, price $50." *Southwest Sentinel,* September 15, 1885.

[43] *Silver City Enterprise,* July 20, 1883.

[44] Ibid. August 22, 1884.

[45] Ibid. August 29, 1884; *Southwest Sentinel,* August 30, 1884.

[46] Grant County Cost and Bond Book. Cause Number 1661. *The Territory vs. Frank Thurmond.* Assault With Intent to Commit Murder.

[47] *Silver City Enterprise,* October 10, 1884.

[48] Ibid. September 27, 1884.

[49] Ibid. September 10, 1886. "Mr. and Mrs. Harrison Thurmond, of Deming, were here Monday. They will soon remove to Silver City."

[50] Ibid. January 11, 1884. "Jim Thurmond and Ed Preston have purchased the Oriental Saloon of Speck & Bagsby at Tombstone." March 22, 1885, "James Thurmond and John McDonald have opened a faro bank in the White House Saloon."

[51] Ibid. November 16, 1883. "J. C. Thurmond has sold the house on Texas street, below Spring, to Kate Stewart." Berry & Russell, *Built to Last: An Architectural History of Silver City, New Mexico.* 32.

[52] Ibid. January 23, 1885.

[53] Ibid. October 29, 1886; December 3, 1886. "The Centennial, which is now under the management of Colonel Harry Newland, a famous mixer known all over the west, and Jim Thurmond, is growing in popularity, and is now a great place of resort. Everybody knows Harry and Jim, and their methods of conducting such a place is in first-class style."

[54] Ibid. December, 10, 1886.

[55] Ibid. November 26, 1886.

[56] Ibid. January 21, 1887; May 13, 1887.

[57] Ibid. May 13, 1887.

[58] *Deming Headlight,* March 5, 1881.

Chapter 11

"They Went Down the Line"

Eighteen-hundred and eighty-seven was not panning out to be a good year for the Thurmonds. Fortunately they were in a financial position to employ a "colored cook." Unfortunately the domestic helpmate, after putting some coal oil in the stove to start a fire, left the kitchen unattended and stepped outside. She had forgotten to place the iron lids on the stove's topside. Flames blazed through the apertures as high as the ceiling. The room was fast engulfed in flames. Soon the whole house was a raging inferno. Luckily there were no injuries. Frank was stunned when he returned from the trip to Lake Valley; finding that his Pine Street residence, the shade fencing and even the windmill and water tank had been destroyed by fire. The Deming dwelling and furnishing were insured for $3000, but the Thurmond's loss doubled that figure.[1] While the house fire may have been snuffed out, another one was not. The mining town of Kingston was scorching hot—economically. Frank and Lottie took notice.

Following the 1887 Christmas holidays, and an exploratory look at Chloride, New Mexico Territory, Frank and Lottie relocated to Kingston. Pleasantly situated in Sierra County nine miles west of Hillsboro in the Black Range's eastern foothills, Kingston was a booming silver camp. Financial backers behind the Kingston Townsite Company had laid out a town, naming it after the well-known Iron King Mine.[2] No doubt the Thurmonds, at least Frank, were already well acquainted with Kingston. The Thurmond brothers were renowned gamblers throughout the Southwest and part of Frank's tour at Kingston is more than satisfactorily documented by both primary and secondary sources. James A. McKenna, a man who was there at the time, as well as the author of *Black Range Tales*, mentions that the Thurmond boys were "big time gamblers" at Kingston.[3] He remarked that Lou Blonger was there, too. *If true*, which lends credit to Mr. Blonger's pension claim that he stayed with Mr. Thurmond at Kingston, it is a black mark on Frank's and Lottie's names. Any linkage to Mr. Lou Blonger is not admirable. Lou was crooked, even if he lived behind the facade of being a gambler and promoter running honest games. Frank was, too, a big time gambler on another front; maintaining heavy financial investments in various southwestern New Mexico Territory mines, such as the Jay Bird in the vicinity of Cooke's Peak, north of Deming.[4]

By the time Frank and Lottie made their appearance at Kingston as permanent residents the town had seen its opening boom. There was yet, however, plenty of cash to claim. Demographics at Kingston should not come as a surprise. It was a rip-roaring mining town, predominantly inhabited by an influx of single men. Of course, close on the miners' heels were the purveyors of pleasure; the sporting men, saloon operators, and shady ladies. One of those Kingston working-girls was madam Kate Stewart, Jim Thurmond's paramour. Exactly just whom they worked for is muddled, but other prostitutes plying their trade of pleasure at Kingston were Lousy Louise, Old Hat, Deaf Carrie, Jew-etta, Big Jennie, Scotty, and Bloody Mary.[5] During Kingston's earliest days it was characterized as a "fun-loving, fast-drinking, and hard-working" mining town.[6]

During a smallpox epidemic, two males volunteered as nurses; their payment a jug of whiskey per day—each. Needless to say the fellows stayed drunk. Soon they were replaced by three gals from the *demimonde* who had volunteered their services to Dr. Guthrie, the only physician in town.[7] Anecdotally it is asserted that during Kingston's infancy, when the town was but a tent city, overnight guests at the scarce places offering a bunk had a preference. The "lower berths were preferred to the upper ones because stray bullets from the nearby saloons sometimes ripped through the canvas walls."[8] At the apex of Kingston's boom the town could boast of twenty-two saloons. One of those was The Monarch, owned by Frank and Lottie Thurmond.[9]

The fact that Lottie had accompanied Frank to Kingston has been clearly established. The exact role she played while there, other than Frank's devoted wife, has not been creditably documented. Whereas Lottie's naughty behavior has been more or less examined at San Antonio, San Angela, Jacksboro, The Flat, Brackettville, and to a lesser extent in Grant County, her sojourn to Kingston is not as transparent. It is not irrational to believe that while Frank may have earned a solid income from their saloon business and in the Kingston gambling halls, Lottie—as she had done at Silver City—was gradually weaning herself from society's undesirable element.

Another Kingston girl was also undergoing the transition. Much like Lottie, this *desmoiselle* had a dreamy, but self-manufactured past. For whatever the reason she, too, had fallen into, been halfheartedly pushed into, or willingly jumped onto the bandwagon leading to the Western frontier's bagnois and beer halls. Her legitimate birth name was Sarah Jane Creech. Old West history knows her best, after she married local stagecoach operator James W. Orchard, as Sadie Orchard.[10] By design Sadie's upbringing and pre-New Mexico Statehood life was a mysterious maize of "deliberate misrepresentations and imaginative role playing."[11] And just like Lottie, sometimes Sadie could spew choice curse words and flaunt a streak of pure naughtiness. By one account, after being spurned by a lover, Sadie went to the man's cabin and purposefully "urinated upon his door step."[12] During another raunchy episode, on a dare, Sadie stripped off her clothing, jumped onto an equine—literally bareback while horseback—and brazenly rode though the town wearing only her birthday suit.[13] Sadie was always cheerful and full of life which made her an undeniable frolicking favorite with the fellows. Sadie didn't seem to have a prejudiced bone in her body, she "took on nearly every man in every camp." In the cumulative that was quite a considerable number of carnal customers. Such iniquitous numeric action allowed Sadie to amass a small fortune.[14] Working her way up the career ladder and breaking the glass ceiling, Sadie assumed the role of a colorful frontier madam, establishing her very own bordello on—of all places—Kingston's Virtue Avenue.[15] Later, while still maintaining the brothel business at Kingston, with an entrepreneurial spirit Sadie opened a second palace of pleasure at nearby Hillsboro.[16] Of course the region's rich history would have to mark Sadie Orchard down as a first-rate whore, but over time she did progress into more traditionally legitimate enterprises like the stagecoach business, as well as becoming a prominent hotel and restaurant proprietor. Her scorecard of sexually satisfied men may be immeasurable, but so are her charitable acts of kindness and philanthropy.[17] Mrs. Lottie Thurmond and Mrs. Sadie Orchard had very much in common: Both were working-gals with a checkered past. Both desperately sought to shed that wicked label and earn acceptance as respectable and upright ladies. In that regard, in the end, they were jubilant winners. Addressing Lottie's newfound prominence an editor for the *Deming Headlight* reported:

> Mr. and Mrs. Frank Thurmond came down from Kingston Wednesday. The ladies of the Social Circle gave their old companion a warm welcome and have induced her to extend her visit for some time, and [she] is stopping with Mrs. Henry Holgate. Mr. Thurmond left for El Paso Wednesday evening.[18]

Lottie's extended visit with the influential ladies of Deming apparently lasted throughout the Thanksgiving Holiday season of 1888. Nostalgia is sometimes the handmaiden for change, and as the Christmas Holidays drew near the Thurmonds were contemplating the prospects of relocating to Deming.

The Thurmonds' plans were no secret. The *Deming Headlight's* editor, even before New Year's Day of 1889, was predicting with high probability that the popular couple would return to the mushrooming municipality. Because, as the full of pride newspaperman beamed: "Like all pioneers of Deming, he [and she] can't stay away, and has [have] unbounded faith in the outlook of this section of New Mexico."[19] The frontier journalist had no crystal ball—but he was right! Still remaining heavily invested in the New Mexico Territory mining business, Frank and Lottie returned to Deming and did what they knew best, opened a saloon. Taking on a new business partner, O. P. Boger, Frank laid plans for welcoming local fellows to The Turf Saloon at Deming. By Spring the establishment was up and running. Since the boys were acknowledged experts at the craft, their efforts were lauded in the local newspaper: "Thurmond and Boger are two of the best known saloon men in Southern New Mexico, whose reputation is a guarantee of good order and fair treatment, in their house. They will keep a fist-class place of resort in every particular, and invite their friends and the public to call on them."[20] Evidently there was a trendy demand for St. Louis keg beer [Budwiser], "the best in the market." Patrons could partake of such a liquid treat at The Turf.[21] Paying for an advertisement in the Deming paper Mr. Thurmond and Mr. Boger "invited comparison," claiming that The Turf strictly maintained only the best brands of imported and domestic wines, liquors and cigars. The same ad mentions The Turf's "Club Rooms," which were "in charge of men of experience" and that the proprietors guaranteed that customers would be treated uniformly fair and courteously.[22] The sporting fellows in charge of those club rooms were not named, and that is history's loss.

By this time Lottie had completely remolded herself. She was no longer an active participant in the sporting life. Unlike so very many of the Southwest's piteously unfortunate prostitutes, Lottie, after her marriage to Frank, had seen the practical wisdom in disassociating herself from a life of sleaze and sin. It was but a troubled pathway leading to nowhere. For a man the saloon and/or gambling business was an acceptable vocation, but not for a lady. If anything in the world mattered to Lottie Thurmond it was being seen—and accepted—as a lady. At Deming her idyllic dream came true. Perchance a touch of Divine intervention played a part, too? Two oldtime buffalo hunters said so. Sam Baldwin noted:

> She got in with Frank Thurman [*sic*], who was a gambler. I knew him well, a fine fellow. Whether they were married then or not, I don't know. They had moved up to Deming. There came on that big revival there, and all the whole bunch, all those gamblers—Old Dick Hudson that didn't know anything but playing poker, and Thruman, and Lottie Deeno [*sic*]—all joined the church. They went down the line, and they staid with their religion, and she died a great church worker. You can ask any of them. They had the highest respect for her there at Deming. I don't know who the

preacher was at that revival. I was away at the time, had
gone to the state of Washington.[23]

Mr. J. Wright Mooar also knew Lottie from her days at Fort Griffin.
Following an early 20th-Century speech to the West Texas Historical
Association, Mooar matter-of-factly mentioned to an inquiring
journalist that he had inadvertently bumped into the graying middle-
aged Gambling Queen of Hearts at El Paso during the early 1890s and
learned during their personal conversation that

> She had quit gambling, had married a New Mexico
> ranchman, joined the church, and had settled down to a
> peaceful life.[24]

Misinformed revisionists sometimes indulge in fanciful efforts to
discount the fact that Fort Griffin's and Brackettville's Lottie Deno and
Mrs. Frank Thurmond were one in the same person. Oldtimers' lucid
remembrances, the Texas criminal and civil courts' records, coupled with
primary source New Mexico Territory marriage records forestall
crediting that fantasy with plausibility. Evidence to the contrary is more
than a little overwhelming. Lottie Thurmond couldn't hide her past
from those who knew her as Lottie Deno, but she did not have to
divulge that name and her tawdry Texas history to new friends at
Deming.

Mrs. Lottie Thurmond became a church going lady. To mistrust her
motivation or to even suggest such is petty. The religious reformation
may have been righteous. The fact that Lottie joined the church is
irrefutable. Mr. Thurmond had mining interest demanding his time.
Frank also enjoyed socializing with "Old Dick Hudson," a prominent
personality throughout the frontier era of southwestern New Mexico
Territory and Grant County's first sheriff. The Hudsons and the
Thurmonds were very well and favorably acquainted.[25] In fact, Olive
Priscilla Whitehill, a daughter of Grant County Sheriff Harvey Howard
Whitehill, wrote a brief history of Deming's St. Luke's Episcopal
Church, a short sketch specifically mentioning Mrs. Lottie Thurmond.
According to Ms Whitehill, Lottie, along with Mrs. George Shepard
[Shepherd], were the two ladies responsible for starting the church's very
first Sunday school. Interestingly they were ably assisted in their efforts
by none other than Dick Hudson's wife, Mary.[26] Another of those
oldtimers drew considerable attention from the press. Dan Tucker had
since moved to southern California, but returned to southwestern New
Mexico Territory for a visit. His appearance was noted in Silver City
and Deming newspapers, as well as Lordsburg's *Western Liberal.*

....During the early days in Grant county, when it was in the transition state, when the rustlers and bad men were giving way to the peaceable citizens, Dan Tucker and his shotgun were two of the greatest civilizers in the county. Dan had a way when he had a warrant for a bad man of killing the man and then reading the warrant....[27]

Dan Tucker and Frank Thurmond were mortals from the same mold. The depths or shallowness of Frank's actual religious beliefs are uncertain. He wasn't a church going man. However, his general outlook on everyday life was uncomplicated. Black and white were not indistinct colors. Mr. Thurmond wronged no man and thought no man should wrong him. It was as simple as that! A particular scenario is illustrative. Amid having his money spread around in various financial ventures, Frank had $1,100 on deposit with the local Deming bank. During a routine audit the bank examiner noticed a particularly damaged $100 bill. Marred money was not remarkable. Until? The very next day, after making a 50 mile train trip to Silver City, the bank examiner found that identical $100 note in the account drawer of another bank; one owned by the very same fellow that held proprietary responsibility for the depository at Deming. The implication was clear. While the auditor had slept, someone had moved all the cash from the Deming bank to the Silver City bank, a covert attempt to make the banks seem solvent, which they weren't. Under orders the banks were closed, all accounts frozen—pending an investigation. Uproarious citizens at Silver City and Deming were outraged. At both towns people were clamoring for action. Frank Thurmond took it! Exactly how he gained entry is unclear, but once inside the Deming bank Frank firmly confronted the clerk, a Mr. Seibold. Mr. Thurmond presented his bank book and demanded his $1,100. Mr. Seibold protested, confidently saying that until the bank examiner released a hold on sequestered funds no money was to change hands. Frank didn't wring his hands in despair, but filled one with a .41 caliber revolver. His reasoning was basic: The bank held his money and he wanted it, not one cent more, nor one cent less. The "dangerous glint" in Frank's eyes and the intimidating presentation of a Colt handgun "convinced the cashier that Thurmond meant business." The bank teller's calculation was painless and easily reached; he handed over $1,100, not one cent more, nor one cent less. Frank pocketed his cash, counting on common sense to prevail. Although Mr. Thurmond was arrested, the criminal case was dismissed after a sensible judge made the determination that a man should not be charged, nor much less could he be convicted of "stealing what rightfully belonged to him," in the first place.[28] Frank Thurmond's life was an open book, that of his wife's

wasn't. Nonetheless, as one turn-of-the-century novelist supposed, both
were book material.

When or just how Alfred Henry Lewis, sometimes using the pen-
name Dan Quin, became acquainted with Frank or Lottie is elusive. A
member of the bar in Ohio and a former prosecuting attorney, Alfred
Henry Lewis was by proclivity a wanderer; having also tasted the
experiences of being a working cowboy, freighter and stagecoach driver
in the Kansas cow towns and on the frontiers of Texas and New
Mexico. However, his real penchant was for journalism.[29] Although it
falls into the realm of but guesswork, the most likely scenario which
introduces the future nationally known writer and the regionally known
faro dealing and poker playing couple—Frank and Lottie—as being
personally acquainted was somewhere, at sometime, along the gaming
circuit in frontier Texas. They were friends, that is indisputable.

While Frank and Lottie Thurmond were pleasantly whiling away
their days at Deming, a raging popularity for all things "Western" was
emerging back "East." Thrilling accounts of hairbreadth escapes from
stalking mountain lions, painted Indians marauding and murdering,
while the gunfighting champions bravely defended besieged frontier
towns from despicable outlaws were captivating stories. Especially for
those readers snug and comfy, safely removed from harm's way. The
20th-Century's moralistic compass had not been set with the future's
niggling social questions; no diktat of political correctness. Measuring
how much astute writer Archibald Clavering Gunter influenced Alfred
Henry Lewis as to the journalistic richness found by fictionalizing real
characters from southwestern New Mexico Territory is blurred. It is
plain that Mr. Gunter had sensibly recognized the possibilities. He knew
where to look. It has been written that, "Few men could lay legitimate
claim to recognition through the medium of contemporary fiction."[30]
During 1890 Mr. Gunter's *Miss Nobody of Nowhere* was released. The
book, an adventurous novel with a love story entwined within, was
geographically set in charming, but yet untamed Silver City. The
imaginary sheriff of the wild New Mexico Territory county was Mr.
Breckenridge "Brick" Garvey, a fictionalized character based in large part
on the life of frontier lawman Harvey Howard Whitehill. There was not
then, nor is there any doubt now, that the very real Mr. Whitehill and
the made-up Mr. Gavey were coequals:

> The people of the West owe Mr. Gunter a debt for
> painting the Indian question in a manner so true and
> accurate, and introducing it into a book which will be
> widely read by the class of people whom Sheriff Garvey
> calls the "cussed philanthropodists." If the book had
> been published last summer and Sheriff Harvey

Whitehill had circulated about fifteen hundred of them through the country, he would have been re-nominated and reelected without a struggle.[31]

Fashioning stories about the wild and woolly west were in vogue. Theodore Roosevelt, who personally knew Alfred Henry Lewis and his younger brother William, had a not subtle suggestion. Mr. Roosevelt encouraged Lewis, who had been turning out human interest newspaper articles for the *Kansas City Times* and the *Kansas City Star*, to continue writing of the Old West. Roosevelt would edit the material, pledging that the noted artist Frederick Remington could be easily induced to supply a Western book's illustrations.[32] The added assertion that William Randolph Hearst cheered Lewis' literary efforts and commissioned the work is not disputed.[33] Alfred Henry Lewis already had two folks in mind to serve as prototypical Western characters. Lewis traveled to Deming. Staying for awhile with his friends Frank and Lottie Thurmond, Mr. Lewis perfected the details of old stories and no doubt concocted recipes for a few fabricated ones. The writer, drawing from his personal experiences and the historical informants retelling of their familiarity with the cardsharps and card rooms and cutthroats was hard work, but an enjoyable and fruitful methodology. The finished product was fiction. Alfred Henry Lewis' imaginary Western characters of Cherokee Hall and the gorgeous Faro Nell in the *Wolfville* series, are, in fact, reincarnations of Mr. Frank Thurmond and his wife, the former Miss Lottie Deno, the Gambling Queen of Hearts.[34] Mr. Lewis nimbly blended a few imaginary place names within the broader context of references to real geographical landmarks. With undisguised mentions of such areas as the very prominent Cooke's Peak, the Florida Mountains, and Palomas [Mexico], thirty miles due south of Deming, there is little doubt that much of his *Wolfville* series takes place on southwestern New Mexico Territory's stage.[35] Publication and smart marketing of the *Wolfville* books propelled Alfred Henry Lewis "into national prominence."[36] Owen Wister in 1902 finished and had published his masterpiece, the *Virginian*. It was literally a book that "turned the American cowboy into a legendary hero."[37] Owen Wister, too, had shrewdly looked to southwestern New Mexico Territory for frontier fellows that would serve as believable models for fictionalized characters in that breakthrough Western novel. The fictionalized Trampas and the Virginian in the classic *Virginian* were, at least in part, based on the very living Dean Duke, an audaciously inclined Diamond A Ranch foreman. Wister seemed to genuinely idolize Duke: "I have never met a man so young who has passed through so many desperate chances."[38]

Previously it was mentioned that John Jacobs of Shackelford County, Texas, wrote about a poker game at Fort Griffin between Lottie Deno and Doc Holliday. During the bluffing contest two steely-eyed competitors seated themselves across from each other, all tell-tale sign drained from their expressionless faces. When the very last hand was played, Mr. Doc Holliday was minus about $3000 and Miss Lottie Deno was daydreaming about spending newfound money on the latest and fanciest Parisian petticoats and pretty dresses. Wild West buffs may find the episode slightly troublesome, a good-timing girl getting ahead of the gunfighting gambler. Acknowledging that a confessed alcoholic and consumptive dentist, one admittedly gone astray, might have actually been forced into forfeiting a pot is not unrealistic. Gambling is a game of chance! Lady Luck generously smiled on Lottie Deno that day. While Mr. Doc Holliday's exaggerated reputation is for the most part a 20th-Century creation, he certainly wasn't an unknown character on the western frontiers, chiefly among the sporting gentry and their stable of whores. By the time Alfred Henry Lewis was stopping over at Deming during 1896—staying with the Thurmonds—Doc Holliday had been dead a number of years, unable to confirm or refute a good story. So, whether or not Mr. Lewis, who wrote of the poker playing match between Faro Nell and Doc Holliday in his near classic 1902 *Wolfville Nights* made up the story from whole cloth or was the recipient of facts straight from the mouths of Frank and/or Lottie is unfathomable.[39]

It is not an enigma, however, that Frank and Lottie moved to a desert ranch near Cambray, twenty-odd miles east of Deming. There Frank added to his diverse investment portfolio by raising cattle.[40] According to several accounts Frank also maintained another ranching property south of Deming near the Florida Mountains. One of Frank's ranching partners in a few business deals was a noted cattleman from the Lone Star State, Simpson "Sim" Holstein. The Texan was an experienced old-time trail driver. Like Frank, Sim was tough-as-nails, having gunned down "desperado" Doughboy Taylor at Kerrville, Texas, during 1871.[41]

Founded during 1892 after the successful drilling of a much needed water well, the community of Cambray became a small railroad village and cattle shipping station. At its population height the little settlement could claim 200 residents. There was a general store, post office, harness shop, railroad and telegraph offices, as well as an extensive network of sturdy plank corrals adjacent to the railroad tracks.[42] Cambray folks were happy folks, evidenced by a snippet in the *Deming Graphic*:

> It is a level plain covered with native grass and very productive. The people are as fine a lot of neighbors as there are anywhere.[43]

There were no gambling halls or saloons or bawdy houses at Cambray. For that type entertainment, or to purchase more legitimate products or obtain the services of a doctor, lawyer, tailor or a preacher, it was but a short westbound train trip to Deming. Although the country surrounding Cambray was open-range—unfenced—when Lottie felt hemmed in she could and did make that quick hop to town for a shopping spree or a fun visit with friends:

> Mrs. Frank Thurmond is here from her new home at Chambray [sic], visiting her many friends. The lady is the guest of Mrs. W. H. Greer.[44]

And:

> Mrs. Frank Thurmond of Chambray [sic], who has been visiting in this city [Deming], took the first train home this week when she learned that Deming had been invaded by Ping Pong. Mrs. Thurmond has always been known as a lady of extraordinary good sense.[45]

Alfred Henry Lewis had good sense too! His writings of the Old West were proving to be a hot ticket to literary success. He returned to southwestern New Mexico Territory during 1901, but Deming and Cambray were no longer situated in Grant County. The territorial legislature had created Luna County, named after the area's most "dominant politician" Solomon Luna. A complete slate of new county officers had been installed by patronage appointments of the Governor, subject to election later.[46] Cipriano Baca, a well-known and well-liked fellow, already with law-enforcement experience in his repertoire was chosen as Luna County's first sheriff.[47] Lottie's husband had played a significant role in creation of the new county:

> Mr. Frank Thurmond, one of the principal mine owners in Cook's Peak, is in Santa Fe interviewing our legislators, and trying to convince them that the people of the proposed county of Florida [later Luna] are able and willing to assume the responsibilities of a separate county government.[48]

Once again author Lewis stayed with Frank and Lottie, this time at the ranch, rekindling the friendship and scavenging delicious tidbits of true-to-life Western lore for his continuing *Wolfville* series.[49] Thinly veiling genuineness with iconic but fictionalized characters and places, and then adding in the melodramatic dialogue, Alfred Henry Lewis demonstrated a master's touch at blending illusory notions with nonfiction. Remembering that Frank Thurmond really had knifed and killed Dan Baxter in Deming during an 1884 saloon squabble is relevant to understanding Mr. Lewis' technique. In the novel *Wolfville*, Cherokee Hall [Frank Thurmond] runs afoul of a mean and terribly nasty fellow nicknamed the Stingin' Lizard. The card game turns sour and

> As the Lizard makes his bluff his hand goes to his artillery like a flash.
> The Lizard's some quick, but Cherokee's too soon for him. With the first move of the Lizard's hand, he searches out a bowie from som'ers back of his neck. I'm some employed placin' myse'f at the time, an' don't decern it none till Cherokee brings it over his shoulder like a stream of white light.
> It's shore great knife-work. Cherokee gives the Lizard aige an p'int, an' all in one motion. Before the Lizard more'n lifts his weepon, Cherokee half slashes his gun-hand off at the wrist; an' then, jest as the Lizard begins to wonder at it, he gets the nine-inch blade plumb through his neck. He's let out right thar.[50]

Frank Thurmond really did kill Dan Baxter! *Wolfville's* Cherokee Hall really didn't kill the Stingin' Lizard! It has been repetitively alleged, but certainly never ever even close to proven, that Doc Holliday while gambling at The Flat killed a scalawag named Ed Bailey with a knife deftly drawn. *Wolfville* was first published in 1897, long before there was any 20th-Century fascination with Mr. Holliday or Mr. Earp. The journalistically hewed skewering of Ed Bailey "just below the brisket" was claimed by Wyatt for an 1896 edition of the *San Francisco Examiner*.[51] Alfred Henry Lewis, then, had two choices to dramatize; one watertight with contemporary evidence, the other as of yet confirmed, contemporaneously or otherwise.[52] Such conundrums made not a difference to Mr. Dan Baxter—or the Stingin' Lizard.

Whereas a fictionalized fellow named Cherokee Hall was making a name for himself in Western novels overstuffed with clichéd dialogue, Mr. Frank Thrumond was recurrently buying and selling mining proprieties. Going over Luna County courthouse records reveals Frank's association with such mines as The Grant, The Black Jack, The Cracker Jack, The Independence, The Crawford, The Golconda, The Monarch, The Fraction, The Song Bird, The Zulu, The Sultan, The Homestead, The Pole Star, The Flat Foot, The Village Smith, and with uninspiring enthusiasm for naming any more mines, The October, The November, and The December.[53] Although she was an equal partner with Frank in the numerous mining claims, Lottie and several of her girlfriends also filed as sole owners on a mine of their very own, The Lucky Joe, located south of Deming in the Tres Hermanas Mining District.[54]

One of those girl mining partners in The Lucky Joe would also wind up playing a significant role in Lottie's story. Why she managed a relocation to Deming from Texas is hazy, but Alle Delle Lowe did just that. Miss Lowe, a Tennesseean by birth and a Mississippiean by parental demand, had come to Deming. Alle Delle Lowe was employed by the school system, having already demonstrated competency as a Spanish teacher in the Lone Star State.[55] Specifics as to how their bond was forged is ambiguous, but unarguably nineteen year-old Alle and Lottie Thurmond were personally close, either by distant blood kinship, a marriage partners' link, or proximity. Not too soon after arriving in southwestern New Mexico Territory, Miss Alle Delle Lowe cascaded head-over-heels in love with an older man. A widower in his late thirties, Pennsylvania born Henry McClure "H. M." Stecker was the freight inspector at Deming for both the Santa Fe and Southern Pacific railroads.[56] Like Frank Thurmond, H. M. Stecker was a member in good stead with the Deming chapter of the Knights of Pythais. Cupid's arrow flew straight and true, pinning H. M. and Alle Delle's hearts together, as evidenced by their Luna County *Certificate of Marriage*.[57] The Thurmonds and the Steckers lives were tightly locked; firmly standing one for the other.

Mrs. Frank Thurmond [Lottie Deno] back row left, with some of her closest friends, the Sigmund Lindeaur family. *Courtesy Deming/Luna Mimbres Museum.*

Mrs. Frank Thurmond [Lottie Deno] far right in front of her Deming residence with unidentified couple. *Courtesy Deming/Luna Mimbres Museum.*

Kingston, New Mexico Territory during the 1880s, when Frank and Lottie were there as proprietors of the Monarch Saloon. *Courtesy Deming/Luna Mimbres Museum.*

Another view of early day Kingston, New Mexico Territory. *Courtesy Deming/Luna Mimbres Museum.*

Mrs. Frank Thurmond [Lottie Deno] center, during a delightful outing on the outskirts of Kingston, New Mexico Territory. *Courtesy Patrick Tidmore.*

Richard "Dick" Hudson the first sheriff of Grant County, New Mexico Territory and the owner of the legendary Hudson's Hot Springs north of Deming. According to Mr. Sam Baldwin, Mr. Hudson "went down the line" during a Deming revival, joining the church, as did Mrs. Lottie Thurmond. *Courtesy Mark Erickson.*

Five of Harvey Whitehill's daughters. Standing L. to. R: Olive Priscilla [who wrote a brief history of Deming's St. Lukes Episcopal Church], Carolyn "Carrie," and Emma Sarah. Seated from L. to R: Mary [Whitehill] Hudson [Mrs. Dick Hudson] and Harriet Jeanette. These girls favorably knew Mrs. Frank Thurmond [Lottie Deno] after she had outlived her dubious and disreputable past. *Courtesy William Bishop.*

St. Lukes Episcopal Church, Deming, New Mexico. Mrs. Frank Thurmond [Lottie Deno] was instrumental in organizing the church's first Sunday school. *Courtesy Deming/Luna Mimbres Museum.*

The Deming Bank. Frank Thurmond robbed the bank to recover his own sequestered funds, but was later judicially exonerated and made the bank's vice-president. *Courtesy Deming/Luna Mimbres Museum.*

CHEROKEE HALL.—*Page 9.*

Lottie's husband Frank Thurmond fictionally depicted as the character Cherokee Hall in the *Wolfville* series by Alfred Henry Lewis: The caricature by renowned Western artist Frederick Remington. *From* Wolfville *[1897], Frederick A. Stokes Company, Publishers.*

Cambray, New Mexico—what's left. *Author's photograph.*

Alle Delle [Lowe] Stecker, a friend and later living companion of Mrs. Frank Thurmond [Lottie Deno]. *Courtesy Lanette and John Shanahan.*

Endnotes Chapter II

1 *Silver City Enterprise*, October 7, 1887.
2 Julyan, *The Place Names of New Mexico*. 184 & 334.
3 McKenna, *Black Range Tales*. "Among the big gamblers of Kingston were the two Bradley brothers, the two Thurman [*sic*] brothers, and Lou Blanger [Blonger]." 132. Admittedly this reference does not specifically identify Frank as being one of the two "Thurman brothers," but contemporaneous newspaper citations place Frank and Lottie Thurmond as a residents of Kingston. That Lou "Blanger" is in fact Lou Blonger is almost irrefutable—and somewhat significant.
4 *Silver City Enterprise*, March 30, 1888.
5 F. Stanley, *The Kingston Story*. 13.
6 Sherman & Sherman, *Ghost Towns and Mining Camps of New Mexico*. 125.
7 Ibid. 124; Michael Jenkinson, *Ghost Towns of New Mexico: Playthings of the Wind*. 136.
8 Ibid. 125; *History of Sierra County, New Mexico* [Sierra County Historical Society], "In the tent-lodging house, lower berths were preferred as stray bullets from nearby saloon brawls often ripped through he canvas walls." 54.
9 Stanley, *The Kingston Story*. "The Monarch Saloon was owned by ." 18; Virginia and George Pete Measday [Compilers], *History of Luna County, New Mexico*. Supplement I. "When Kingston became a bustling mining town, the Thurmonds moved into the Black Range to operate their own gambling house with varied success." 22.
10 Patsy Crow King, *Sadie Orchard: The Time of Her Life*. Author King discredits Sadie's assertion that she was born in England, spotlighting her place of birth as Mills County, Iowa. 23. That Sarah Creech married James W. Orchard may be found in the Sierra County, New Mexico, Probate Court Records: photocopied in King's biography. 33.
11 Jacqueline Meketa, *From Martyrs To Murderers: The Old Southwest's Saints, Sinners, Scalawags*. "As a result of her secrecy, deliberate misrepresentations, and imaginative role playing while alive, it is difficult to separate fact from fiction when researching Sadie's life, nonetheless, her story is a tantalizing one." 147.
12 Bill Rakocy, *Ghosts of Kingston and Hillsboro, New Mexico: A Pictorial Documentary of the Great Black Range Country*. 24.
13 Jay Moynahan, *Soiled Doves, Sportin' Women and Other Fallen Flowers— Prostitution on the American Frontier*. 68.
14 Rakocy, *Ghosts of Kingston and Hillsboro, New Mexico: A Pictorial Documentary of the Great Black Range Country*. 50.
15 King, *Sadie Orchard: The Time of Her Life*. "She established her brothel on Virtue Avenue." 2.
16 Ibid. 32.
17 Meketa, *From Martyrs To Murderers: The Old Southwest's Saints, Sinners & Scalawags*. "She was a prostitute and a madam, but initiated a drive to raise money to build a church and used her vigor and stamina to achieve many charitable works." 148; F. Stanley, *The Hillsboro Story*. "Mrs. S. J. Orchard owned the Hillsboro hotel....Sadie has been a much abused person, for she was very much a lady." 14-15.
18 *Deming Headlight*, November, 16, 1888.
19 Ibid. December 14, 1888.
20 Ibid. April 5, 1889.
21 Ibid. May 19, 1889.

[22] Ibid. June 9, 1889.

[23] Sam Baldwin to Earl Vandale and Hervey Chesley. Nita Stewart Memorial Library.

[24] Hunter, "The Lottie Deno I Knew." 34. With a view toward protective prudence, the author opted to delete Lottie's married name from the article; referring to her post gambling life as Mrs. _____. For biography of the truly remarkable Mooar refer to Charles G. Anderson's *In Search Of The Buffalo: The Story of J. Wright Mooar.*

[25] *Southwest Sentinel,* August 9, 1884. "Col Head, Col [Dick] Hudson, Frank Thrumond and a number of other congenial spirits help enliven the corridors of the Timmer House."

[26] Typescript from handwritten history of St. Luke's Episcopal Church, by Olive Whitehill. Courtesy, Deming/Luna Mimbres Museum. Deming, New Mexico.

[27] *Silver City Enterprise* repeat of story carried in the Lordsburg *Western Liberal,* April 15, 1892.

[28] Hunter, *The Story of Lottie Deno: Her Life and Times.* 140-141; Alexander, *Sheriff Harvey Whitehill: Silver City Stalwart.* 266-267; Metz, *Encyclopedia of Lawmen, Outlaws, and Gunfighters.* 248; Rose, *Lottie Deno: Gambling Queen of Hearts.* 84.

[29] DeArment, *Broadway Bat, Gunfighter in Gotham: The New York City Years of Bat Masterson.* 51.

[30] Alexander, *Sheriff Harvey Whitehill: Silver City Stalwart.* 247.

[31] Archibald Clavering Gunter, *Miss Nobody of Nowhere.* Title page; *La Ventura Magazine,* July 27, 1968. "Under the name of 'Brick Garvey' he [Whitehill] was one of the principal characters in Archibald Clavering Gunter's novel, *Miss Nobody of Nowhere.*"; *Silver City Enterprise,* January 3, 1902. "Mr. Whitehill whose record as a doughty officer is preserved in literature as the will-known character of 'Garvey' in Archibald Clavering Gunter's clever novel, *Miss Nobody of Nowhere.*"

[32] DeArment, *Broadway Bat, Gunfighter in Gotham: The New York Years of Bat Masterson.* "Several years later, Roosevelt, who had read and enjoyed Lewis's western stories, suggested the author gather them into a volume that he would edit and have illustrated by his artist friend, Frederic Remington. The resulting book appeared in 1897 under the title *Wolfville* and catapulted Alfred Henry Lewis into national prominence." 52.

[33] Rose, *Lottie Deno: Gambling Queen of Hearts.* 88.

[34] DeArment, *Knights of the Green Cloth: The Saga of Frontier Gamblers.* "Alfred Henry Lewis, a popular turn-of-the-century novelist and author of many short stores [sic] of western color, knew the Thurmonds in New Mexico and based several of his fictional tales on the real-life experiences of the gambling couple. In his *Wolfville* tales, published between 1897 and 1908, Lewis featured gambling man 'Cherokee Hall' and a woman he called 'Faro Nell,' based upon his friends Frank and Charlotte Thurmond." 264; *Deming Headlight,* April 18, 1963, "Alfred Henry Lewis repeated and unmistakably described the Thurmonds in his books comprising the 'Wolfville' series. The Thurmonds were then known as 'Cherokee Hall' and 'Faro Nell.' Wolfville was an imaginary town, probably a composite of many wild and woolly town of the early west." Rose, *Lottie Deno: Gambling Queen of Hearts.* 87.

[35] Rose, *Lottie Deno: Gambling Queen of Hearts.* 88. Author Rose capably handles the geographical comparisons between real southwestern New Mexico locations and places cited in the *Wolfville* books.

[36] DeArment, *Broadway Bat, Gunfighter in Gotham: The New York City Years of Bat Masterson.* 52

[37] Keith Wheeler, *The Chroniclers.* 203

[38] George Hilliard, *A Hundred Years Of Horse Tracks: The Story of the Gray Ranch.* 36-37.

[39] Alfred Henry Lewis, *Wolfville Nights*. 57-65.

[40] *By-Laws, Rules, Regulations and Names of Members of the Cattle Raisers Association of Texas.* 29 & 121. Courtesy, Susan Wagner, Editor, *The Cattleman.* Fort Worth, Texas.

[41] Ibid. "T. J. Cook, Sim Holstein, Frank Thurmond." 29; Hunter, "The Deming I knew 44 Years Ago." "I did not know until I came to Bandera in 1921 that Sim Holstein was the slayer of Doughboy Taylor, a desperado, in Kerrville, in the 1880s." 349; J. Marvin Hunter, [ed.] *The Trail Drivers of Texas.* "During the fall we branded 'Mavericks' and put up trail herds and in the spring of 1873 Olley Treadwell came through with a herd for Kansas belonging to Sim Holstein of Gonzales [Texas]. 405; "Good trail bosses who made quick time with stock in good shape were always in demand. Ab Blocker, Gus Black, Mac Stewart, Fayette Butler, Pleas Bulter, Jim Byler, Sim Holstein, Henry Clair, Jones Glenn, Jesse McCoy, Bob Jennings and Bob Lauterday were all record-breakers in taking herds through in quick time and fine shape...." 442-443; While Mr. Hunter was correct in saying Mr. Holstein killed Mr. Taylor it was in 1871, rather than during the "1880s, " according to a noted authority on the Sutton-Taylor feud, Mr. Chuck Parsons: Parsons to author, May 29, 2007.

[42] Charles G. Finke, "Cambray." *The New Mexico Philatelist.* July-August 1986. 4-5; Julyan, *The Place Names of New Mexico.* 55; Pearce, *New Mexico Place Names.* 23.

[43] *Deming Graphic,* November 1, 1912.

[44] Hunter, *The Story of Lottie Deno: Her Life and Times.* Quoting the *Deming Herald* of January 28, 1902. 132.

[45] Ibid. Quoting the *Deming Headlight* of August 16, 1902. 131; Both Julyan, *The Place Names of New Mexico* and Pearce, *New Mexico Place Names* do not show entries for "Chambray" but do for "Cambray.

[46] Julyan, The *Place Names of New Mexico.* 215;

[47] Charles Jensen, "Cipriano Baca: Famous New Mexico Lawman." *New Mexico Genealogist.* December 2004. 206.

[48] *Deming Headlight,* January 14, 1898.

[49] Hunter, *The Story of Lottie Deno: Her Life and Times.* 157. Author Hunter places the Thurmond ranch as 30 miles south of Deming. Frank may have also had ranching interest in that section, as well as Cambray east of Deming. Certainly he was invested heavily in mines south of Deming; Alexander, *Sheriff Harvey Whitehill: Silver City Stalwart.* "The Wolfville series included *Wolfville; Sandburs; Wolfville Nights; Wolfville Days; The Black Lion Inn; Wolfville Folks* and *Faro Nell and Her Friends.*" 253, n. 63.

[50] Alfred Henry Lewis, *Wolfville.* 16.

[51] Neil B. Carmony [Ed.], *How I Routed A Gang Of Arizona Outlaws.* Quoting the *San Francisco Examiner* of August 2, 1896. 8. Editor Carmony, an authority in this field of study, interestingly notes that despite Mr. Wyatt Earp's "tendency to doctor the facts about his law enforcement career, in his prime he was without doubt a tough *hombre.*" 4; Alford E. Turner[Editor], *The Earps Talk.* Quoting the *San Francisco Examiner.* 3.

[52] Roberts, *Doc Holliday: The Life And The Legend.* The author, in dealing with the supposed death of Ed Bailey, analytically acknowledges the scarcity of evidence, and places the episode in a speculative realm: "Still, Earp, who told the story more than once, did not claim to be an eyewitness to the Bailey stabbing and sometimes confused names, place, and details in his recollections, so that it is possible that the incident in question happened somewhere else in Texas. For example Brackett, the town near Fort Clark, had a murderous reputation....Given Holliday's peregrinations and Earp's known movements the Bailey episode could have happened somewhere other than Fort

Griffin at some place like Brackett or San Angela, whose records are scare or nonexistent and whose township had no newspapers." 86-88.

[53] Records of the Thurmonds mining claims may be located at the Luna County Clerk's Office, Luna County Courthouse, Deming, New Mexico. See, *Indirect Index of Mining Claims* and *Transcribed Mining Deed Books.*

[54] Notice Of Mining Location. *Mining Book I.* Page 511. Luna County Clerk's Office, Luna County Courthouse, Deming, New Mexico.

[55] Unidentified newsclip from California obituary for Alle Dell [Lowe] Stecker. "Mrs. Stecker was born December 9, 1884, in Tiptonville, Tenn. She moved to Texas as a teenager and taught Mexicans to read and write English."; Twelfth United States Census [1900], Pearl River, Mississippi. There are numerous mentions of Mrs. Alle Delle [Lowe] Stecker's teaching assignments in the local papers. *Deming Graphic,* September 6, 1907; May 8, 1908; September 10, 1909; and the *Deming Headlight* September 12, 1913.

[56] *Deming Headlight,* February 22, 1906. This issue of the newspaper refers to Mr. Stecker as "Harry" rather than "Henry" as reflected in numerous Luna County Probate Records.

[57] Marriage Book I, Direct Index. [Filed] July 27, 1903, H. M. Stecker to Allie D. Lowe; Certificate of Marriage, Territory of New Mexico, County of Luna, H. M. Stecker to Allie D. Lowe, July 23, 1903. Courtesy, Luna County Clerk, Luna County Courthouse, Deming, New Mexico. Other official court documents refer to Mrs. Stecker's correctly: "Alle Delle."

Chapter 12

"She Shushed and Giggled"

While in Deming another aspiring journalist had also seen the advisability of visiting with Mrs. Lottie Thurmond. Alfred Henry Lewis had sparked a story. Somewhat curiously the intuitive writer bypassed an opportunity to interview Mr. Frank Thurmond, the extraordinarily well-known saloonkeeper, frontier gambler and knife-fighter. At least Mr. J. Marvin Hunter makes no mention regarding such a consultation though he was acquainted with Frank. Mr. Hunter, at the time a tenderfoot newsman working for the *Deming Headlight* and later the founder of *Frontier Times* magazine, asserts

> I knew Lottie Deno in Deming in 1900 and became well acquainted with her. She was a charming and gracious lady, and being a young man of inquiring nature, I soon persuaded her to tell me about her early life in Kentucky, though she never did tell me her maiden name, for which I have searched these many long years.[1]

Remembering that Mr. Hunter's remarks are found in *The Story of Lottie Deno: Her Life and Times* which was published posthumously during 1959 is crucial for understanding bewildering truths.[2] Too, making due note of the book's subtitle, *The Story of the Mysterious Aristocrat Whom Became a Lady Gambler and Female Daredevil of Frontier Days*, is a precursor for previewing the book's predisposed thesis. The appetizer is a foretaste of the repast to come. The tease fits the theme and vice versa. While he was yet alive, Mr. Hunter published three major articles in periodicals mentioning Lottie Deno, discounting any newspaper citations. Even as J. Marvin Hunter acknowledges knowing the oldtime gambling girl at Deming, he makes no mention whatsoever of conducting any interviews with her in those informative pieces. Nor in any of these articles is the state of Kentucky or Lottie's childhood even mentioned, although he had "persuaded" Aunt Lottie to tell him "about her early life in Kentucky." The first article, a 1910 *San Angelo Standard* newspaper story written by his father, John Warren Hunter, who was not acquainted with Miss Lottie, "The Mystery Woman of Fort Concho" was republished in the January 1927 edition of *Frontier Times*. The story more-or-less forwards the traditional dreamscape concerning Miss Deno and her gambling days in Texas, but there is no citation at all regarding any interviews with her by J. Marvin

231

Hunter—or his father.[3] For *Frontier Times* [May 1944] J. Marvin
Hunter penned some of his best remembrances in an edifying article
titled "The Deming I Knew 44 Years Ago." Pertinently, Mr. Hunter
comments that he knew Aunt Lottie while living in Deming, but a
circumspect reading fails to pinpoint any mention of a face-to-face
interview. Publisher Hunter's remark that he "afterwards learned" is
informative:

> Another character I knew well in Deming, I afterwards
> learned was the famous Lottie Denno [*sic*], who
> operated a gambling house at old Fort Griffin during
> buffalo hunting days. She had reformed, and was an
> active church worker in Deming, and everybody loved
> her. She was a beautiful woman, even in her old age, and
> during the time I lived next door to her home I never
> suspected that she had ever trod the "primrose path" or
> had had such a colorful life. She was highly respected
> and a very cultured and refined woman. She married a
> New Mexico ranchman, and forgot that she was ever
> known at [as] Lottie Denno.[4]

Three years later [1947] J. Marvin Hunter's article "The Lottie Deno I
Knew" appeared in *The West Texas Historical Association Yearbook.*
Once again Mr. Hunter divulges that he knew Lottie while at Deming
nearly a half-century earlier, but strikingly there is not any declaration of
a fact-finding interview. Mr. Hunter's very own comments—with the
blank spaces now filled—seems to refute that he ever talked with Lottie
Thurmond about her genealogical background, much less her previous
exciting life as a lady gambler:

> I then recalled that I knew a Mr. and Mrs. [Thurmond]
> in Deming, New Mexico, back in 1900, and that Mr.
> [Thurmond] called his wife "Lottie." For nearly two
> years I lived next door to this elderly couple, and they
> were splendid neighbors. Everybody in Deming loved
> Mrs. [Thurmond]. She was a beautiful woman, and a
> delightful conversationalist. Her hair was snow white,
> and she had bright sparkling black eyes. I do not know
> what age she was when I knew her, but she must have
> been in her late sixties. She was an active, energetic
> church worker, and devoted much time to charitable
> work, in visiting the sick, looking after cases of distress,
> and took a leading part in the social activities of the
> town. I had heard it whispered around that she at one

time operated a gambling house at Silver City but I did not believe the rumor, for I could not feature Mrs. [Thurmond] as being that type of woman, so dismissed it from my thoughts.[5]

Mr. Hunter's inexplicably omitting details of a 1900 face-to-face interview with Mrs. Lottie Thurmond in magazine or journal pieces penned while he was alive, only to have that fine point emerge fifty-nine years later and posthumously, is for the 21st-Century researcher perplexing. Tracing the source of any remarks concerning Lottie's upbringing and early history is problematical. J. Marvin Hunter accepting a frontier newspaper job under the editorship of George L. Shakespeare at the *Deming Headlight* is not in doubt; photographs accompanying this text provide conformation. Accepting as fact that for awhile Mr. Hunter lived next door to Frank and Lottie Thurmond at Deming is not unreasonable. Establishing just how he learned of Aunt Lottie's childhood and pre-Texas life is the conundrum. There is a more than interesting clue, but it necessitates that distasteful chronological leap

After the appearance of Lewis' fictionalized Faro Nell in the *Wolfville* series and Rye's tangible Lottie Deno in *The Quirt and the Spur*, followed by his father's interesting 1910 piece and the 1927 reprint of that account in *Frontier Times*, Mr. J. Marvin Hunter was tuned to the possibilities of a good Western story, one featuring a female protagonist. The tales were of sufficient merit to ignite a creative project. Years before his own 1940s articles about Lottie Deno appeared in print, Mr. Hunter had arranged an appointment for groundwork at Deming during "1936 or so."[6] Interestingly, Margaret Mitchell's epic tale of a Civil War era Southern Belle, *Gone With The Wind*, had also been published during 1936; winning the Pulitzer Prize in 1937.[7] Eloquently, renaissance impressions of the Old South had been reset—the idyllic foundation poured. With her "seventeen-inch waist, the smallest in three counties," her "magnolia-white skin" and perfect upturned "breasts well matured" Scarlett O'Hara had spun her tangled web of possessiveness and greed. On the spot a world-wide readership was infatuated with the drama.[8] Was a nonfiction writer also obsessively entangled in Scarlett's web? At Deming, J. Marvin Hunter talked with one of Mrs. Thurmond's closest lady friends, Mr. Andrew Jackson "Jack" Tidmore's wife, Susie, the mother of Lottie Deno's goddaughter Margaret Roberta Tidmore.[9] Roberta and her younger brother Morris Brantley Tidmore were two of Lottie's especial favorites among Deming's throng of schoolchildren. Mr. Tidmore was a successful and respected mercantile owner, having "a very large following among the Anglo and Spanish-American people in this section

[Deming], being greatly trusted and beloved by them."[10] The Tidmores were beloved by Lottie, too. And she by them.

Mrs. Tidmore was a natural choice for an inquisitive biographer searching for elusive clues. Mrs. Lottie Thurmond had told Mrs. Susie Tidmore many things, not necessarily true things, though. When politely pressed about her previous life, Lottie had to sometimes account for that past, generating enough of a nice and benign tale for a real lady to get by on. Susie, a bosom friend of Lottie's listened, perhaps naively, but certainly not cynically. After all, Mrs. Lottie Thumond was a gentlewoman from Kentucky, a cultured lady, the sophisticated daughter of a wealthy plantation owner—that admired breeder of top-quality Thoroughbreds. What about her family? Where were they? Did they ever come to Deming for a visit? Did she go to Kentucky for reunions? Well, no, they had shunned her after the ill-advised marriage to gambler Frank Thurmond. Mrs. Tidmore should have picked up on small inconsistencies but she didn't: Like Lottie saying her father affectionately taught her to bet and bluff, but the parents had disowned her because she married a sporting man.[11] The expressed purpose of J. Marvin Hunter's extraordinary 1936 trip to Deming and his face to face interview with the conversant Mrs. Tidmore was for gathering needed biographical and background data about Mrs. Lottie Thurmond.[12] Mrs. Tidmore cheerfully and willingly shared with Mr. Hunter what she knew—or thought she knew! J. Marvin Hunter jotted it down in his notebook. This sparks a glimmer of peculiarity when recalling Mr. Hunter's avow that he had already interviewed Lottie about such matters during 1900, thirty-six years before. Mr. Hunter returned to Texas. Curiously, his knowledge about Lottie Deno—in book form—lay dormant. Twenty-three years later [1959] J. Marvin Hunter's posthumously published book *The Story of Lottie Deno: Her Life and Times* was released. Apparently after Mrs. Susie Tidmore saw a copy she was not too happy, because

....it quoted her by name and the quotes were largely incorrect.[13]

The Tidmore family believed, which they somewhat based on Mr. Hunter's own words, that in large part much of *The Story of Lottie Deno: Her Life and Times* was just "surmise." Roberta [Tidmore] Wilcox, in writing of her mother's evident disgust, said: "Mr. Hunter knew Mrs. Thurmond in Deming in 1900 when he was 20 and she was 56, and said he guessed at her past then."[14] Guesswork aside, returning to the chronological story is fitting.

Truthfulness about one of Deming's best loved pioneer couples is revealing. Mr. and Mrs. Thurmond were important cogs in Deming's community affairs. Frank was a respected businessman in the community. He had risen above earning an income from sporting fraternity dealings. The lucrative portfolio—aside from his mining and cattle interests—may be authenticated by two disclosures. First, Frank Thurmond attained the position of vice-president of the Deming National Bank, the very same institution he had earlier made a forced withdrawal from.[15] Secondly, he was the driving force bringing new technology to Deming, a fact clearly demonstrated by adoption of City Ordinance No. 25:

> Be it ordered by the Board of Trustees of the Village of Deming: Section I. That for the considerations hereinafter specified, the right, privilege and franchise is hereby given and granted to Frank Thurmond, his associates and assigns, to the right of way over, across, under and along the streets, highways and bridges in the Village of Deming, in the County of Luna and Territory of New Mexico, including any and all territory and additions that may hereafter be annexed to said Village of Deming, for the purpose of erecting, constructing, equipping, maintaining and operating an Electric Street Railway and Power System in said Village of Deming and to that end to generate, transmit and supply electricity and electric power for any and all purposes which may be necessary, convenient or incident to the proper carrying into effect and enjoyment of said right, privilege and franchise.[16]

Having at long last attained a desirable level of respectably Frank and Lottie Thrumond played parts in Deming's lively social doings. The couple were frequent participants at picnics and enjoyable overnight excursions in the region's picturesque mountain country. The gorgeous Upper Gila country above Silver City was a really a good spot for extended camping vacations. Children could run and play—and ride horses. Men could hunt and fish—and around the campfires tell tall tales about the area's wild and woolly days. Contented ladies could visit, gossip—and much to Lottie's delight—play cards. Camaraderie and fun were contagious. And all could, smilingly or not, sit still long enough for a photographer to capture the moment. Another favorite spot for shorter trips was the Mimbres Hot Springs situated north of Deming and south of Silver City, not too far from Fort Cummings.

Frank, now a true entrepreneur, still maintained a reputation for toughness. It is a fact exemplified by the impressionable voice of a child, Herman Lindauer. Herman was the son of Sigmund Lindauer, one of

Deming's leading merchants and an extremely close personal friend of the Thurmonds. Herman recalled:

> He [Frank Thurmond] and my father had some mining properties in the Tres Hermanas Mountains and once on a trip out there with Frank when I was just a small boy, a horse almost bit my thumb off. Uncle Frank got a basin of cold water and had me stick my thumb in it and the way he looked at me, I knew I just couldn't cry. He wasn't the kind of a guy you could cry in front of. All Indian, he was faster with a bowie knife than anybody with a gun.[17]

Herman Lindauer's reference to "Uncle Frank" is noteworthy. Having no brood of their own, the childless Thurmonds took an active interest in Deming's youngsters. Throughout the neighborhood the outgoing couple were known to almost everyone as "Aunt Lottie" and "Uncle Frank." Considering her talents from bygone days it is not surprising that Aunt Lottie especially enjoyed playing innocent card games with the kids. After school they would stop by the Thurmond's residence, 408 West Pine Street, learning lessons not taught in the classrooms.[18] Of the several photographs depicting Frank and Lottie in recreational settings, children are pivotal components of the gaiety.

Frank and Lottie Thurmonds' moments of jollity were robbed when tasked with benevolently consoling Alle Delle Stecker during July 1906. Without warning H. M. Stecker had been stricken with an intestinal disorder, one leading to heart failure.[19] Mr. Stecker expired; married less than three years. Too, he died intestate, without a *Last Will and Testament*. First things were tended to first. Mr. Henry McClure Stecker, under auspices of the Knights of Pythias, with ancillary arrangements provided by Mahoney Mortuary, was laid to rest in Deming's Mountain View Cemetery.[20] Mrs. Alle Delle Stecker was now a twenty-one year old widow, in need of help emotionally and legally. The Thurmonds filled that void, Lottie as a loving friend, Frank as a financial surety, a guarantor on Alle Delle's petition to be named administratrix of her husband's estate.[21] For Mrs. Alle Delle, though saddened by the tragic loss, there was finally a pinch of good news. After taking the drawn out steps of legality she was named administratrix; the sole beneficiary of Mr. Stecker's estate, $2391.12 less the money he owed, $499.61, netting Alle Delle $1,891.51.[22] Alle Delle began coming out from under the fog of mourning.

There was some not so nice news on the horizon, however. At age 70, Frank Thurmond began fighting the hopeless battle with an "incurable malady of the throat," cancer![23] Undergoing a surgical procedure failed to check the disease, it had progressed too far.[24] On the 5th of June 1908, Mr. Frank Thurmond peacefully surrendered his last breath, dying at his Deming home.[25] Obituaries were published in local newspapers, the *Deming Headlight* and the *Silver City Enterprise*.[26] In a later edition of the *Headlight*, "A Friend" offered discerning thoughts about Frank's character, herein repeated in part:

> He was a man of deep and abiding convictions, and seldom or never lost confidence in a friend. In person he was tall, slender and wiry, and capable of great endurance. He was emotional and enthusiastic by nature, yet possessed of great self-control and calm in all his physical movements, and ready and willing at all times to lose his life, if necessary, in defense of what he believed to be right. In the presence of men the tenderness and warmth of his real nature was seldom revealed by any physical demonstrations, but at home and among the many little children about town who he loved his unconscious smiles came as sparkles from his heart....For several years Mr. Thurmond was engaged in the cattle business, and was at all times engaged in the fascinating business of mining, which he pursued with varying fortune, but no matter whether rich or poor he never betrayed a friend and performed all his obligations with scrupulous fidelity, his word being as good as the written bond....[27]

Frank Thurmond, an authentic Western character of note and a frontier fighter of the old school was laid to rest in the Knight's of Pythias section at Deming's Mountain View Cemetery. A grave site was reserved for Lottie between Frank and H. M. Stecker.[28] In his *Last Will and Testament* of February 8, 1904, Frank had named his wife executrix of the estate, bequeathing all of his "real, personal, and mixed property" to her; "for her sole use and benefit."[29] At Deming on 24th day of August 1908 The Probate Court probated Frank's *Will*.[30] Although Frank's death had been untimely, it was not unexpected. When Uncle Frank wagered all the chips for that last game with cancer, the surgery, he knew the odds were slim. Frank Thurmond was a gambler, he'd played the last hand—all in! Frank wasn't a quitter! Nor was Aunt Lottie!

With abandon after Frank's death Lottie lost herself in church work and social affairs. Lottie participated in charitable projects and community service tasks conducted by the Episcopal Ladies' Guild. There were other activities, too. Lottie was a charter member—some say the founder—of Deming's Golden Gossip Club. The membership was limited to but a dozen local women. Vacancies were filled only when someone relocated to another town—or after they had been eulogized. When a rare opening did occur, it was Aunt Lottie who was tasked with naming the replacement. *If true*, it is an unmistakable indication that Lottie was a powerful force. Or, that the other eleven ladies wanted to avoid hurting rejected applicants' feelings. The waiting list of aspirants was not short, nor was the envy of hopeful candidates. The club's motto was straightforward. It was said in unison at every meeting: "To tell the best things, to make the best of the bad things, and to straighten [out] mistakes," that was the group's shared goal. Luncheon meetings were scheduled for every Tuesday afternoon, because according to local folklore "the wind doesn't blow on Tuesday at Deming." There were no dues, nor club officers, nor bylaws, nor persnickety bookkeeping requirements. The original chatty dozen were some of Deming's very finest ladies: Mrs. P. M. Steed, Mrs. Samuel W. Swope, Mrs. C. O. Donaldson, Mrs. W. E. Holt, Mrs. J. B. Taylor, Mrs. Newton A. Bolich, Mrs. Alice Smith, Mrs. Joseph A. Mahoney, Mrs. John Corbett, Mrs. George Shepard, Mrs. A. W. Pollard and Mrs. Frank Thurmond.[31] The girls met weekly to sew, eat, and gossip:

> The afternoon is spent reviewing local happenings with particular emphasis on those items not generally covered by local newspapers. Each member is [was] expected to provide an exclusive tidbit for the edification of the other members. Unfortunately, no minutes are recorded and the best source of "hot" news in the Mimbres Valley is not made available to [the] local news media.[32]

Besides eating and loquaciously chirping about other people's private business, part of the membership indulged in another pastime, playing cards. That was Aunt Lottie's forte. Lottie had several idiosyncrasies. When it came to playing cards she was determined to win at all costs, cheating if necessary. Lottie's little quirk was not undetected. It was well known to the Golden Gossips, as well as other social sponsors throughout Deming. Ensuring club harmony the other eleven girlfriends formulated a workable plan. According to Lottie's goddaughter, Roberta Tidmore Wilcox, "As she got older she'd cheat on her score card at bridges parties. The women knew she did this, so they often would have an extra little prize for her. They loved her and indulged her eccentricity."[33] Patty Israel was up to the aging Mrs. Thurmond's tricks, "Lottie was always a winner at card parties. She hated to lose so much that the hostess would have an extra present for her if she lost."[34]

Cheating at cards wasn't Lottie's solitary peculiarity. Another was that she proudly boasted of something none besides her possessed; Lottie had the only carpeted outhouse in Deming, a not unwise or impractical touch it would seem.[35] An added eccentricity is that Aunt Lottie, accompanied by Aunt Mary, Dick Hudson's widow, sometimes made an appearance at the upscale Deming Club, always carrying dancing shoes in their handbags, just "in case" someone might ask them to sashay across the dance floor.[36] Less sensible, however, was another of Mrs. Thurmond's recurring personal practices. When it snowed Lottie would disrobe and while wearing but her birthday suit playfully bathe in the snow—in her backyard of course! Deming was short on secrets.[37]

Something that was not hush-hush was that Lottie no longer liked to cook. And she didn't! The days of running a restaurant were days gone by. A respectable lady of means did not need to do that. Preparing meals for money and tending to Odd Fellows' galas or the Ancient Order of United Workmen's celebrations for pay were now beneath her dignified strata. When it came to the cookstove she was missing in action. Aunt Lottie had worked out a routine that suited her quite well. In the morning she would take breakfast at the Pollard residence, at noontime she would make her presence known at yard-gates with screeching "hoo-hoos" and partake of dinner [lunch] at the Lindauer or Tidmore homes. For evening supper she stopped in at J. A. Mahoney's house, a local businessman and the town's undertaker. "No one minded this because Lottie was so well-liked. Besides she hated to do housework & cooking."[38] Aunt Lottie seldom stayed home alone and was in on the planning of parties and family reunions, but not the hands-on baking and cleaning chores.[39] Domestic drudgery was not in Aunt Lottie's deck.

With her beautiful and premature graying, nearly pure white hair, Aunt Lottie was known throughout Deming as a lady with refined habits and a dainty approach to personal grooming. Frequently she would shampoo at someone else's residence, making sure that they had a "linen" towel to dry with; otherwise there would be a trace of lint. Afterwards she'd generously douse with talcum powder. Aunt Lottie always looked very nice and smelled very nice. Kids didn't like that old-person smell. Even Roberta's little dog, Chubbie, liked Aunt Lottie. Often the drooling little pet escorted Lottie home after her delicious lunch at the Tidmore's, then returned home to protect his own front yard.[40] Aunt Lottie Thurmond was truly a Deming treasure. Neighborhood children had their own grandmothers, but everybody felt loved by Aunt Lottie.[41] Putting a genuine human face on Aunt Lottie is not challenging. She sometimes regressed to childlike giddiness, as her goddaughter Roberta detected:

On Christmas Eve she stayed all night at our house and helped put the toys under the tree when we children had gone to bed. I remember not being really asleep on Christmas and hearing her get a doll out of Mother's closet, picking it up so the doll said "ma ma" and she and Mother shushed and giggled.[42]

Aside from her dexterity with a deck of cards, Aunt Lottie was a master at needlework, excelling at crocheting and embroidering. Where she picked up such proficiency would be but guesswork, though she asserted it was an acquired skill learned while attending a convent in Kentucky.[43] She wasn't stingy with sharing her talent, recurrently taking young girls under her motherly wing for an instructive session. One lady, Wandra Smalley, remembered that she and a friend—as young girls—eagerly learned to "tat" from Aunt Lottie. During the sewing lessons Aunt Lottie mesmerized them with "gory tales of Geronimo attacking ranchers."[44] Aunt Lottie was not shy. She was no shrinking violet as evidenced by the handbill promoting a performance by local thespians in Deming's Rialto Theater; Aunt Lottie was a cast member of the amateur production.

Mrs. Lottie Thurmond, in addition to making area children feel at ease, provided support for her friend, the Widow Stecker. Alle Delle moved in with Aunt Lottie, sharing the commodious and comfortably furnished Pine Street home.[45] Examination of Luna County's Assessment Rolls corroborates that while Aunt Lottie may not have been classed as a wealthy widow, she was substantially well fixed—enough to keep her taxes paid.[46] Loved by all who knew her, Aunt Lottie was a whirlwind of social activity, aptly earning a descriptive term many used to characterize her; she was just "peppy." All good things must come to an end. As the years went by Aunt Lottie's peppiness began to fade. Feebleness began taking its place. As the 1930s approached Aunt Lottie began thinking of her mortality.

Whether it was due to age or her degree of literacy is not knowable, but on the 24th day of February 1930, Aunt Lottie hen-scratched her signature on a handwritten piece of paper, executing her *Last Will and Testament*. The document had been drawn up by Arthur A. Temke and witnessed by Mrs. O. E. Howell, Superintendent of the Deming Hospital Association, Inc.[47] The signing may have taken place in the hospital. Aunt Lottie was so confined for a few days during 1930; although the sickness she suffered is not specified, the bill for $25 is.[48]

One writer has claimed, absent any source citation, that Mrs. Stecker was in fact Aunt Lottie's younger sister.[49] Their forty-plus year age difference suggests otherwise. Alle Delle's date of birth would be of relevance for sustaining such an assertion. It also speaks to the myth.

Mrs. Alle Delle Stecker was born on the 9th day of December 1884.[50] Therefore it makes any unthinking contention that Aunt Lottie ventured west during the mid-1860s as sole support for her only sister's education in Kentucky's finest private schools illogical. It sounded nice though. Important, too, are Aunt Lottie's own words:

> *I give and bequeath all of my personal effects, furniture, jewelry, clothing in my residence at 408 West Pine Street in Deming New Mexico or Elsewhere, to my dear friend Mrs. Alle B[D]elle Stecker, now a resident of San Luis Obispo, California.*[51]

The Pine Street residence? Lottie Thurmond bequeathed that to Mrs. Alle Delle Stecker, Mr. Sigmund Lindauer and Mr. Joseph A. Mahoney, "the survivor or survivors of them, share and share alike, absolutely and forever."[52]

Mrs. Alle Delle Stecker had moved from Deming to San Luis Obispo, California. There she had accepted employment as a high-school teacher. And there Mrs. Stecker would remain until she retired, never to remarry. Mrs. Stecker would live out her retirement years residing with "school families or school board members."[53] Esteemed by the students and faculty alike, Mrs. Stecker was especially recognized when the San Luis Obispo High School annual *Tiger Tales* was dedicated in her honor:

Dedication

In appreciation of her devoted interest in the students and their activities, in respect for her ability and knowledge as a teacher, and in warm regard for her clear, honest judgment and her sympathetic understanding, this volume is dedicated to Mrs. Alle Dell Stecker.[54]

For a diverse accumulation of justifiable reasons Mrs. Stecker did not mention too much about her life at Deming or her close relationship with Mrs. Lottie Thurmond. What she knew for a fact or suspected Mrs. Stecker kept to herself. At San Luis Obispo, Alle Delle Stecker passed to the other side on January 8, 1988, at age 103.[55] Oh, but to have interviewed her!

As Aunt Lottie aged her admissions to the Deming Hospital became more frequent; the overnight stays longer. During the summer of 1933, one trip necessitated a visit of 39 days, at $5 per day. Another medical stay that same year in September was but for one night.[56]

After the Christmas Holiday season of 1933, Aunt Lottie's health began taking a worsening downturn. On February 3, 1934 she was admitted to the hospital at Deming. Doctor J. G. Moir was Mrs. Thurmond's attending physician, aided by the hospital's Supervising Nurse, Mrs. Reagor.[57] Suffering from Uremia—blood in the urine—and the complications of "old age," the health fading progression had commenced. It was an irreversible course. The once so peppy Aunt Lottie, now 89 years old, was nearing the end. Six days later on Friday the 9th at high noon Mrs. Charlotte J. Thurmond peacefully closed her eyes and quietly slipped away.[58] Whatever secrets Aunt Lottie had, and she had plenty, stayed with her.

The following Sunday afternoon at 2:30 a large crowd gathered at Deming's St. Luke's Episcopal Church. The touching funeral service was conducted by pipe-smoking Harvard educated preacher, Reverend Ross R. Calvin, who would later author *Sky Determines: An Interpretation of the Southwest* and *River of the Sun: Stories of the Storied Gila.*[59] At the Mountain View Cemetery graveside services were conducted by the Reverend William Sickel. After the last farewell and prayer, Aunt Lottie was tenderly lowered into the grave reserved for her; between her devoted husband Frank Thurmond and Henry McClure Stecker. The crowd disbursed. The last shovel of dirt sealed the tomb—and the truth.

As a sidebar, Aunt Lottie's personal property, of which there were a great number of items, was inventoried by order of Luna County's Probate Court. One of the many things enumerated was a scuffed leather-covered trunk.[60] Mr. J. Marvin Hunter believed, and there's no good reason for argument, that it was the trunk once belonging to lawman John C. Jacobs at Fort Griffin, then to Lottie Deno. The trunk was sold in the estate sale when Aunt Lottie's personal property was disposed of. According to Mr. Hunter, Reverend J. E. Fuller, a Methodist Minister, had been the pastor of a church in Deming at the time. It was the good Rev. Fuller who purchased the leather-bound trunk at auction.[61] Somewhat later, after his transfer to Stockdale, Texas, Minister Fuller sold the trunk to Mr. Hunter.[62] There were no fancy Parisian fashions folded inside, at least none were mentioned. Now the trunk is on public display in the Texas Hill Country at the Frontier Times Museum at Bandera.

Mentioned earlier in this text, the photograph so often used as a youthful image of Lottie Deno, the one on the cover of Mr. Hunter's *The Story of Lottie Deno: Her Life and Times* and Mrs. Rose's *Lottie Deno: Gambling Queen of Hearts* simply is not an image of Lottie. Such being the case it is but fair to say—at least for this photo—there is not any evidence whatsoever of intentional deception on anyone's part. Mr. Hunter's book was posthumously published by his children, The 4 Hunters; John Warren Hunter, Myra Jennette Saul, J. Marvin Hunter,

Jr. and Susie Rachel Short. They complied and edited the material from their father's vast collection of personal notes, documents and period photographs. Confusion about and misidentification of oldtime photographs is not new, nor an unusual phenomenon. When the image was first published they believed it was Miss Lottie Deno. Scores have been the writers following suit. None were knowingly palming off fraudulent work. Mislabeled or missing a label, the delightful photo made it into the book. Hopefully, some day the pretty girl will step forward with a name—and a story.

Such a fascinating tale of our beloved Lottie Deno, the female gambling princess of the Southwest's frontiers, must come to a close. Absent penning a lengthy list of the iconic Wild West tough cookies, safely it may be said that Lottie knew—in one way or the other—many of those guys and gals that now have names recognizable in many American households. Some of those folks were not very nice people. A fraction of that menagerie straightened up their acts, ultimately leading respectful and productive lives, or at least they tried to leave that impression. Most of them died in bed. A few of them, boots on, died laying in the pools of blood and gore varnishing barroom floors. Unlike Lottie Deno, a mainstream of the sporting ladies could not or would not—and did not—extricate themselves from scandalous behavior, sexual depravity and years spent living in squalor. Recognizing their depressing plight may be factually demonstrated; sociologically admitting that societal contributions hastened their downfall is saddening. Puritanical standards prevented Aunt Lottie from truthfully revealing too much detail about her previous card playing and cavorting life, that questionable portion of the story prior to becoming Mrs. Frank Thurmond. Those tasteless Texas days and routine arrests, were days best swept under the Deming rug—totally erased. Propriety and good manners demanded Aunt Lottie fill in those blank spaces with particulars befitting a genuine lady—a gentlewoman of the Old South—and she did. Would it have been wise for the sweet old girl to have revealed the real truth about her upbringing, her family, the uncertainties, her not so lonesome travels throughout the Southwest, and the raw people she frequented the saloons, dance halls and disorderly houses with? Well, if she had, the genre of Old West history would have been rewarded. Understandably she didn't! That truthfulness, if everybody in Deming had known, might not have worked too well for the adored and admired Aunt Lottie. She was, after all, a respectable lady. Perhaps her goddaughter Roberta, more than anyone else, and who loved her unconditionally, said it the very best: "So probably when she kept her secret, Aunt Lottie knew exactly what she was doing, and she did it with great success. Her last years may have been dull, but they were respectable. Oh my, yes!"[63]

George Shakespeare and family. At the *Deming Headlight* J. Marvin Hunter, a budding newspaperman and future publisher of *Frontier Times Magazine*, worked for Mr. Shakespeare. *Courtesy Deming/Luna Mimbres Museum.*

Headquarters for the *Deming Headlight*. L. to R: John Ellis, Willie Shakespeare and Mr. J. Marvin Hunter. *Courtesy Deming/Luna Mimbres Museum.*

Folks on an extended camping trip at the Gila Hot Springs north of Silver City, New Mexico Territory. Mrs. Frank Thurmond [Lottie Deno] seated at card table on left, with Helen Swope resting her hand on Lottie's shoulder. Frank Thurmond standing at far right holding the hand of Esther Brisley. *Courtesy Deming/Luna Mimbres Museum.*

Mrs. Frank Thurmond [Lottie Deno] horseback, second from right, with little Alice Bolich peeking over her shoulder. Mr. Frank Thurmond barely visible at extreme right. *Courtesy Deming/Luna Mimbres Museum.*

At Deming, L. to. R: Lillian Lindauer, "Aunt Lottie," and Herman Lindauer. *Courtesy Deming/Luna Mimbres Museum.*

"Aunt Lottie" Thurmond far left, flanking young Herman Lindauer, with "Uncle Frank" Thurmond on Lindauer's left wearing hat. Others are not positively identified. *Courtesy Deming/Luna Mimbres Museum.*

Herman Lindauer as he appeared in uniform at Harvard Military School in Los Angles, California. Herman frequently wrote letters to "Aunt Lottie" Thurmond. *Courtesy, Deming/Luna Mimbres Museum.*

Deming's original Golden Gossip Club. The founder, Mrs. Charlotte Thurmond ["Aunt Lottie"] seated at extreme left. *Courtesy Patrick Tidmore.*

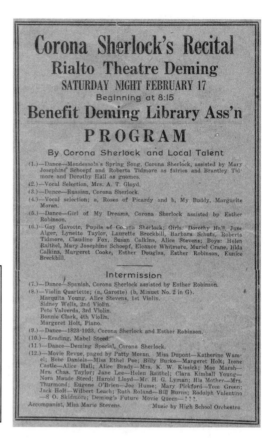

Corona Sherlock's Recital
Rialto Theatre Deming
SATURDAY NIGHT FEBRUARY 17
Beginning at 8:15
Benefit Deming Library Ass'n

PROGRAM
By Corona Sherlock and Local Talent

(1.)—Dance—Mendessohn's Spring Song, Corona Sherlock, assisted by Mary Josephine Schoepf and Roberta Tidmore as fairies and Brantley Tidmore and Dorothy Hall as gnomes.
(2.)—Vocal Selection, Mrs. A. T. Gloyd.
(3.)—Dance—Russian, Corona Sherlock.
(4.)—Vocal selection; a, Roses of Picardy and b, My Buddy, Margurite Moran.
(5.)—Dance—Girl of My Dreams, Corona Sherlock assisted by Esther Robinson.
(6.)—Gay Gavotte, Pupils of Corona Sherlock; Girls: Dorothy Hall, June Alger, Lynette Taylor, Laurette Breckbill, Barbara Schutz, Roberta Tidmore, Claudine Fox, Susan Calkins, Alice Stevens; Boys: Helen Raithel, Mary Josephine Schoepf, Eleanor Whitmore, Muriel Crane, Hilda Calkins, Margeret Cooke, Esther Douglas, Esther Robinson, Eunice Breckbill.

Intermission
(7.)—Dance—Spanish, Corona Sherlock assisted by Esther Robinson.
(8.)—Violin Quartette; (a, Garotte) (b, Minuet No. 2 in G).
Marquita Stevens, Alice Stevens, 1st Violin.
Sidney Wells, 2nd Violin.
Pete Valverda, 3rd Violin.
Bonnie Clark, 4th Violin.
Margeret Holt, Piano.
(9.)—Dance—1823-1923, Corona Sherlock and Esther Robinson.
(10.)—Reading, Mabel Steed.
(11.)—Dance—Deming Special, Corona Sherlock.
(12.)—Movie Revue, paged by Patty Moran. Miss Dupont—Katherine Wammel; Bebe Daniels—Miss Ethel Poe; Billy Burke—Margeret Holt; Irene Castle—Alice Hall; Alice Brady—Mrs. K. W. Kissick; Mae Marsh—Mrs. Chas. Taylor; Jane Lee—Helen Raithel; Clara Kimball Young—Nora Maude Steed; Harold Lloyd—Mr. H. G. Lyman; His Mother—Mrs. Thurmond; Eugene O'Brien—Joe Hume; Mary Pickford—Tom Green; Jack Holt—Wilbert Leach; Ruth Roland—Bill Burns; Rodolph Valentino —S O. Skidmore; Deming's Future Movie Queen—???.
Accompanist, Miss Marie Stevens.   Music by High School Orchestra.

Handbill for performance at Deming's Rialto Theater. "Aunt Lottie's" assigned role highlighted in last paragraph. Though not conclusive, the photograph of Mrs. Thurmond may be as she dressed for the part. *Handbill and photograph courtesy Patrick Tidmore.*

Alle Delle Stecker, seated second row from top, far left, with one of her high-school classes at San Luis Obispo, California. Mrs. Stecker was one of three heirs to Lottie Thurmond's estate. *Courtesy Lanette and John Shanahan.*

Another heir to Lottie Thurmond's estate, a close personal friend, Sigmund Lindauer. *Courtesy Deming/Luna Mimbres Museum.*

Joseph A. Mahoney, local Deming businessman and friend of Mrs. Lottie Thurmond. Mr. Mahoney was the third beneficiary listed in Lottie's *Last Will and Testament.* Before her death "Aunt Lottie" regularly took her evening meals with the Mahoneys. *Courtesy Deming/Luna Mimbres Museum.*

Susie Tidmore and "Aunt Lottie." Mr. J. Marvin Hunter interviewed Mrs. Tidmore about "Aunt Lottie's" childhood days. There is little doubt that much of what has been written about Lottie Deno's early life and Kentucky upbringing was slyly embellished by Lottie, repeated to Mrs. Tidmore who didn't question the tale's veracity, and then when asked passed the information along to an inquiring Mr. Hunter. *Courtesy Patrick Tidmore.*

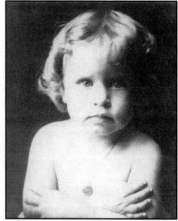

Roberta Tidmore [Wilcox], Lottie's goddaughter. *Courtesy Patrick Tidmore.*

Abby Carney, Roberta Tidmore [Lottie's goddaughter] and "Aunt Lottie" Thurmond. *Courtesy Patrick Tidmore.*

The Angel of San Antonio; Mystic Maude; *Lotta Dinero*; The Frozen Heart of Fort Griffin; or Miss Lottie Deno. Mrs. Charlotte Thurmond had her secrets—and she kept them! *Courtesy Patrick Tidmore.*

Purportedly Lottie Deno's scuffed leather trunk. On display at the Frontier Times Museum, Bandera, Texas. *Author's photo.*

The author at the Deming grave site of Charlotte Thurmond [Lottie Deno]. *Courtesy Bob Alexander.*

Endnotes Chapter 12

[1] Hunter, *The Story of Lottie Deno: Her Life and Times*. 1.

[2] Browning and McCravy, *A Complete Guide To Hunter's Frontier Times*. "His [J. Marvin Hunter] last book, *The Story of Lottie Deno*, was published after his death by my brother and sisters and me [J. Marvin Hunter, Jr.]. I printed it in my print shop in Grand Prairie. It gives factual information about the 'lady gambler' he knew in Deming, New Mexico." x.

[3] Hunter, "The Lottie Deno I Knew." Frequently it has been written, though misinterpreted, that John Warren Hunter who wrote "The Mystery Woman of Fort Concho," actually knew Miss Lottie Deno. This error may be dispelled by a careful review of Mr. J. Marvin Hunter's remarks, with emphasis added: "In the issue of *Frontier Times* for January, 1927, I published a short article about "The Mystery Woman of Fort Concho," written by my father, John Warren Hunter, in 1910. Father was at that time on the editorial staff of the San Angelo Standard, and *gathered his information about the mystery woman from old timers who were living there at the time the incidents mentioned took place*." 30.

[4] Hunter, "The Deming I Knew 44 Years Ago." 349.

[5] Hunter, "The Lottie Deno I Knew." 34.

[6] Wilcox, "Aunt Lottie." 87.

[7] Margaret Mitchell, *Gone With The Wind*. Copyright 1936, Macmillian Publishing Company.

[8] Ibid. 25; Pyron, *Southern Daughter: The Life of Margaret Mitchell*. "And by now, too, foreign presses were milling out their translations by the thousands and the tens of thousands." 435.

[9] Wilcox, "Aunt Lottie." "Aunt Lottie wasn't really my aunt. She was my godmother, and I still have her beautiful old ivory-covered prayer book which she gave me when I was confirmed. It has a black leather case, lined with white moiré, and fastened with an etched silver clasp. I was taught to call her 'aunt' as I did several of my mother's closest friends." 87.

[10] Unidentified newsclip [Jack Tidmore's obituary] 1933.

[11] Wilcox, "Aunt Lottie." "She [Lottie] told Mother [Susie Tidmore] that she had been wealthy and influential, but that her family had disowned her because they disapproved of her marriage to Mr. Thurmond." 87.

[12] Ibid. "A man named Mr. [J. Marvin] Hunter had called and asked if he could come visit with her to ask her [Susie Tidmore] about Aunt Lottie. This was in 1936 or so, several years after she [Lottie Thurmond] died. He said that he wrote books about people and events of the frontier west. She had said that he could come, mainly, I think, because she was curious. Then when he came...." 85.

[13] Ibid.

[14] Ibid. "It is difficult to tell how much of his [J. Marvin Hunter's] story is surmise. Mr. Hunter knew Mrs. Thurmond in Deming in 1900 when he was 20 and she was 56, and said he guessed at her past then."

[15] *Deming Headlight*, June 11, 1908. "...Mr. Thurmond was vice-president of the Deming National Bank, and in comfortable circumstances financially...."

[16] Section I, of 7 section Deming City Ordinance Number 25. 1905.

[17] Bill McGaw, "Deming Woman 'Took' Holliday For $70,000." *The Southwesterner*. May. 1962. 2.

[18] Measday, *History of Luna County, New Mexico*. Supplement I. "Most widely known residents of early Deming, without doubt, were Mr. and Mrs. Frank

Thurmond. In Deming, the Thurmonds were known as a quiet cultured couple in moderate financial circumstances. 'Aunt Lottie,' as Charlotte Thurmond was called by every child in the village...." "The couple also purchased a house in the village in which they lived until their deaths. (This house is owned today by Ora Perkins at 408 West Pine....)" 22.

[19] *Deming Headlight*, February 22, 1906.

[20] Ibid.; Virginia Woodward Measday, Deloris Measday Ruebush and Carol Measday Wootton, *Death Records From Mahoney Mortuary, Deming, Luna County, New Mexico, 1894-1907.*

[21] Administrator's Bond And Oath. Alle Delle Stecker of the Estate of Henry M. Stecker. April 4, 1906. Frank Thurmond and J. G. Moir, Sureties in the amount of $5000 each. Courtesy, Luna County Clerk, Luna County Courthouse, Deming, New Mexico.

[22] Final Account, Probate Court. Estate of Henry McClure Stecker. Luna County Clerk, Luna County Courthouse, Deming, New Mexioc.

[23] *Silver City Enterprise*, June 5, 1908.

[24] Ibid.

[25] Ibid; *Certificate Of Death*. Number 1510995. Frank Thurman [sic], June 5, 1908, Deming, Territory of New Mexico, County of Luna. Courtesy, New Mexico Vital Records and Health Statistics. Santa Fe. The official death certificate places Mr. Thurmond's age at 69, rather than 70 years old, as cited in the *Silver City Enterprise*; Measday, Ruebush and Wootton, *Death Records From Mahoney Mortuary, Deming, Luna County, New Mexico*. n. p.

[26] Ibid.; *Deming Headlight*, June 5, 1908.

[27] *Deming Headlight*, June 11, 1908.

[28] James A. Browning, *Violence Was No Stranger: A Guide to the Grave Sites of Famous Westerners.* 255.

[29] *Last Will and Testament of Frank Thurmond*. February 8, 1904. Courtesy, Luna County Clerk, Luna County Courthouse, Deming, New Mexico.

[30] *Certificate of Proof of Will*. Estate of Frank Thurmond, deceased. Probate Court, County of Luna, Territory of New Mexico. August 24, 1908. Courtesy, Luna County Clerk, Luna County Courthouse, Deming, New Mexico.

[31] *Deming Headlight*, Old-Timer's Edition, April 18, 1963; LaPorta, ed., *The History of Luna County*. 50.

[32] Ibid., [??], 1988; *The Southwesterner*, May 1962.

[33] Wilcox, "Aunt Lottie." 88.

[34] Handwritten manuscript, Patty Israel. Courtesy, Deming/Luna Mimbres Museum Archives. Deming, New Mexico.

[35] Measday, *History of Luna County*. Supplement I. "....reported to have had the only carpeted outhouse in Deming in the early days." 22; Helen Swope Carroll [Contributor] *History of Luna County*. "...as far as I know they [Frank and Lottie Thurmond] had the only carpeted outhouse in town—a fact learned during a short stay with them." 102.

[36] Wandra P. Smalley [Contributor], *The History of Luna County*. 136.

[37] Wilcox, "Aunt Lottie." 88; Dorothy A. Mathews [Contributor] *History of Luna County*. "One time I asked her [Aunt Lottie] how she stayed so pretty and well. She told me that in the winter, when it would snow, she took a bath in the snow in her back yard." 103.

[38] Handwritten manuscript, Martha Pollard Smalley. Courtesy Deming/Luna Mimbres Museum Archives, Deming, New Mexico; Wilcox, "Aunt Lottie." 88; Wandra P. Smalley [Contributor] *The History of Luna County*. "'Aunt' Lottie with a 'hoo-hoo'

would appear at lunchtime to eat with us, or at Mr. Lindauer's or at the A. J. Mahoney's." 136.

[39] Wilcox, "Aunt Lottie." 88.

[40] Ibid; Roberta Tidomre Wilcox [Contributor], *The History of Luna County*. 183.

[41] Ibid.

[42] Ibid.

[43] Ibid. "She had leaned fancywork from the nuns at the convent school where she had been sent as a girl, she said." 87.

[44] LaPorta, ed., *The History of Luna County*. 50; Smalley [Contributor] *The History of Luna County*. 136.

[45] Untied States Census. 1910. Deming, Luna County, New Mexico Territory.

[46] Assessment Roll, 1910. Luna County. Treasurer and Ex-Officio Collector's Office. Courtesy, Luna County Clerk, Luna County Courthouse, Deming, New Mexico.

[47] Certification of Charlotte J. Thurmond's *Last Will and Testament*. Probate No. 480. Probate Court, Luna County, Deming New Mexico.

[48] *Deming Hospital Assn. Inc., Claimant vs. Joseph A. Mahoney and Sigmund Lindauer*, Executors of the Estate of Charlotte J. Thurmond, Deceased. Probate Court. Probate No. 480. Luna County, Deming, New Mexico. This legal filing was not adversarial, but a perfunctory step in settling Aunt Lottie's outstanding debts.

[49] Rose, *Lottie Deno: Gambling Queen of Hearts*. 113.

[50] *Certificate of Death*, No. 8055447063. Alle Dell Stecker, Deceased. DOB December 9, 1884; DOD January 8, 1988. State of California, County of San Luis Obispo.

[51] *Last Will and Testament*, Charlotte J. Thurmond. Luna County Clerk, Luna County Courthouse, Deming, New Mexico.

[52] Ibid.

[53] Especial thanks must be extended to Lynette & John Shanahan, Templeton, California, for their gracious, thorough, and prompt historical research into the life of Mrs. Stecker's tenure as a highly respected San Luis Obispo High School teacher. Amiably they ferreted out primary source data and delightful photos.

[54] San Luis Obispo High School Annual—*Tiger Tales*—1941. Courtesy Lynette & John Shanahan.

[55] *Certificate of Death*, State of California. Alle Delle Stecker, January 8, 1988; J. Horner, Reference Dept. San Luis Obispo City-County Library, San Luis Obispo, California, to author, February 9, 2006; San Luis Obispo *Telegram Tribune*, January 13, 1988.

[56] *Deming Hospital Association, Inc., vs. Joseph A. Mahoney and Sigmund Lindauer*, Executors of the Estate of Charlotte J. Thurmond, Deceased. Probate Court Luna County, Deming, New Mexico.

[57] Ibid.

[58] *Certificate Of Death*, Number 1459372. Lottie Thurmond, February 9, 1934, Deming, New Mexico.

[59] *Deming Headlight*, February 16, 1934; Ross Calvin, *River of the Sun: Stories of the Storied Gila*.

[60] Inventory of Property. The Estate of Charlotte Thurmond, Deceased. Luna County Probate Court. No. 480. Luna County Courthouse, Deming, New Mexico.

[61] Hunter, "The Lottie Deno I Knew." "I am convinced that it is the same little leather-bound trunk that she carried away from Fort Griffin when she departed for parts unknown." 35.

[62] Hunter, *The Story of Lottie Deno: Her Life and Times*. 46.

[63] Wilcox, "Aunt Lottie." 88.

Bibliography

Non-Published Sources:

Non-Published sources—manuscripts, official documents, court records, tax rolls, correspondence, census records, interviews, etc., are cited with specificity in chapter endnotes. Primary and secondary source materials obtained from the following accommodating institutions:

Old Jail Art Center and Archives. Albany, Texas.
Fort Griffin State Park, Fort Griffin, Texas.
Nita Stewart Haley Memorial Library & J. Evetts Haley History Center. Midland.
Texas State Library & Archives Commission. Austin.
University of Maryland, College Park, Maryland.
Harold B. Simpson History Complex—Confederate Research Center. Hillsboro, Texas.
Panhandle-Plains Historical Museum. Canyon, Texas.
Southwest Collection. Texas Tech University. Lubbock.
National Ranching Heritage Center. Lubbock.
The Texas Collection. Baylor University. Waco.
West Texas Collection. Porter Henderson Library. Angelo State University. San Angelo.
Fort Concho Historic Site and Museum Archives. San Angelo.
Texas Ranger Hall of Fame and Museum. Waco.
Waco Public Library. Waco.
Frontier Times Museum, Bandara, Texas.
The Center for American History. University of Texas. Austin.
Arizona Historical Society—Yuma. Yuma, Arizona.
Texana/Genealogy Dept. San Antonio Public Library. San Antonio.
Periodicals Department. El Paso Public Library. El Paso.
Hardin-Simmons University. Abilene, Texas.
Shackelford County Clerk. Albany, Texas.
Jack County Clerk. Jacksboro, Texas.
Kinney County Clerk's Office, Brackettville, Texas.
Kinney County Appraisal Office, Brackettville, Texas.
G. J. Ritchie Public Library, Jacksboro, Texas.
New Mexico Commission of Public Records—State Record Center & Archives. Santa Fe.
New Mexico Vital Records and Health Statistics. Santa Fe.
Miller Library. Western New Mexico University. Silver City, New Mexico.
Grant County Clerk. Silver City, New Mexico
Silver City Museum. Silver City. New Mexico
Silver City Public Library, Silver City New Mexico.
Luna County Clerk. Deming, New Mexico
Deming Luna/Mimbres Museum. Deming, New Mexico.
Deming Public Library. Deming, New Mexico.
Deming City Clerk's Office. Deming, New Mexico
The Magazine House. La Pine, Oregon

Books:

Adams, Ramon F. *Six-Guns and Saddle Leather—A Bibliography of Books and Pamphlets On Western Outlaws and Gunmen.* Dover Publications, Inc. New York. 1969.

Ailman, H. B. (Lundwall, Helen, ed.) *Pioneering in Territorial Silver City—H. B. Ailman's Recollections of Silver City and the Southwest, 1871-1892.* University of New Mexico. Albuquerque. 1983.

Alexander, Bob *Dangerous Dan Tucker—New Mexico's Deadly Lawman.* High-Lonesome Books. Silver City. 2001.

_____. *Harvey Whitehill: Silver City Stalwart—An Old West Lawman on the New Mexico Frontier.* High-Lonesome Books. Silver City. 2005.

_____. *Lawmen, Outlaws and S. O. Bs—Gunfighters of the Old Southwest.* High-Lonesome Books. Silver City. 2004.

_____. *Six-Guns and Single-Jacks: A History of Silver City and Southwestern New Mexico.* Gila Books. Silver City. 2005.

_____. *Desert Desperadoes: The Banditti of Southwestern New Mexico.* Gila Books. Silver City. 2006.

_____. *Lawmen, Outlaws, and S. O. Bs.* Volume II. High-Lonesome Books. Silver City. 2007.

Anderson, Charles G. *In Search Of The Buffalo: The Story of J. Wright Mooar.* Pioneer Press. Union City, Tennessee. 1996.

Austerman, Wayne R. *Sharps Rifles and Spanish Mules—The San Antonio/El Paso Mail, 1851-1881.* Texas A & M University Press. College Station. 1985.

Awbrey, Betty Dooley (with Dooley) *Why Stop?—A Guide to Texas Historical Roadside Markers.* Lone Star Books. Houston. 1999.

Ball, Larry D. *Desert Lawmen: The High Sheriffs of New Mexico and Arizona, 1846-1912.* University of New Mexico. Albuquerque. 1992.

Bartholomew, Ed *Wyatt Earp—The Man and the Myth.* Frontier Book Co. Toyahavle, Texas. 1964.

_____. *Western Hard-Cases: Or, Gunfighters Named Smith.* Frontier Book Co. Ruidoso, New Mexico. 1960.

Barton, Barbara *Pistol Packin' Preachers: Circuit Riders of Texas.* Republic of Texas Press. Taylor Trade Publishing. Lanham, Maryland. 2005.

Battey, F. A. [& Company] *Biographical Souvenir of the State of Texas.* Donohue & Henneberry. Chicago. 1889.

Bell, Bob Boze *The Illustrated Life and Times of Doc Holliday.* Tri-Star—Boze Publications. Phoenix. 1994.

Berry, Susan (with Russell) *Built to Last—An Architectural History of Silver City, New Mexico.* Silver City Museum Society. Silver City. 1995.

Biggers, Don H. (Farmer, Joan, ed.) *Shackelford County Sketches.* The Clear Fork Press. Albany & Fort Griffin. 1974.

_____. *Buffalo Guns & Barbed Wire.* Texas Tech University Press. Lubbock. 1991.

Blanton, Joseph Edwin *John Larn.* Venture Press. Albany, Texas. 1994.

Blevins, Don *From Angels to Hellcats—Legendary Texas Women, 1836 to 1880.* Mountain Press Publishing Company. Missoula, Montana. 2001.

Bowser, David *West of the Creek: Murder, Mayhem and Vice in Old San Antonio.* Maverick Publishing Company. San Antonio. 2003.

Brown, Richard Maxwell *No Duty To Retreat.* University of Oklahoma. Norman. 1991.

Brown, Robert L. *Saloons of the American West.* Sundance Books. Silverton, Colorado. 1978.

Browning, James A. *Violence Was No Stranger—A Guide to the Grave Sites of Famous Westerners*. Vol. I. Barbed Wire Press. Stillwater, Oklahoma. 1993.
_____. *Violence Was No Stranger*. Vol. II. Published by Janice B. McCravy. 2004
_____. [with Janice B. McCravy] *Hunters's Frontier Times*. Eakin Press. Austin. 2000.

Burrows, William E. *Vigilante!—The Story of Americans…Then and Now…Guarding Each Other*. Harcourt Brace Jovanovich. New York. 1976.

Butler, Anne M. *Daughters of Joy, Sisters of Misery—Prostitutes in the American West—1865-90*. University of Illinois Press. Urbana and Chicago. 1985.

Butts, J. Lee *Texas Bad Girls—Hussies, Harlots and Horse Thieves*. Republic of Texas Press. Plano, Texas. 2001.

Caldwell, Clifton *Fort Davis: A Family Frontier Fort*. Clear Fork Press. Albany, Texas. 1986

Caldwell, Shirley (with Green & Nail) *For 500 Years—The Shackelford County Courthouse*. Bright Sky Press. Albany, Texas and New York, New York. 2001.

Carmony, Neil B. (ed.) *How I Routed A Gang Of Arizona Outlaws*. Trail to Yesterday Books. Tucson. 1995.

Carter, Robert G. *On the Border with Mackenzie or Winning West Texas from the Comanches*. Texas State Historical Association. Austin. 2007'

Casey, Robert J. *The Texas Border And Some Borderliners*. The Bobbs-Merrill Company, Inc. Indianapolis. 1950.

Cashion, Ty *A Texas Frontier—The Clear Fork Country and Fort Griffin, 1849-1887*. University of Oklahoma Press. Norman. 1996.

Chase, C. M. *The Editor's Run in Colorado and New Mexico*. Frontier Book Co. Fort Davis, Texas. 1950.

Chesley, Hervey E. *Trails Traveled—Tales Told*. Nita Stewart Haley Memorial Library. Midland. 1979.

Clarke, Mary Whatley *A Century of Cow Business—The First Hundred Years of the Texas and Southwestern Cattle Raisers Association*. Fort Worth.
_____. *The Palo Pinto Story*. The Manney Company. Fort Worth, Texas. 1956.

Clayton, Lawrence (ed., with Farmer) *Tracks Along the Clear Fork—Stories from Shackelford and Throckmorton Counties*. McWhiney Foundation Press. Abilene, Texas. 2000.

Clemens, Gus. *The Concho Country*. Ethicon, Inc. 1994.

Collinson, Frank (Clarke, Mary Whatley, ed.) *Life in the Saddle*. University of Oklahoma Press. Norman. 1963.

Cook, James H. *Fifty Years on the Old Frontier*. University of Oklahoma Press. Norman. 1957.

Cook, John R. *The Border and The Buffalo*. State House Press. Austin. 1989.

Cook, Michael L. [with Glenda K. Trapp] *Kentucky Genealogical Index*. Volume I & 3. Cook Publications. Evansville, Indiana. n. d.

Couchman, Donald Howard *Cook's Peak—Pasaron Por Aqui: A Focus On United States History In Southwestern New Mexico*. New Mexico Bureau of Land Management. Las Cruces. 1990.

Crouch, Carrie J. *A History of Young County*, Texas. Texas State Historical Association. Austin, Texas. 1956.

Cunningham, Sharon (ed., with Gilbert & Reminger) *Encyclopedia of Buffalo Hunters and Skinner Volume I*. Pioneer Press. Union City, Tennessee. 2003.

Curry, W. Hubert *Sun Rising on the West: The Saga of Henry Clay and Elizabeth Smith*. Crosby County Pioneer Memorial (Quality Printers & Typographers) Crosbyton, Texas. 1979.

Cusack, Michael F. (with Pirtle) *The Lonely Sentinel—Fort Clark: On Texas's Western Frontier*. Eakin Press. Austin. 1985.

Dary, David *Seeking Pleasure in the Old West*. Alfred A. Knopf, Inc. New York. 1995.

DeArment, Robert K. *Knights of the Green Cloth—The Saga of the Frontier Gamblers*. University of Oklahoma Press. Norman. 1982.

_____. *Bravo of the Brazos—John Larn of Fort Griffin, Texas*. University of Oklahoma Press. Norman. 2002.

_____. *Alias Frank Canton*. University of Oklahoma Press. Norman.1996.

_____. *George Scarborough—The Life And Death of a Lawman on the Closing Frontier*. University of Oklahoma Press. Norman. 1992.

_____. *Broadway Bat: Gunfighter in Gotham, The New York City Years of Bat Masterson*. Talei Publishers. Honolulu. 2005.

Dobie, J. Frank *Rattlesnakes*. Little Brown and Company. Boston. 1965.

_____. *Coronado's Children: Tales of Lost Mines and Buried Treasure of the Southwest*. University of Texas Press. Austin. 1930.

Dooley, Claude (with Awbrey). *Why Stop?—A Guide to Texas Historical Roadside Markers*. Lone Star Books. Houston. 1999.

Drago, Harry Sinclair *Great American Cattle Trails—The Story of the Old Cow Paths of the East and the Longhorn Highways of the Plains*. Bramhall House. New York. 1965.

Dunlay, Thomas W. *Wolves for the Blue Soldiers—Indian Scouts and Auxiliaries with the United States Army, 1860-90*. University of Nebraska Press. Lincoln. 1982.

Eckhardt, C. F. *Tales of Badmen, Bad Women, and Bad Places*. Texas Tech University Press. Lubbock. 1999.

Enss, Chris *How the West Was Worn: Bustles and Buckskins on the Wild Frontier*. Twodot. Helena, MT. 2006.

_____. *The Lady Was a Gambler: True Stories of Notorious Women of the Old West*. Twodot, Helena, MT. 2008.

Erodoes, Richard *Saloons of the Old West*. Gramercy Books. New York. 1997.

Erwin, Richard E. *The Truth About Wyatt Earp*. The O. K. Press. Carpinteria, California. 1993.

Everett, Donald *San Antonio Legacy*. Trinity University Press. San Antonio. 1979.

Farmer, Joan Halford (ed., with Clayton) *Tracks Along the Clear Fork—Stories from Shackelford and Throckmorton Counties*. McWhiney Foundation Press. Abilene, Texas.2000.

_____. *Fort Griffin: Wildest Town on the Prairie*. Self. Albany, Texas. 2004.

Fehrenbach, T. R. *Lone Star—A History of Texas and the Texans*. Macmillan Publishing Co., Inc. New York. 1968.

Ferris, Robert G. (Series Editor) *Soldier And Brave—Historic Places Associated With Indian Affairs and the Indian Wars in the Trans-Mississippi West*. National Park Service. Washington, D. C. 1971.

Findlay, John M. *People of Chance—Gambling In American Society From Jamestown to Las Vegas*. Oxford University Press. New York. 1986.

Frazier, Robert W. *Forts Of The West—Military Forts and Presidios and Posts Commonly Called Forts West of the Mississippi River to 1898*. University of Oklahoma Press. Norman. 1965

Frost, H. Gordon *The Gentlemen's Club: The Story of Prostitution In El Paso*. Mangan Books. El Paso. 1983.

Galbreath, Lester W. *Fort Griffin and the Clear Fork Country*. By Author. 1997.

_____. *Campfire Tales: True Stories From The Western Frontier*. Bright Sky Press. Albany, Texas. 2005.

Gard, Wayne *The Great Buffalo Hunt—Its History and Drama, and its Role in the Opening of the West*. University of Nebraska Press. Lincoln. 1959.

_____. *Frontier Justice*. University of Oklahoma Press. Norman. 1949.

Gilbert, Miles (ed., with Reminger & Cunningham) *Encyclopedia of Buffalo Hunters and Skinners Volume I*. Pioneer Press. Union City, Tennessee. 2003.

Gillett, James B. *Fugitives From Justice*. State House Press. Austin. 1997. Gournay, Luke *Texas Boundaries—Evolution of the State's Counties*. Texas A & M University Press. College Station. 1995.

Green, Bill *The Dancing was Lively—Fort Concho, Texas: A Social History, 1867 to 1882*. Fort Concho Sketches Publishing Co. San Angelo. 1974.

Green, Bob (with Caldwell & Nail). *For 500 Years—The Shackelford County Courthouse*. Bright Sky Press. Albany, Texas and New York, New York. 2001.

Green, Karen Mauer *The Kentucky Gazette, 1801-1820*. Gateway Press, Inc. Baltimore. 1985.

Greene, A. C. *A Personal Country*. University of North Texas Press. Denton. 1969.

_____. *900 Miles On The Butterfield Trail*. University of North Texas Press. Denton. 1994.

Gregory, J. N. *Fort Concho—Its Why and Wherefore*. Newsfoto Yearbooks. San Angelo. 1957.

Gunter, Archibald Clavering *Miss Nobody of Nowhere* The Home Publishing Co. New York. 1890.

Hackler, George *The Butterfield Trail In New Mexico*. Yucca Enterprises. Las Cruces. 2005.

Haenn, William F. *Images of America: Fort Clark and Brackettville, Land of Heroes*. Arcadia Publishing. Charleston, South Carolina. 2002.

Haley, J. Evetts *Jeff Milton—A Good Man With A Gun*. University of Oklahoma Press. Norman. 1948.

_____. *Fort Concho and the Texas Frontier*. San Angelo Standard-Times. San Angelo. Texas 1952.

Haley, James L. *The Buffalo War—The History of the Red River Indian Uprising of 1874*. Doubleday & Company, Inc. New York. 1976.

Hamilton, Allen Lee *Sentinel of the Southern Plains—Fort Richardson and the Northwest Texas Frontier, 1866-1878*. Texas Christian University Press. Fort Worth. 1988.

Henderson, Eva Pendleton *Wild Horses, A Turn-Of-The Century Prairie Girlhood*. Sunstone Press. Santa Fe. 1983.

Hertzog, Peter *Outlaws of New Mexico*. Sunstone Press. Santa Fe. 1984.

Hewett, Janet B. (ed.) *Supplement To The Official Records Of The Union And Confederate Armies*. Part III—Correspondence. Volume 3. Serial No. 95. Broadfoot Publishing Company Wilmington, North Carolina. 1999.

Hicks, Jim. (ed.) *The Gamblers*. Time-Life Books. New York. 1978.

Hilliard, George *A Hundred Years of Horse Tracks—The Story of the Gray Ranch*. High-Lonesome Books. Silver City. 1996.

Holden, Frances Mayhugh *Lambshead Before Interwoven—A Texas Range Chronicle, 1848-1878*. Texas A & M University Press. College Station. 1982.

Holden, W. C. *Rollie Burns or An Account of the Ranching Industry on the South Plains*. Texas A & M University Press. College Station. (1932) 1986.

_____. *Alkali Trails*. Texas Tech University Press. Lubbock. 1930.

Hooker, Forrestine C. (Steve Wilson, ed.) *Child of the Fighting Tenth: On The Frontier With The Buffalo Soldiers*. Oxford University Press. Oxford, New York. 2003.

Huckaby, Ida Lasater *Ninety-Four Years In Jack County*. Steck Company. Austin. 1949.

Hunter, J. Marvin *The Story of Lottie Deno—Her Life and Times*. The Four Hunters. Bandera. 1959.

_____. (ed.). *The Trail Drivers of Texas.* University of Texas Press. Austin. 1985.

Hyams, Jay *The Life and Times of the Western Movie.* Gallery Books. New York. 1983.

Jack County Genealogical Society. *The History of Jack County Texas.* Curtis Media Corp. 1985.

Jahns, Pat *The Frontier World of Doc Holliday.* Hastings House Publishers. New York. 1957.

Jenkinson, Michael *Ghost Towns of New Mexico: Playthings of the Wind.* University of New Mexico. Albuquerque. 1967.

Jillson, Willard Rouse *Old Kentucky Entries And Deeds.* The Standard Printing Co. Louisville. 1926.

Johnson, David *John Ringo.* Barbed Wire Press. Stillwater, Oklahoma. 1996.

Julyan, Robert *The Place Names of New Mexico.* University of New Mexico. Albuquerque. 1996.

Kentucky, State of *Report of the Adjutant General of the State of Kentucky, 1866.* Kentucky Yeoman Office, John H. Harney, Public Printer. Frankfort, Kentucky. 1866.

Kinevan, Marcos *Frontier Cavalryman: Lieutenant John Bigelow With The Buffalo Soldiers In Texas.* Texas Western Press. El Paso, Texas. 1998.

King, Patsy Crow *Sadie Orchard: The Time of Her Life.* Self. (PDX Printing) El Paso. 2006.

Kleber, John E. [ed.] *The Kentucky Encyclopedia.* University of Kentucky Press. Lexington. 1992.

Knight, Oliver *Life and Manners in the Frontier Army.* University of Oklahoma Press. Norman. 1978.

Koop, Waldo E. (with Rosa). *Rowdy Joe Lowe—Gambler With A Gun.* University of Oklahoma Press. Norman. 1989.

Kraisinger, Gary & Margaret *The Western: The Greatest Texas Cattle Trail, 1874-1886.* Self. Halstead, Kansas. 2004.

Leckie, Shirley A. (ed.) *The Colonel's Lady on the Western Frontier—The Correspondence of   Alice Kirk Grierson.* University of Nebraska Press. Lincoln. 1989.

Leckie, William H. *The Buffalo Soldiers—A Narrative of the Negro Cavalry in the West.* University of Oklahoma Press. Norman. 1967.

_____. & Leckie, Shirley A. *Unlikely Warriors—General Benjamin Grierson and His Family* University of Oklahoma Press. Norman. 1984.

Ledbetter, Barbra A. Neal *Fort Belknap, Frontier Saga—Indians, Negroes and Anglo Americans On the Texas Border.* Lavender Books. 1982.

Lewis, Alfred Henry *Wolfville.* (Grosset & Dunlap) Frederick A. Stokes Company. New York. 1897.

_____. *Wolfville Days.* (Grossett & Dunlap) Frederick A. Stokes Company. New York. 1902.

_____. *Wolfville Nights.* (Grosset & Dunlap) Frederick A. Stokes Company. New York. 1902.

Lewis, Preston *The Lady and Doc Holliday.* Diamond Books. Austin. 1989.

Luna County Historical Society *The History of Luna County.* Deming. 1978.

Lynch, Sylvia D. *Aristocracy's Outlaw—The Doc Holliday Story.* Iris Press. New Tazewell, TN. 1994.

McAdams, Mrs. Harry Kennett *Kentucky Pioneer And Court Records.* Genealogical Publishing Company. Baltimore. 1967.

McConnell, H. H. *Five Years A Cavalryman or, Sketches of Regular Army Life on the Texas Frontier, 1866-1871.* University of Oklahoma Press. Norman. 1996.

McConnell, Joseph Carroll *The West Texas Frontier or a Descriptive History of Early Times In Western Texas*. Gazette Printing. Jacksboro.

McCravy, Janice B. [with James A. Browning] *Hunter's Frontier Times*. Eakin Press. Austin. 2000.

McIntire, Jim (DeArment, Robert, ed.) *Early Days In Texas*. University of Oklahoma Press. Norman. 1992.

McKenna, James A. *Black Range Tales*. The Rio Grande Press. Glorieta, New Mexico. 1963.

McLaird, James D. *Calamity Jane: The Woman and the Legend*. University of Oklahoma. Norman. 2005.

McLoughlin, Denis *Wild & Woolly—Encyclopedia of the Old West*. Doubleday & Company, Inc. Garden City, New York. 1975.

McMinus, J. *Bexar County, Texas, Marriage Records, 1837-1866*. n. p. n. d.

Marshall, Jim *Swinging Doors*. Frank McCaffrey Publishers. Seattle. 1949.

Masterson, W. B. (Bat) *Famous Gunfighters of the Western Frontier*. (1907 *Human Life* series). VistaBooks. Silverthorne, Colorado. 1996.

Matthews, Sallie Reynolds *Interwoven—A Pioneer Chronicle*. Texas A & M University Press. College Station. (1936) 1997.

Meketa, Jacqueline *From Martyrs To Murderers: The Old Southwest's Saints, Sinners & Scalawags*. Yucca Tree Press. Las Cruces. 1993.

Metz, Leon Claire *The Encyclopedia of Lawmen, Outlaws, and Gunfighters*. Facts on File, Inc. New York. 2003.

_____. *John Selman, Texas Gunfighter*. Hastings House Publishers. New York. 1966.

_____. *The Shooters*. Mangan Books. El Paso. (1976) 1986.

_____. *Pat Garrett: The Story Of A Western Lawman*. University of Oklahoma. Norman. 1974.

Michener, James A. *Texas*. Random House. New York. 1985.

Michno, Gregory F. *Encyclopedia of Indian Wars—Western Battles and Skirmishes, 1850-1890*. Mountain Press Publishing Company. Missoula. 2003.

Miles, Susan *Fort Concho In 1877*. The Bradley Co. San Angelo. 1972.

Monahan, Sherry *The Wicked West: Boozers, Cruisers, Gamblers, and more*. Rio Nuevo Publishers. Tucson. 2005.

Moynahan, Jay *Talkin' About Sportin' Women—A Dictionary of Terms Related to Prostitution on The American Frontier*. Chickadee Publishing. Spokane. 2002.

_____. *Soiled Doves, Sportin' Women and Other Fallen Flowers—Prostitution on the American Frontier*. Chicadee Publishing. Spokane. 2005.

_____. *Photographs of Red Light Ladies, 1863-1920*. Chickadee Publishing. Spokane. 2005.

_____. *Fifty Years of Prostitute Photos, 1870-1920*. Vols. I, II, III. Chickadee Publishing. Spokane. 2004 and 2005.

_____. *Just Call Me Kate: Four Kates of Negotiable Virtue*. Chickadee Publishing. Spokane. 2005

Mulroy, Kevin *Freedom on the Border: The Seminole Maroons in Florida, the Indian Territory, Coahuila, And Texas*. Texas Tech University Press. Lubbock. 1993.

Myers, John Myers *Doc Holliday*. University of Nebraska Press. Lincoln. 1955.

Myrick, David F. *New Mexico's Railroads—A Historical Survey*. University of New Mexico Press. Albuquerque. 1970.

Nail, Reilly (with Caldwell & Green). *For 500 Years—The Shacckelford County Courthouse*. Bright Sky Press. Albany, Texas and New York, New York. 2001.

Nash, Jay Robert *Encyclopedia of Western Lawmen & Outlaws*. Da Capo Press, Inc. New York. 1992.

Neal, Jr., Charles M. *Valor Across The Lone Star: The Congressional Medal of Honor in Frontier Texas.* Texas State Historical Association. 2002.

Nelson, Susan & David *The Silver City Book I—"Wild and Woolly Days"* Silver Star Publications. Silver City. 1978.

Newcomb, Jr., W. W. *The Indians of Texas—From Prehistoric to Modern Times.* University of Texas Press. Austin. 1961.

Nolan, Frederick *Tascosa: Its Life and Gaudy Times.* Texas Tech University. Lubbock. 2007.

_____. *The West of Billy the Kid.* University of Oklahoma Press. Norman. 1998.

Nordyke, Lewis *Great Roundup—The Story of Texas and Southwestern Cowmen.* William Morrow &Company. New York. 1955.

Northcott, Dennis. *Indiana Civil War Veterans.* By author. St. Louis, Missouri. 2005.

Notson, William M. *Fort Concho Medical History.* Fort Concho Preservation & Museum. San Angelo.1974.

O'Neal, Bill. *Encyclopedia of Western Gunfighters.* University of Oklahoma Press. Norman. 1979.

_____. *Fighting Men of the Indian Wars.* Barbed Wire Press. Stillwater, Oklahoma. 1991.

Pearce, T. M. *New Mexico Place Names: A Geographical Dictionary.* University of New Mexico. Albuquerque. 1965.

Perkins, Doug (with Ward) *Brave Men & Cold Steel—A History of Range Detectives and Their Peacemakers.* Texas & Southwestern Cattle Raisers Foundation. Fort Worth. 1984.

Pierce, Michael D. *The Most Promising Young Officer—A Life of Ranald Slidell Mackenzie.* University of Oklahoma Press. Norman. 1993.

Pirtle III, Caleb (with Cusack) *The Lonely Sentinel—Fort Clark: On Texas's Western Frontier.* Eakin Press. Austin. 1985.

Poe, Sophie A. *Buckboard Days.* University of New Mexico Press. Albuquerque. 1936.

Poling-Kempes, Lesley, *The Harvey Girls: Women Who Opened the West.* Marlowe & Company. New York. 1991.

Prassel, Frank Richard *The Western Peace Officer—A Legacy o f Law and Order.* University of Oklahoma Press. Norman. 1972.

Rakocy, Bill *Ghosts of Kingstron and Hillsboro, New Mexico.* Bravo Press. El Paso. 1983.

Rath, Ida Ellen *The Rath Trail.* McCormick-Armstrong Co., Inc. Wichita, Kansas. 1961.

Rathjen, Frederick W. *The Texas Panhandle Frontier.* University of Texas Press. Austin. 1973.

Reiter, Joan Swallow *The Women.* Time-Life Books. Alexandria, Virginia. 1978.

Reminger, Leo (ed., with Gilbert & Cunningham) *Encyclopedia of Buffalo Hunters and Skinners.* Volume I. Pioneer Press. Union City, Tennessee. 2003.

Richardson, Rupert Norval *Comanche Barrier to South Plains Settlement.* Eakin Press. Austin. 1996.

Rickey, Jr., Don *Forty Miles a Day on Beans and Hay.* University of Oklahoma Press. Norman. 1963.

Ringgold, Jennie Parks *Frontier Days In The Southwest.* The Naylor Company. San Antonio. 1952.

Rister, Carl Coke *Fort Griffin on the Texas Frontier.* University of Oklahoma Press. Norman. 1956.

Roberts, Gary L. *Doc Holliday: The Life and Legend.* John Wiley & Sons, Inc. Hoboken, N. J. 2006.

Robertson, Pauline Durrett and R. L. Robertson. *Panhandle Pilgrimage: Illustrated Tales Tracing History In The Texas Panhandle.* Paramount Publishing Company. 1978.

Robinson III, Charles *The Frontier World of Fort Griffin—The Life and Death of a Western Town.* Arthur H. Clark Company. Spokane. 1992.

_____. *Bad Hand—A Biography Of General Ranald S. Mackenzie.* State House Press. Austin. 1993.

_____. *Frontier Forts of Texas.* Lone Star Books. Houston. 1986.

_____. *The Buffalo Hunters.* State House Press. Austin. 1995.

Rosa, Joseph G. (with Koop) *Rowdy Joe Lowe—Gambler With A Gun.* University of Oklahoma Press. Norman. 1989.

Rose, Cynthia *Lottie Deno—Gambling Queen of Hearts.* Clear Light Publishers. Santa Fe. 1994.

Russell, Sharman Apt (with Berry) *Built to Last—An Architectural History of Silver City, New Mexico* Silver City Historical Society. Silver City. 1995.

Rutter, Michael *Upstairs Girls: Prostitution in the American West.* Farcountry Press. Helena, MT. 2005.

Rye, Edgar *The Quirt and the Spur.* Texas Tech University Press. Lubbock. 2000.

Sandoz, Mari *The Buffalo Hunters—The Story of the Hide Men.* Hasting House. New York. 1954.

San Antonio Genealogical & Historical Society *Marriages of Bexar County Texas— Books E & F, August 27, 1866-May 29, 1879.* San Antonio, Texas. n. d.

Sauer, Else (ed.) *Kinney County. 1852-1977* Kinney County Historical Society. Brackettville, Texas. n. d.

Seagraves, Anne *Soiled Doves—Prostitution in the Early West.* Wesanne Publictions. Hayden, Idaho. 1994.

Severa, Joan *Dressed for the Photographer: Ordinary Americans & Fashion, 1840-1900.* Kent State University Press. Kent, Ohio. 1995.

Sherman, James E. & Barbara H. *Ghost Towns and Mining Camps of New Mexico.* University of Oklahoma Press. Norman. 1975.

Skogen, Larry C. *Indian Depredation Claims, 1796-1920.* University of Oklahoma Press. Norman 1996.

Smith, Thomas T. *The Old Army In Texas—A Research Guide to the U. S. Army in Nineteenth-Century Texas.* Texas State Historical Association. Austin. 2000.

Sonnichen, C. L. *I'll Die Before I'll Run—The Story of the Great Feuds of Texas.* University of Nebraska Press. Lincoln. 1951.

Stallard, Patricia Y. *Glittering Misery—Dependents of the Indian Fighting Army.* University of Oklahoma Press. Norman. 1978.

Stanley, F. (Stanley Crocchiola) *The Deming New Mexico Story.* Pantex, Texas. 1962.

_____. *The Lake Valley Story.* Pep, Texas. 1964.

_____. *The Kingston Story.* Pantex, Texas. 1961.

_____. *The Shakespeare Story.* Pantex, Texas. 1961.

_____. *The Georgetown Story.* Pep, Texas. 1963.

_____. *The Hillsboro Story.* Pep, Texas. 1964.

Steckmesser, Kent Ladd *The Western Hero In History And Legend.* University of Oklahoma Press. Norman. 1965.

Stephens, John Richard (ed.) *Wyatt Earp Speaks.* Fern Canyon Press. Cambria, California. 1998.

Swartley, Ron *Fort Cummings and Massacre Canyon: Rugged Duty in the Old Southwest.* Frontier Image Press. Silver City, New Mexico. 2004.

Tanner, Karen Holliday *Doc Holliday—A Family Portrait.* University of Oklahoma Press. Norman. 1998.

_____. *Doc's Holliday's Las Vegas Career.* Self. Fallbrook, California. 2005.

_____. [with John D. Tanner, Jr.] *Directory Of Inmates: New Mexico Territorial Penitentiary, 1884-1912.* Runnin' Iron. Fallbrook, California. 2006.

Tefetiller, Casey *Wyatt Earp—The Life Behind The Legend.* John Wiley & Sons, Inc. New York. 1997.

Thrapp, Dan L. *Encyclopedia of Frontier Biography.* Three Volumes. University of Nebraska Press. Lincoln. 1988.

Tise, Sammy *Texas County Sheriffs.* Tise Genealogical Research. Hallettsville, Texas. 1989.

Tom Green County Historical Preservation League, Inc. *Tom Green County: Chronicles of Our Heritage.* Volume One. H. V. Chapman & Sons. Abilene, Texas.1993.

Tórrez, Robert J. *New Mexico in 1876-1877 A Newspaperman's View: The Travels & Reports of William D. Dawson.* Rio Grande Books. Albuquerque. 2007.

Trapp, Glenda K. [with Michael L. Cook] *Kentucky Genealogical Index.* Volume I. Cook Publications. Evansville, Indiana. n. d.

Traywick, Ben T. *John Henry (The "Doc" Holliday Story).* Red Marie's Bookstore. Tombstone. 1996.

Turner, Alford E. *The Earps Talk.* Creative Publishing. College Station, Texas. 1982.

Uglow, Loyd M. *Standing In The Gap—Army Outposts, Picket Stations, And the Pacification of the Texas Frontier 1866-1886.* Texas Christian University Press. Fort Worth. 2001.

Utley, Robert M. *High Noon In Lincoln: Violence on the Western Frontier.* University of New Mexico Albuquerque. 1987.

Van Cise, Philip *Fighting the Underworld.* The Riverside Press. Cambridge Massachusetts. 1936.

Ward, Nancy (with Perkins) *Brave Men & Cold Steel—A History of Range Detectives and Their Peacemakers.* Texas & Southwestern Cattle Raisers Foundation. Fort Worth. 1984.

Waugh, Julia Nott *The Silver Cradle* University of Texas Press. Austin. 1955.

Watts, Peter *A Dictionary of the Old West.* Promontory Press. New York. 1977.

Wheeler, Keith *The Chroniclers.* Time-Life Books. New York. 1976.

White, Gifford, *1840 Citizens Of Texas. Land Grants.* Volumes 1 & 3. Ericson Books. Nacogdoches, Texas. 1988.

Wjote. Virgil D. *Index To Texas CSA Pension Files.* National Historical Publishing Company. Waynesboro, Tennessee. 1989.

Williams, Clayton W. (Wallace, Ernest, ed.) *Texas' Last Frontier—Fort Stockton and the Trans-Pecos, 1861-1895.* Texas A & M University Press. College Station. 1982.

Williams, J. W. (Neighbours, Kenneth F., ed.) *Old Texas Trails.* Eakin Press. Austin.1979.

Williams, O. W. (Myres, S. D., ed.) *Pioneer Surveyor & Frontier Lawyer—The Personal Narrative of O. W. Williams, 1877-1902.* Texas Western Press. El Paso. 1966.

Wilson Club *Jefferson County Kentucky: Early Marriages.* Book III [June 1837-May 10, 1842] McDowell Publications. Utica, Kentucky. n. d.

Wooster, Robert *Soldiers, Sutlers, and Settlers—Garrison Life on the Texas Frontier.* Texas A & M University. College Station. 1987.

Periodicals:

Alexander, Bob "Comanchero Nightmare: John N. Hittson." National Association
    For Outlaw And Lawman History, Inc. (NOLA) *Quarterly.* April – June 2004.
_____."Guns. Girls & Gamblers: Silver City's Wilder Side." Western Outlaw-
    Lawman History Association (WOLA) *Journal.* #Winter 2005.
Andrews, Emily K. (Sandra L. Myres, ed.) "Woman's View of the Texas Frontier,
    1874: The Diary of Emily K. Andrews." *Southwestern Historical Quarterly.* Vol.
    LXXXVI. No. 1. July 1982.
Aranda, Daniel D. "An Episode From Victorio's War." *Real West.* February 1984.
_____. "Apache Depredations in Doña Ana County: An Incident in Victorio's
    War." *Southern New Mexico Historical Review.* January 1996.
Ballenger, Dean "Poker Alice Was Too Much For The West's Slickest Card Sharps."
    Frontier West. October 1972.
Bell, Bob Boze "Clash Of The Madams: Alice Abbott vs. Etta Clark." *True West.* July
    2003.
Bello, Nino Lo, "Poker Alice." *True West.* October 1956.
Bergdale, Vince "Lottie Deno—Queen of the Pasteboards." *Trail's End Magazine.*
    Aug/Sept. 1998.
Biffle, Kent "Lottie Deno Was Odd Jewel in Rough West." *Dallas Morning News.*
    January 7, 1990.
Biggers, Don H. "The Old Stone Ranch." *Frontier Times.* July 1946.
_____. "The Famous Brock Case." *Frontier Times.* May 1946.
_____. " On the Buffalo Range of Texas." *Frontier Times.* May 1949.
Biggers, Don L. "On the Buffalo Range of Texas." *Frontier Times.* May 1941.
Blalock, Fred Frank "J. Wright Mooar and the Decade of Destruction." *Real West.*
    January 1974.
Boessenecker, John "Lawman Bob Paul's Doc and Wyatt Connection." *Wild West.*
    August 2003.
Bork A. W. (with Boyer, Glen) "The O. K. Corral Fight At Tombstone: A Footnote
    By Kate Elder." *Arizona and the West.* Spring 1977.
Bowmaster, Patrick A. "A Fresh Look at 'Big Nose Kate'." National Association For
    Outlaw and Lawman History, Inc., (NOLA) *Quarterly.* July-September. 1998.
Bragg, J. J. "Days of Peril on the Clear Fork." *Frontier Times.* April 1926.
Campbell, Suzanne "The Nasworthy Family." *Angelo State University President's
    Report.* May 2001.
Cashion, Ty "Rewriting the Wild West for a New History." *Journal of the West .*
    October 1995.
_____. "(Gun) Smoke Gets in Your Eyes: A Revisionist Look at 'Violent' Fort
    Griffin." *Southwestern Historical Quarterly.* July 1995.
Cerveri, Doris "La Tules: Gambling Lady." *Real West.* March 1973.
Cheney, Louise "The Frozen Heart of Fort Griffin." *Real West.* September 1973.
_____. "Poker Alice." *Pioneer West.* July 1967.
_____. "La Tules Of Old Santa Fe." *Golden West.* January 1967.
_____. "The Petticoat Gambler Made Faro A Lethal Game." *Frontier West.* October
    1973.
_____. "Picturesque Old Fort Griffin." *Real West.* October 1972.
Coriell, Marian M. "Madame Moustache: The Perfumed Dove Who Mined The
    Miners." *Great West.* September 1969.
Crane, R. C. "Stage-Coaching in the Concho Country." *West Texas Historical
    Association Year Book.* 1934.

Crimmons, M. L. "Camp Cooper and Fort Griffin, Texas." *West Texas Historical Association Year Book.* 1941.
_____. "Old Fort Richardson." *Frontier Times.* July 1940.
Cross, Cora Melton "Life on the On Cattle Range in Texas." *Frontier Times.* May 1929.
Crum, Tom "Camp Cooper, A Different Look." *West Texas Historical Association Year Book. 1992.*
Cunningham, Sharon "Yellow House Canyon Fight—Buffalo Hunters vs. Plains Indians." *Wild West.* June 2003.
Darby, Ray "Poker Alice: Queen of Gamblers." *True Western Adventures.* June 1961/
Dealey, Edward M. "The Story of Old Tascosa." *Frontier Times.* October 1926.
DeArment, Robert K. "John Shanssey, From Prize Ring to Politics." *True West.* March 1999.
_____. "Horse Thief—'Hurricane Bill' Martin." *True West.* June 1991.
_____. "The Frontier Adventures of Jim McIntire." *True West.* February 1999.
_____. "Western Lore—Bat Masterson Myths." *Wild West.* June 2004.
_____. "John Larn's Bloody Trail Drive." *True West.* January 1997.
_____. "The Bloody McDonalds." National Association for Outlaw and Lawman History, Inc. (NOLA) *Quarterly.* October-December 1992.
_____. "Deadly Deputy." *True West.* February 1999.
_____. "Badmen of the Wild and Woolly West had a handle on some of the more colorful nicknames." *Wild West.* June 2003.
Devereaux, Jan "Jagville." National Association for Outlaw and Lawman History, Inc. (NOLA) *Quarterly.* January-March 2004.
_____. "Gentle Woman, Tough Medicine." National Association for Outlaw and Lawman History Inc. (NOLA) *Quarterly.* April-June 2003.
Dinges, Bruce J., "The San Angelo Riot of 1881: The Army, Race Relations, and Settlement on the Texas Frontier." *Journal of the West.* Vol. 41, No. 3. Summer 2002.
Dobie, J. Frank "Fifty Years of Battling for Interest of Range Cattlemen." *The Cattleman.* March 1927.
Dorkin, Mark "Wyatt Earp's 1897 Yuma and Cibola Sojourns." Western Outlaw-Lawman History Association (WOLA) *Journal.* Spring 2005.
Eckhart, Jerry "Rath City: Texas Hide Town." *True West.* September 1992.
Evans, W. L. "A Journey to Fort Griffin in 1876." *Frontier Times.* May 1926.
Ewing Jr., Floyd F. "Unionist Sentiment of the Northwest Texas Frontier." *West Texas Historical Association Year Book.* 1957.
Farmer, L. E. (Mrs.) "Fort Davis on the Clear Fork of the Brazos." *West Texas Historical Association Year Book.* 1957.
Felchner, William J. "The Manly Art in the Old West." *True West.* April 1992.
Finke, Charles G. "Cambray." *New Mexico Philatelist.* July-August 1986.
Ford, Gary "Rath City—A Brief But Important Time in History." *Back to Rath's Trail.* June 2000.
Fauntleroy, J. D. "Old Stage Routes of Texas." *Frontier Times.* July 1929.
Ginger, Lewis "'Rowdy Joe Lowe.' A Character." *Frontier Times.* December 1926.
Grant, Ben O. "Citizen Law Enforcement Bodies: A Little More About Vigilantes." *West Texas Historical Association Year Book.* 1963.
_____. & Webb, J. R. "On the Cattle Trail and Buffalo Range, Joe S. McCombs." *West Texas Historical Association Year Book.* 1935.
_____. "Life in Old Fort Griffin." *West Texas Historical Association Year Book.* 1934.

_____. "Explorers and Early Settlers of Shackelford County." *West Texas Historical Association Year Book.* 1935.

Greever, William S. "Railway Development In the Southwest." *New Mexico Historical Review.* Volume 32. 1937.

Gustafson, C. A. "Dan Tucker: Deming's Lethal Lawman." *Destination Deming.* 1999 Luna County Visitors' Guide.

Haskew, Eula "Stribling and Kirkland of Fort Griffin." *West Texas Historical Association Year Book.* 1956.

Hatfield, Dot Ferguson "J. Marvin Hunter, Pioneer Printer." *True West.* March 1999.

Hatley, Allen G. "Old West Adventurer, John W. Poe." *True West,* June 1999.

_____. "Cap Arrington—Adventurer, Ranger and Sheriff." *Wild West,* June 2001.

Hathaway, Seth "The Adventures of a Buffalo Hunter." *Frontier Times.* December 1931.

Holden, W. C. "Law and Lawlessness on the Texas Frontier, 1875-1890." *Southwestern Historical Quarterly.* 1940.

Hornung, Chuck (with Roberts) "The Split: Did Doc & Wyatt Split Because of a Racial Slur?" *True West.* December 2001.

Humphrey, David C., "Prostitution and Public Policy in Austin, Texas, 1870-1915." *Southwestern Historical Quarterly.* Vol. LXXXVI, No. 4. April 1983.

Hunter, J. Marvin (ed.) "The Mystery Woman at Fort Concho." *Frontier Times.* January 1927.

_____. "J. Wright Mooar and John W. Mooar." *Old West.* Spring 1967.

_____. "The Lottie Deno I Knew." *West Texas Historical Association Year Book.* 1947.

_____. "The Deming I Knew 44 Years Ago." *Frontier Times.* May 1944.

_____. (ed.) "Bracketville and Old Fort Clark." *Frontier Times.* May 1935.

_____. (ed.) "Picturesque Characters Among Women of Wild West." *Frontier Times.* September 1932.

Hutto, John R. "Mrs. Elizabeth (Aunt Hank) Smith." *West Texas Historical Association Year Book.* 1939.

Jay, Roger "The Peoria Bummer: Wyatt Earp's Lost Year." *Wild West.* August 2003.

Johnson, David "The Fifth Ace: H. F. Sills and His Testimony." National Outlaw and Lawman History Association, Ind. (NOLA) *Quarterly.* April-June 2007.

Kincaid, N. H. "True Stories of West Texas." *Frontier Times.* November 1947.

_____. "Rath City." *West Texas Historical Association Year Book.* 1948.

_____. "Saved By A Rattlesnake." *Frontier Times.* February 1948.

Lewis, Preston "Lottie Deno, Gambler." *True West.* September 1987.

_____. "FARO—Is A Four-Letter Word." *True West.* October. 1989.

_____. "Bluster's Last Stand—The Battle of Yellowhouse Canyon." *True West.* April 1992.

Lipscomb, Millie Gene "The Saga of Lottie Deno." *The Junior Historian.* December 1946.

McGaw, Bill "Deming Woman 'Took' Holliday for $70,000." *The Southwesterner.* May 1962.

Martin, Cy "Klondike Gold Rush Girlies." *Real West.* 1968.

Martin, Jeannie "Poker Alice: Fabulous Lady Gambler." *Real West.* November 1970.

Meketa, Jacqueline Dorgan "A Plethora of Purple Prose." *True West.* August 1991.

Miles, Susan "Fort Concho in 1877." *West Texas Historical Association Year Book.* 1959.

Mooar, J. Wright "Frontier Experiences of J. Wright Mooar." *West Texas Historical Association Year Book.* 1928.

Myres, Roger "Between Wichita and Dodge: The Travels and Friends of Kate Elder." National Outlaw Lawman History Association, Inc. (NOLA) *Quarterly*. April-June 2007.

Myres, Sandra L., "A Woman's View of the Texas Frontier, 1874: The Diary of Emily K. Andrews." *Southwestern Historical Quarterly*. Vol. LXXXVI, No. 1. July 1982.

Neighbours, Kenneth F. "Tonkawa Scouts and Guides." *West Texas Historical Association Year Book*. 1973.

Newcomb, Diedra "Life in Old Fort Griffin." *Old Timer*. May 1981.

Notson, W. M. "Fort Concho in 1870." *Frontier Times*. May 1926.

Owens, Valarie "The Frozen Face of Fort Griffin." *Texas Co-op Power*. February 1969

Parsons, Chuck "James W. Grahame—From Birmingham, England to Fort Griffin: An Englishman Finds Adventure in Texas." *English-Westerners Brand Book*. 50th Anniversary Edition. 2005.

Rainman, Philip "The Legend of Lottie Deno." *The West*. December 1965.

Rasch, Phillip J. "Six Shooter and Three Shooter' Smith." National Association of Outlaw and Lawman History Association, Inc. (NOLA) *Quarterly*. Winter. 1985.

Richardson, Rupert N. "The Saga of Camp Cooper." *West Texas Historical Association Year Book*. 1980.

_____. "The Comanche Reservation in Texas." *West Texas Historical Association Year Book*. 1929.

Rickards, Colin "The Cowboy From Yorkshire." *True West*. June 1969.

Rister, Carl C. "Fort Griffin." *West Texas Historical Association Year Book*. 1925.

Robbins, Lance "Poker Alice." *Real West*. January 1967.

_____. "La Tules, The Notorious Redhead." *Real West*. June 1968.

Roberts, Emmett "Frontier Experiences of Emmett Roberts of Nugent, Texas." *West Texas Historical Association Yearbook*. 1927.

Roberts, Gary L. "Mrs. John Holliday?", *True West*. December 2001.

_____. (with Hornung) "The Split: Did Doc & Wyatt Split Because of a Racial Slur?" *True West*. December 2001.

Robinson III, Charles M., "Buffalo Hunting at Fort Griffin." *True West*. March 1988.

_____. "John Larn." *True West*. October 1989.

_____. "J. Wright Mooar and the Great Buffalo Hunt." *Old West*. Winter 1989.

_____. "From Billy the Kid to Bank President: John William Poe." *True West*. September 1992

Russell, Sharman Apt "Russian Bill: the True Story of an Outlaw." *Journal of the West*. April 1984.

Rybolt, Bob "Whispering Smith Still a Mystery." National Association for Outlaw and Lawman History, Inc. (NOLA) *Quarterly*. Spring. 1985.

Schmid, Vernon "Hides and Bones." *Roundup Magazine*. December 2006,

Schubert, Frank N. "Gunfire at San Angela: When 10th Cavalry troopers from Fort Concho Retaliated against Texas civilians." *Wild West*. February 2004.

Selcer, Richard F. "Fort Worth and the Fraternity of Strange Women." *Southwestern Historical Quarterly*. Vol. XCVI, No. 1. July 1992.

Sherman, Jean Dale "A Century With the Texas Rangers." *The Cattleman*. March 1937.

Smith, Glenn "Some Early Runnels County History, 1858-185." *West Texas Historical Association Year Book*. 1966.

Smith, Ralph A. "The West Texas Bone Business." *West Texas Historical Association Year Book*. 1979.

Smither, Harriet, ed. "The Diary of Adolphus Sterne." *Southwestern Historical Quarterly.* October 1933.

_____. "The Diary of Adolphus Sterne." *Southwestern Historical Quarterly.* July 1934.

Sonnichsen, C. L. "Justice After Dark." *True West.* January-February. 1966.

Strickland, Rex W. (ed.) "The Recollections of W. S. Glenn, Buffalo Hunter." *Panhandle-Plains Historical Review.* Vol. XXII. 1949.

Syers, Ed. "Lottie Deno Added Color To Fort Griffin Gambling." *The Abilene Reporter-News.* November 23, 1971.

Tanner, Karen Holliday and John D., Jr. "The Case of Ada Hulmes: Murder and Scandal in New Mexico." *Wild West.* December 2003.

Tanner, John D. "Violence in New Mexico Territory—A Penitentiary Analysis." Western Outlaw-Lawman History Association (WOLA), *Journal.* Summer 2003.

Thomas, Robert. "Lady Luck." *Ranch Magazine.* August 1983.

Tolbert, Frank X. "The Lieutenant's Letter." *Argosy Magazine.* September 1956.

Traywick, Ben T. "The Real Doc Holliday." *Wild West.* October 1997.

Trendall, Norm "Poker Alice." *Westerner.* September-October 1969.

Young, Bob "He Whipped Rowdy Denison Into Shape." National Association and Center for Outlaw and Lawman History [NOLA] *Quarterly.* Vol. XII, No. 2. Fall 1987.

Young, Bob & Jan. "Madame Moustache." *True West.* June 1956.

Webb, J. R. "Henry Herron, Pioneer and Peace Officer During Fort Griffin Days." *West Texas Historical Association Year Book.* 1944.

_____. "Chapters From the Frontier Life of Phin W. Reynolds." *West Texas Historical Association Year Book.* 1945.

_____ & Grant, Ben O. "On the Cattle Trail and Buffalo Range, Joe S. McCombs." *West Texas Historical Association Year Book.* 1935.

Webb, Walter Prescott "Buffalo Hunt." *True West.* January-February 1961.

Weiss Jr., Harold J. "Overdosing and Underestimating: A Look at a Violent and Not-so-Violent American West." National Association for Outlaw and Lawman History, Inc. (NOLA) *Quarterly.* April-June 2003.

Whisenhunt, Donald W. "Frontier Military Life at Fort Richardson." *West Texas Historical Association Year Book.* 1966.

Wilcox, Roberta Tidmore, "Aunt Lottie." *Password.* Summer. 1982.

Williams, O. W. "From Dallas to the Site of Lubbock in 1877." *West Texas Historical Association Year Book.* 1939.

Newspapers

Abilene Reporter News
Arizona Sentinel
Kansas City Star
Dallas Weekly Herald
Albuquerque Journal
Weatherford Exponent
Las Cruces Sun-News
Albany Echo
Deming Headlight
Albany News
Deming Graphic
Galveston Daily News
San Antonio Daily Express
New Southwest & Grant County
   Herald
The Frontier Echo
Silver City Enterprise
Dallas Morning News
Silver City Independent
Fort Griffin Echo
Southwest Sentinel

El Paso Lone Sta
Santa Fe New Mexican
Wichita Daily Eagle
Tombstone Epitaph
Douglas Daily International
Arizona Star
Denver Post
Deming Herald
The Deming Tribune & Lake Valley
   Herald
San Francisco Examiner
San Luis Obispo Telegram Tribune
Las Vegas Optic
Newman's Semi-Weekly
Colorado Miner
Fairplay Flume
Denver Tribune
Schulenberg Argus
Daily Fort Worth Democra
Western Liberal

Index

272

ABOUT THE AUTHOR

Although a native Texan, Jan Devereaux spent many of her formative years in southeastern New Mexico and, in fact, graduated from high-school at Carlsbad. Her full-time job as the Outpatient Supervisor for Baylor Hospital at Waxahachie, Texas, somewhat restricts the time she can allot for Western history projects, one of her true passions. Jan particularly enjoys meeting with and interviewing oldtimers, the descendants of the fascinating Old West characters she writes about. In 2005 Jan received national recognition for two of her journal pieces published the preceding year. The Western Outlaw-Lawman History Association awarded her article "Jagville" the coveted Outsanding Article of the Year Award. The National Association for Outlaw and Lawman History Association honored Jan's work with its prestigious Best Western Article Award for "Settlin' a Grudge." Jan Devereaux is an ardent Wild West History Association supporter, and serves on the Board of Directors. Jan is frequently a guest speaker at conferences and seminars focusing on the Old West. *Pistols, Petticoats, & Poker* is Jan Devereaux's first book, a culmination of five years historical study and exploration. Jan has a number of exciting writing projects currently underway. Besides the Wild West History Association, Jan is also an active member of Oklahombres and the National Ranching Heritage Center. When not on the job at her home near Maypearl in the Central Texas ranch country, Jan relaxes caring for her horses—and enthusiastically pursuing the trails of historic personalities—especially the women who made their contributions during America's westward expansion.